ONE MAN'S EUROPE

Gordon Nicholas

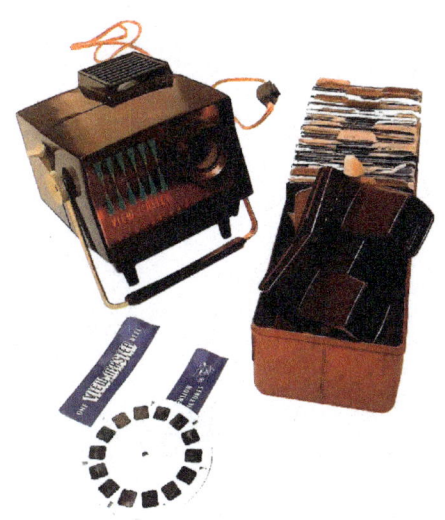

Supplied for the Public Service

Code 28-614

https://www.onemanseurope.com

ISBN: 978-1-916604-02-5

This book is a travel memoir based on true events. It reflects the author's recollections of experiences over time, his personal views and opinions. Some names and characteristics may have been changed, and others' recollections of the period and events may be different.

ONE MAN'S EUROPE

Introduction by Gordon Nicholas, 1970

I dedicate these notes to my three lovely children, of whom I am so proud. When I started out on my travels around Europe, I had no idea that I would ever have a family. I found even the idea of settling down difficult and it laughable that anyone would want to settle down with me. I have been fortunate that my line of work has permitted me to travel so freely, but my travels have also taught me the importance of being able to come 'home'. Unlikely though it seems, 'home', and finding oneself, is what this book is really about.

I was born in 1923, so, by the time I finished school, the Second World War was in full swing, and Bristol University was closed. My studies had to be postponed until a couple of years after the war, when I graduated as part of the ex-service scheme. Despite the cold, the damp and the cramped digs, I hugely enjoyed my time in university. The people and ideas I met there were to shape much of my life. It was there that I first fell in love, so I have always loved university towns. I extended my stay for as long as I could, so it wasn't until 1953 that I finally emerged with letters after my name, a reshaped person, emerging into a new world. 'Stundezero '– Zero Hour as the Germans would say.

I have always prided myself on being a man of the world in general, beyond the notion of belonging to just one place and, for the majority of the period covered in this travelogue, I had no real place that I called home. I had children very late in life, an indescribable blessing, but one I knew for too short a time. I know

now that my family is my home, wherever they may be in the world, but a home has to have a context to sit in, in the same way that a house sits in its landscape, and I feel many people today have lost sight of their contexts.

I have seen rich and poor communities, East and West, Christian, Muslim and atheist states. I have sat with old academics playing chess, danced with youngsters in bars, chewed tobacco with goat herders high on the mountains and inspected factory production lines with industrialists. I have been blessed with the time and opportunity to see the world as it is for myself and, as a bookseller, to read how others saw it first-hand too. My conclusions are clear.

The world is a wonderful place, full of wonderful people who are, on the whole, just like you and me. They do the best with what they have and try and make life better for their children. People are kind, welcoming and generous by default. Make a little effort to get to know them and you'll be greatly rewarded. Most of us know this, most of the time. All cultures are a mix of influences and all cultures evolve over time. Our language, laws, culture and our histories are completely intertwined with those of our brothers and sisters across the sea. We are all part of one great family. A Union.

I am grateful that my children will be spared the terrible poverty and horrific violence that tore through Europe during my lifetime; it continues to shape our world even now. But we will only avoid such catastrophes in the future if we learn that there is no such thing as nationality, no such behaviour as foreign, no such place as abroad. I hope I have passed this message on to my children. I believe that, even if we experience moments of darkness, as we are at the moment, the sun will continue to shine on our wider family, our Union.

FOREWORD

By William (Nicholas) Hyde, 2023

I t's been nearly fifty years since my father started writing this book, and the world has changed, almost beyond recognition, since then. In that time, not only have regimes, political systems and even countries disappeared but, more significantly, people's aspirations and expectations have changed too. The ability to travel abroad is no longer an exotic business for the well-off requiring significant planning. Today most working-class families can book a holiday online with a few clicks and jet off to the sun within hours.

My father would think this a good thing. Despite the westernisation of local cultures, he would love the fact that you can now swipe your mobile phone to buy fries in Bucharest or be able to slurp cream topped coffee in a Starbucks in the heart of Bratislava.

He would however slightly miss what he called the "connection to the people and their land" that was there in the days before mass tourism. This book gives us a few brief glimpses of that innocent world that existed in the short window between the end of the war and our modern age.

My father was the "manager" of a wonderful bookshop in Bath that was owned by city socialite and Admiralty darling, Miss Seawright. The title of manager seems a little inappropriate given the chaotic and non-commercial way the bookshop operated, but for years he was the shop's front man. I can see him now sitting in his little office in the attic, maps, booklets and travel guides all around him. His desk, which took up nearly half the tiny room, was always covered in a mountain of notes and letters, many with intriguing stamps and postmarks from overseas. In my mind I see a half-typed application for a visa, or something similar, protruding from the mouth of the huge metal typewriter that I used to play with and that he hated so much. By the time I arrived on the scene, he had ceased to travel, but he was a person whose brain refused to be constrained by the walls of that small room, of Bath society or domestic wedded bliss. He, like the mysterious Miss Seawright who actually owned the shop, was passionate about the concept of Europe and the causes he believed in, causes that he, like many others of that generation, were willing to die for. He died far too soon, but he has been the inspiration for most of my life and all of my own travels.

He spent twenty years travelling around Europe by himself before finally marrying my mother in 1970 and settling down. Life before her was a taboo subject in our household when I was growing up, so quite where all those maps and booklets went, I do not know. Only his Dutch coffee percolator and his collection of View-Master reels were allowed in the house. View-Master reels are paper disks the size of beer mats, containing seven pairs of small colour photos. When placed in the View-Master and held up to the light, they produce a 3D image, immersing you in a completely different world. It is surprisingly effective. They were very popular in the fifties and sixties, so everywhere he went he purchased them as souvenirs. I grew up with him handing me the heavy Bakelite View-Master with its fragile paper disk, and carefully clicking the lever, a fascinating story behind every scene. Now it's virtually all I have left of him.

Time, modesty, and his dislike of that officious typewriter, that silently sat judging whatever it was you had typed before even considering committing it to paper, prevented him from ever finishing his travelogue. His travels inspired my own, and it has always been one of my main missions in life to finish it for him, introducing others to a fascinating man and his enigmatic and eccentric employer. But life often gets in the way, and only when faced with my own mortality was I able to seriously begin the task of piecing together the bits that I have left.

Over the years I have made my own jottings about what he said, copied down the dates of visas in passports that have long since disappeared, researched the publication dates of each View-Master slide and documented his thoughts before I visited the same places. I have a few notes in old exercise books containing his thoughts as he looked back on his travels, as well as my own vivid childhood memories of him and Miss Seawright in their peculiarly uncommercial bookshop.

As I lay in a hospital bed, full of all manner of drugs, these items helped guide many conversations with him that I wished I had had when he was alive.

You will understand that it has taken a long time to put this book together. Even after all these years, I am not even vaguely able to come to terms with his passing. However, I have enjoyed spending time with him, chatting almost, teasing other bits of information out of him. Every now and again, I have added a few contextual comments of my own, while he takes a sip of tea or a bite from a sticky bun. These are all denoted by italicised text.

My father's unshakable faith in people and in the future has helped me cope with cancer, his dry humour, childlike spirit and obvious love of food have made me smile during dark times. I was too young when he died, but he remains the best father that I could ever possibly wish to have.

The world has changed dramatically since 1953, or since 1970, and it has unquestionably changed for the better, but my father's message, so clearly set out in his introduction and conclusion, is surely as relevant now as it was back then. We need the input of previous generations, of people like him and Miss Seawright, to help resolve the problems we currently face. We need to build the future on the foundations of the past.

Whether you choose to dip into each chapter to visit a place with him and wander curiously through the back streets of a famous location, or work chronologically through it watching him, and Europe itself, mature, I hope that you enjoy spending a little bit of time with my father. Perhaps if you are ever in the city of Bath, you'll take a walk down New Bond Street and see his shop, or better still buy a sticky bun and think what a wonderful place Europe is.

CONTENTS

The Weir at Bath with Pulteney Bridge.

BATH

Introduction, May 1970[1]

I t was a glorious morning. The sun was already high in the sky, warming the honey-coloured eighteenth-century buildings for which the city was famous and sparkling off the surface of the water as it leapt joyously over the steps of the weir. The parks were full of daffodils and baskets, bursting with primroses and begonias, hung from every lamppost. I beamed with delight as I walked down the raised pavements of Milsom Street, smelling first the sharp tang of cheeses drifting out from the department store 'Jolly's' food section, and then the delicious aroma of coffee as I passed Old Bond Street where a shop with the three coffee grinders in the window was roasting beans. A quick detour took me into the arcade, where I hastily acquired a brown paper bag containing a sticky bun, which made its way into my suit pocket for later. All was well with the world, and I was a happy man.

A customer once confided in me that she had walked along the length of Stall Street and not heard a word of English, suggesting that Bath had somehow suddenly changed for the worse. Bath is a beautiful and elegant city nestled amongst Somerset's sleepy green hills, a showcase of Georgian and Roman architecture. The entire city is a UNESCO World Heritage site. But it has been an international tourist destination for over two thousand years and foreign languages have been bouncing of the walls of the buildings

---

Opposite: *I have stood with my father looking at the weir thousands of times, yet he has not left us a single painting of it. This picture has him scurrying over an architecturally well-defined bridge, which appears in a blur, towards the restaurant at the centre, before a post-lunch haze of trees blinking in the sun.*

on Stall Street for that entire time. Everything that you see here, from the baths themselves, the Abbey, the Pumproom, and the sweeping Palladian Crescents were all designed and built with international tourism in mind. Bath exists because people were meant to visit it, and of course to spend their money while they were doing so, in its many gambling houses, public houses and even the odd bookshop.

My bookshop was tucked away down one of Bath's medieval side lanes, barely wide enough for two horses to pass, with worn down stones and an ancient drainage channel down the middle. I say, 'my shop', but I didn't own it and it wasn't really a shop in the sense that you'd expect today. We never made any money, but that wasn't the point of the place. It was an old-fashioned bookshop, a haven of calm and culture. In an effort to give a little back to the community, I had set up a lending service of sorts and so, after going through the complex ceremony of assembling my coffee pot and tapping down the ground beans, I was soon busy readying a series of poetry primers for posting. Ted Hughes to a man at Porton Down, a bit of Philip Larkin to a chap working at Plymouth Docks and a collection of Sylvia Plath for a lovely lady working at RAF Filton. Sometimes the books came back, sometimes they didn't. It didn't matter if they gave someone a little enjoyment.

You will see that I am a man happy with my own company, indeed there is nothing like the presence of a loitering customer to spoil a good morning's reading, so when the bell attached to the back of the door sang out and a smartly dressed lady entered, I put my cup of Douwe Egberts' coffee down with a slight frown. The visitor was none other than a famous British actress who had made her name in America after the war. She entered, slightly fussily I recall, in the way people who like to draw attention to themselves often do. I bowed low and offered her a cup of tea. It was the type of shop where good manners came a long way ahead of good commerce.

"It's a lovely May morning and here I am, once again in the gorgeous city of Bath!" she exclaimed, needlessly, as it turned out, as I had already noticed both of those things. She was obviously excited, far too excited for tea, fortunately, which I am notoriously bad at making, besides which the urn was on the third floor, up two flights of vertiginous and highly treacherous stairs. I'm sure something could be done about them, but I do try and discourage my customers from exploring the shop too much.

I wondered what my celebrated guest wanted and feared that such a heightened level of expectation could only lead to disappointment when it came to my services. I was in the city every morning and, while it is indeed often lovely, I was rarely excited to be there. I had, however, spent the last twenty years roaming round Europe, and I knew that I would un-questionably have felt the same way as she did if I were somewhere else, such as Paris or Rome. It was not so much the city that caused her excitement therefore, but her relationship and unfamiliarity with it. Although I had ceased to travel by then, my mind instantly fluttered away to a series of exotic locations around the world where I might like to have spent a morning in May; places that I had not yet been. Under Nepal's duck-egg-blue skies perhaps, staring up at another famous mountain range, celebrating the Festival of the Roses in Morocco's dusty Todra Gorge, or even simply enjoying a salt-beef bagel in New York's Central Park.

She was, of course, after a book about Bath as a souvenir of her travels.

For almost two decades after the war I spent every moment that I could wandering around Europe, visiting its great cities, eating the local food and peeking behind the official façades. Not comprehensively, not particularly systematically or logically, but just as the opportunity presented. I have been fortunate to have visited far more places and seen many more things than the average man on the street, and yet the list of things and places that I wish to see still continues to grow rather than get smaller. For me, the poring over maps and the comparison of brochures is great sport and, although I have now ceased to travel, I still plan future journeys, launching great itineraries across the globe from the maps on the wall of my pokey office above the shop. Photographs of the major sites of cities various are pinned to my walls, timetables and hotel booklets are linked together with webs of string, while relevant reading material is piled carefully beneath each destination. Travelling only so far as the Old Green Tree Pub, which is just around the corner from my shop and where I found myself later in the day munching on a spot of trout on toast and sipping slowly at a half-pint glass of Butcombe bitter from the seclusion of a wood panelled booth, I asked myself why? What was the attraction that so many people find in travelling, what is it that we are searching for when we go abroad?

I believe that the delight of travel is strongly connected to the emotion of surprise and delight in experiencing something new or different. Would that same lady have felt as excited if she were back at home in Vermont reading Walter Ison's 'Georgian Buildings of Bath'? No, because she would only be experiencing a very small part of it, even if the book were very good. For the record, it is a very thorough piece of work architecturally, but with a rather emotionless analysis. It spends far too long on the frost resistance of limestone and makes no mention of how the buildings reflect the warmth of the sun or seem to 'smile' at you in the rain. The fact of being in a place, the difficulties of getting there, what the weather was like and how tired or hungry you were when you saw it, alters a place, making the experience unique to you. A delicious lunch, the sound of a brass band playing in the distance, even, dare I say it, a conversation with a friendly bookseller, these are the things that make up memories of a city, while a well-known classical façade, frost resistant or not, can be completely forgettable.

Then there is the matter of scale. If man is the measure of all things, then some things can make a man feel very small indeed. A book from Bath would be a minuscule item back in my American friend's world, lost in the shadows of Mount Mansfield and the sights and sounds of Burlington's markets, which, to her would be very dull, but which might delight me as a tourist. A photograph of the Pont du Gard, displayed in the Middlebury College Museum (that's a photography museum, also in Vermont – I've done my research) may reveal its structure and method of construction perfectly well. But to stand before it is something completely different. Only when one becomes aware of its colossal size dominating the landscape can one understand the incredible feat that the building of it really was. So, there is beauty that is permanent and beauty that is experiential. Either can lead to the firing of the imagination that becomes the sense of enrichment that we choose to remember, but most often it's a combination of the two. Sometimes it takes the act of doing something mundane or childish in front of a great site, that allows us to bond with it. Drinking a coffee or licking an ice-cream in front of a great sculpture or outside a cathedral for example can bring an otherwise cold piece of art to life. Looking Leonardo da Vinci square in the eye and saying 'chocolate please' makes him part of our history and us part of his world.

A Fiat 500 in front of the Pont du Gard, see also page 112.

For me, in the image above, the fact that a tiny, unreliable little Italian car has been parked in front of this monumental Roman marvel is what completes this picture. The juxtaposition of ancient, outstanding engineering with modern, poor-quality engineering is clear to see. The photograph would be empty without the Fiat and have no message for the viewer. The fact that the car's owner cares not two hoots for the bridge's history or construction technique and simply uses it as a garage, makes me smile. A sense of humility and perspective is important after all.

On a lesser level, there is also excitement in the planning before the journey itself, the reading of many books, some perhaps purchased from your local bookstore, I hope. I keep them on the ground floor with the books for tourists, just in case it floods, as it often does in Bath. As a general rule, the higher the quality of the item, the further from the floods, the front door and the public in general it will be. The process of acquiring visas, finding connections and patching together workarounds takes time. It was a little easier in my day, I must confess, when the world was not so ideologically divided, and nylons were tradable for accommodation and even a civilian like me could hitch a free ride on a DC3 in exchange for a packet of Dunhill or Embassy. I got a lot of help too from people behind the scenes and am supremely grateful to all of those who made my adventures possible and who trusted in me. We must remember that many people have died preserving our ability to travel freely, while others are still prevented from doing so by the systems in which they live. It is a privilege to have travelled as I have done, across Europe and across the 'Iron Curtain'.

For our children it may be difficult to comprehend, but the period immediately after the war was a time of great austerity, poverty and constraint. By the beginning of the nineteen-fifties, everything was still militarised, rationing was still in place. Famous tourist hot spots like Florence's sun-drenched Piazza della Signoria, were just rain-filled bombsites. It was another world entirely, a tired war-torn world, but prosperity was beginning to return all across Europe, as was hope for the future. For a while, Europe was a single community of comradeship, slowly recovering from a shared trauma, and travel throughout it was unrestricted. Tourism was not as industrialised as it is now and although that meant items such as Kodak film and aspirin were often hard to get hold of, it also meant that travellers like myself experienced a closer connection to the land than would be possible today.

After years of studying and pottering around our own fair isle, I was persuaded to go and have a look at the Swiss Alps, slap bang in the middle of Europe, in a neutral state that was relatively untouched by the war.

Why would I not go, seeing as I could? For all my reading, for all the research, nothing – nothing – prepared me for the shock of actually seeing, no being, amongst the Alps. The enormous size, the stillness of the lower hills, the blinding bluish-white light, the gentle clanging of cowbells or the hair-raising roar of an avalanche across the valley. All of these were totally different from anything that I had experienced before and things that I could not get from a painting, a photograph, or a book.

The Swiss Alps as remembered by my father.

But what struck me most on my travels were not the many differences that I get so excited about in this journal, but the similarities and the inter-connectedness of things. Standing at the foot of those mountains, as far from wartime Bristol as you could imagine, I was, in fact, surrounded by my own past, my own thought processes and a large percentage of our science and art. A decision taken a thousand miles away and five hundred years ago affects us still and I find a perverse pleasure in that. Our fastest, most modern trains have the same wheel width decided by the chariot makers of ancient Rome and our cars the same dimensions as their carriages. On a bridge in beautiful Sarajevo a young man fires a gun in protest and, at the other end of Europe, two of my uncles die. In a small chapel, in a small town, high up in the Apennines, a grumpy old man paints a fresco and the whole future of art, the whole extent of visual representation, is altered. The world never looks at anything the same way again. All of this is influence. This interrelatedness takes place on a small and overcrowded continent with an incredible diversity of natural beauty and such a range of architectural styles that the eye is constantly delighted, the spirit refreshed, and the imagination enriched. All this we share with our fellow Europeans.

I resolved then that I would try and see as much of Europe as I could, with the resources available to a simple soul. This is a record of those years; not a complete travelogue – that would be tedious for us both – but it is a reflection on what stands out in my mind, now that my travels are over. I have made no reference to any books, maps or writings of my own, so place names may occasionally be incorrect or dates and sequences in the wrong order. It does not matter. They are what I remember most vividly and what was of most value to me. It is a mere reflection of what Europe meant to one European.

I am delighted that my eldest son, who is more of a European than I could ever hope to be, has decided to join me on this journey and add a few thoughts of his own. I will have to leave to him the difficult task of making my ramblings more relevant and readable as well as all of the help with my photographs.

I hope that, regardless of your situation or nationality, you all eventually settle in a happy context, wherever that may be. The best of luck to you all.

Gordon Nicholas
Manager (of sorts) Seawright's Bookshop
New Bond Street,
Bath,
Europe

SWITZERLAND

On Insignificance, Summer 1953

For me, graduation coincided almost exactly with my thirtieth birthday and I knew exactly how I wanted to celebrate. Not with luxuries, cake, or a lavish party, but by spending time alone after years of communal living in close proximity to others and an opportunity to challenge myself physically after years of academia. As an only child, I have always been a solitary person, happy with my own company and, whilst I find it easy to be cheerful and friendly in public, it is just a shopkeeper's mask. The army and then university did a lot to correct this insularity. They forced me to share personal possessions and personal space, sleeping on thin mattresses next to my comrades, six of us crammed into a tent, twelve of us into a small damp apartment. In that way it had done me the world of good. I knew I would miss my university chums, but right then, spending time by myself was definitely what I wanted.

Perhaps you have the image of me as a dusty academic, tall and thin, possibly physically frail. I was both of the former, but the latter I was not. Army rations and university canteens had left me far fitter and better nourished than at any other time in my life. Nor was I a complete novice when it came to mountain climbing. By 1953 I had already climbed most of the summits that Britain had to offer: Snowdon and Garnedd Ugain in '46 with like-minded army pals, Ben Nevis in '47. The Alps seemed a logical next step, a return to form.

With my haversack packed to capacity and my old army boots lovingly polished, I caught the frightfully early 04:20 train from Bristol to London. I must have looked a frightful mess, dressed in my old khaki battle dress trousers and ex-submarine service cable knit jumper, but, at the time, there were many such transient figures going about in ex-service or 'demob' clothing with their large kit bags, sleeping on benches or wherever they could, and I did not stand out at all. The cavernous engine shed loomed over me in the darkness reflecting in some way my anxious anticipation of the adventure that lay ahead.

There was a breakfast of sorts in the 'Moo Cow Milk Bar' in Victoria; I remember powdered eggs in various forms. Despite its name, fresh milk was definitely not its speciality. Then a filthy steam train packed with morose people and heavy cases on the long, slow run to Folkstone Quay, where I got my first glimpse of the grey, storm-tossed sea. The smell of the sea, whatever the weather, is a distinctive one that we all enjoy, but it was the absence of the smell of the land that was more noticeable. The war had left every city smelling of dust, soot and rubble, an acid taste that burned the back of the throat all the time until you no longer noticed it. No amount of alcohol could wash it away, but standing here beside the carriages on Folkstone Quay, the cold, wet, salty air blew it away in seconds.

My goal was the famous Eiger mountain that towers over the Bernese Oberland in Switzerland. Just under four thousand metres high, it is not the tallest mountain in the Alps, but is one of the most dangerous, its imposing north face remains one of the most technically difficult ascents in the region, only being conquered in 1938. After years of military checkpoints, where you couldn't go from one end of the platform to the other without having your papers checked three times, the idea of travelling abroad and testing myself in this way seemed fantastical. The thought that I could tackle the mighty 'Ogre' was at best naïve bravado.

[WH] Neutrality during the Second World War protected Switzerland, but at a significant cost that was not immediately obvious. The country had not been invaded by Germany, nor had any fighting occurred on its soil. As a result, unlike most of Europe, all of its infrastructure, including its railway network, and its economy, including the hospitality industry with its hotel and catering sectors, were still fully functional. America was clear that wartime neutrality meant complicit support of the Nazis and was equally clear that Switzerland was going to pay (quite literally) for its

inaction. The Swiss, it was decided, were to be a major contributor to the Marshall Plan and to finance the recovery in Europe, not least through the famous Schweizer Spende fund. It was important, therefore, that Switzerland's economy expanded rapidly after the war. So almost overnight it became the favourite holiday destination for American military personnel serving in Europe, with official tours of duty being amended to include respite in cities such as Lucerne, where streets of hotels were taken over by the military. Translators and chefs were flown in to make the Americans feel at home and many local culinary peculiarities persist in this region to this day, such as Hawaii toast, hash browns and Swiss apple pie. American soldiers, just like the German ones before them, loved taking part in the physical activities available such as hiking, canoeing, mountain climbing and skiing. In towns such as Interlaken, which were connected to the main railway network, huge numbers of hotels and conference centres suddenly sprang up. Special trains were laid on, such as the overnight service from Boulogne to Interlaken, to bring soldiers from bases all over Europe and, of course, other tourists, such as my father, to Swiss destinations. Thomas Cook has offered package holidays to Interlaken since 1951 and this is how his trip was arranged.

I don't want to get into politics in this memoir, as politics date very quickly and are not relevant to my story, but the British Government had apparently been advised that trains were a redundant method of transport in the emerging age of motorways and family cars, so, while the rest of Europe was using the opportunity (and Swiss funding) to electrify railway lines and build new public infrastructure, Britain had frozen investment in trains and was continuing to rely on steam engines built in the twenties and thirties. It was a shabby and broken country back then, exhausted by the war, almost entirely reliant on its previous reputation and a very 'hit and miss' war record. Britain was, and in my view still is, far too focused on an imagined, but historically inaccurate, glorious past. I find such John Bull tub-thumping obnoxious and tiresome and I was, in truth, quite glad to see the back of the country for a while. Britain barely survived the war let alone won it alone.

If I thought the train packed, the boat was even more so, seemingly already full before our train arrived. With no space to sit and every obvious perch already occupied, I roamed around for the duration of the crossing, squatting on the floor to read whenever I got the chance. I don't mind 'roughing it' in the slightest, but the ticket had been expensive. I would have gone outside, but the weather did not bode well. The decks were already sopping and not just with sea water. This was, of course, at the beginning of the era of cheap popular travel; the charter air business was still getting going, so this great exodus by train and sea was apparently fairly normal. The crossing itself, however, was not.

I have heard many a tale of rough crossings, but this time it happened to be true. Those who knew far more about such things than I doubted whether the ferry would sail at all. But we were a maritime nation and the "Blitz spirit" was still with us, so, perhaps foolishly, cheerfully in denial about the reality of our situation, we pressed on. The dark waves towered above us, plunging us into shadow in much the same way as the ship had dwarfed the train back on the quay. The screams of passengers mingled with those of the gulls in the wind. People were sick everywhere and I think that only the heady excitement of the experience prevented me from joining them. I can still see the bows of the 'Canterbury' going up and up, then, after a slight hesitation, plunging down for an eternity.

As we neared the French coast, the water turned yellowish green with the sand churned up by the waves. I still sometimes dream about those waves, flung high up in the air and then an enormous boom, heard clearly over the shrieking of the wind, as they crashed back down against the breakwater. Finally, we backed gingerly into the harbour.

The TS Canterbury (opposite) was clearly a tough old bird and has a colourful history and an honourable war record. She was built in 1928 and had a top speed of 21 knots. She was delivered to Southern Railways to serve the Dover Calais rail link. At the start of the war, she was converted to a troop ship and armed. She took part in the Dunkirk evacuation where she made five trips into enemy waters and served as a target and training ship for two years before taking part in the Normandy landings, running four missions. She was the first ship out of Dieppe and Folkestone after the war and the first civilian ship to be equipped with RADAR. Incredibly, she was in service with British Rail until 1965.

The TS Canterbury

My first steps on French soil were anticlimactic, stumbling over the railway sleepers to find Coach 57 of an infinitely long train. And what a find it was! Hard upright wooden backs, equally hard leather bench seats, four-a-side with no leg room for squat Frenchmen, let alone tall English tourists. I decided to give my 'seat' such as it was, to someone else. It wasn't simply magnanimity; I thought that I was going to be more comfortable sitting on my kitbag in the carriage connections. It was clearly going to be a long night. I had been given a voucher for a meal in the station restaurant. It was still a time of food stamps and rationing and food could not simply be purchased by anyone in the way we would expect today. Any expectations of fine dining were soon dashed. My first taste of French cooking was a soulless, industrial affair and the restaurant was clearly overworked, understaffed and underfunded. Rationing officially ended in France in 1949 and in Britain only in 1954, but in both countries many even basic goods, such as meat and dairy products, continued to be, as the Russians would say, 'defisitnii', in deficit, for many decades afterwards. But I was used to eating modestly.

Whilst the meal was instantly unforgettable, the small bottle of French wine that I had with it I remember being absolutely awful. I am by no means an expert on such matters and would not normally have dreamed of ordering such a luxury, but it was explicitly included on my voucher, authorised by the 'Ministère de l'agriculture' themselves with no little fanfare. Did they know how bad it tasted or was this punishment for such extravagance and self-indulgence? How quickly we forget the six years of war that we had all just lived through, or even my time as a student, when such a meal would have been reserved for kings and generals.

The train did not leave until midnight, so, fortified by my dinner, I sallied forth into the Boulogne night. Up on its hilltop, Boulogne's Hautville had looked interesting as the ferry had come in, the octagonal tower of the 'Marie' and the dome of Notre Dame poking out above the tiled rooftops. I made my way up the steep hill from the harbour to the old, fortified village. Here I found the France that I had read about in the novels of Zola and Dumas and seen in the landscape paintings of Boudin. Narrow cobbled streets with drainage ditches, high stone walls, arched alleyways and cast-iron streetlamps. I expected to see Jean Gabin or Commissioner Maigret come walking out of the shadows. Boulogne was exactly as I had wanted France to be, but something was missing. Its deserted streets seemed dull and lifeless on a wet night, as monochrome and empty as the illustrations in Georges Simenon's novels.

I turned around and started making my way back down the hill, following the old town wall, treading carefully on the slippery cobbles. That was when I saw a bunch of red roses, almost shining in the darkness, a splash of intense colour that focused the eye. They had been arranged carefully in an old, chipped, porcelain jug and placed beneath a brass plaque on the wall. Another reminder of the war that had engulfed everything. 'Here were shot seven members of the Resistance.' These were not members of some strange military organisation; these were ordinary people, brave citizens of this town, husbands, wives, brothers, aunts. Not soldiers or reservists, they had been fishermen and bakers, booksellers, sommeliers for local restaurants perhaps. They had given their lives to overthrow the Nazi invasion of their hometown.

This resistance to hostile invasion and residual terror of rape and pillage is not a collective memory for us. Not since the Norman Conquest have we endured an experience that the rest of Europe knows well. In the cold and darkness of that hill in Boulogne I realised for the first time that I was truly 'abroad'.

Memorial to the members of the Resistance in Boulogne.

The port of Boulogne fell quickly to the Germans in May 1940 after a minimal fight. It remained in German control until September 1944. It was one of several Channel ports selected by Adolf Hitler to be a fortress city. The idea was that these would be heavily fortified towns manned by troops prepared to fight to the end. The geography of Boulogne is naturally suited to defence, with numerous artillery batteries on high ground, fortified over centuries, surrounding the town. The town's fortifications were strong, but never completed. The French Resistance continually disrupted work and the flow of supplies. Fishermen from the town sabotaged the sea defences too, removing submerged obstacles, chains and even live mines.

On 16th September 1944, the 3rd Canadian Division, which had landed at Normandy, surrounded the port, cutting it off from German supply lines. For the next few days, a massive bombardment of the city took place with shells raining down day and night. Although the level of material damage done was not that great, the Resistance sowed the seeds of despair amongst the German troops, exaggerating the amount of coordination between the air force, army and navy units attacking. The Germans decided to surrender the "fortress city" just six days later.

A large diesel engine roared in the darkness, and we were off, the plates that connected the carriages lurching around, sending my kitbag squirming at every join in the rails. Shadowy figures, illuminated only by a single dull amber bulb, came and went during the night, cupping their trembling hands around paper cigarettes as if the warm glow was the last remaining vestige of civilisation.

My ice axe and crampons instantly made their way to the top of my bag and refused to be cushioned. There was nothing that I could do but sit it out.

The night passed, as all nights and even wars eventually do. The dawn came up, pink I remember, over the rolling hills of the Haute-Savoie revealing a new world. In my mind, I see a lone farmer ploughing with two oxen in that early light on an emerald-green slope so vertiginous that I was amazed that it held soil, let alone animals of such weight. The shady characters had long since deserted the train, so I could finally stretch out on the floor. Sticky though it was with mud, beer slops and cigarette ash, it felt like heaven to me, so I lay there letting the warm air from the open windows wash over me. At the border, the scruffy unshaven French guards disappeared too, and the SNCF diesel locomotive was changed for an electric one. Smiling Swiss officials in impeccable uniforms climbed back into the coaches and welcomed us into the magic that was Switzerland.

The train wound its way quietly through the rolling pastures and narrow cuttings, as if trying not to wake me from an incredible dream. Castles and lakes in brilliant colours appeared from behind veils of mist. Then a great peak pierced through the clouds. I caught my breath at the sheer size of it and its harsh outline, such violence captured in rock form. I wondered which of the great names this one bore, the clouds broke open completely and I saw that my "great peak" was no more than a shoulder, and a lesser shoulder at that, of the real mountains that soared higher and higher behind it. I should like to have recorded that moment: my first glimpse of the ceiling of

Europe; the sheer beauty of the scene; the balance of greens and greys in the foreground; the purples and blues stretching off to infinity; the immensity of the scale all perfectly framed for a second by the carriage window. But a photograph can never capture the sheer shock of witnessing such a scene. There was a freshness, almost a naivety about the scene outside the window. Here was a part of Europe that had somehow escaped the madness of centuries of failed empire building and wars. It was a place of hope, a place of purity, a place from which we could rebuild in a better, simpler way.

The Bernese Oberland continued to unfold in front of me as the train ran down along the side of the lake at Spiez. Never have I seen water so green, almost luminous in the sunlight, against a backdrop of hills so dark. I had seen photographs, of course, coloured ones, too, but nothing had prepared me for this. The roof of the boxlike schloss was bright red, as if the colour were chosen to be deliberately pleasing in such a landscape. Brightly coloured chalets surrounded it, nestling into the emerald slopes like wildflowers. It was a fairy tale land. The bells of the level crossings rang out, as if in greeting, one after another, as we crossed the many roads that led into Interlaken and the sun smiled down upon it all.

Interlaken in 1953.

From the already commercial holiday centre of Interlaken up to Grindelwald itself on the electric mountain railway, little wooden carts, as happy to carry climbers, local cheeses, or sheep, twisted their way slowly up into the hills. The air was fresh here and burned slightly like vodka in the lungs. There was such an intense level of light that I already had brown lenses clipped onto my glasses. I could have sat on that cart trundling through the rolling countryside all day, but all too soon, we lurched to the right and a tarmac platform slid alongside. Two large Alpen hotels, both six storeys high, dominated the village, but, towering over them and making them look like toys, was the black face of the Eiger itself.

The 'Bellevue' and 'Des Alpes' hotels in 1953, the Eiger behind them.

The hotel was extremely efficient and much larger than I had expected. It was pleasantly orientated, so, although a wall of cold air drained constantly from the mountain, the rest was bathed in sun the whole day. The hotels shared a breakfast terrace, which became a curling rink in winter, and one of my greatest joys was to sit out on it with a Moka coffee pot blinking in the sun, looking across at that iconic shadowy north face. It was so very different a place from anything that I had experienced before. I could barely believe that it was real.

Dinner, humble but delicious fare. Rosti, with calves' liver and a great dollop of cream. A glass of cherry schnapps over fresh fruit for dessert. How different from my last ropey meal back in Boulogne! I imagined my round-faced university chums deliriously licking the plates clean and rolled happily into bed.

Breakfast was to be an even greater surprise. I was, in truth, shocked, almost angry, to see such an exotic spread of items that simply could not be obtained on a continent only starting to recover from six years of war and decades of poverty. Fresh pastries, slices of fresh meat and sausage, waffles, mountain cheese, bacon and eggs, yoghurt, and sausage from Gimmelwald, were all piled up to be consumed. I was torn: I wanted to try everything, maybe all at once, but I wanted to take it back to my family and friends, too. There in front of me was the tangible evidence of Swiss neutrality, the result of their refusal to do the decent thing and make the same sacrifice that every other country in Europe had. Everyone had lost family: Britain 450,000, France 560,000, Germany 9,000,000, Russia 24,000,000. The Swiss had lost no one at all. I felt sick and staggered off with a bowl of porridge. There had to be changes in the world.

In order to acclimatise, I did several high-level walks and then decided on a first climb of the Schwarzhorn. Apart from being a straightforward climb, it had the advantage of having a chairlift part of the way, so I soared upwards accompanied only by a milk churn, which did not speak to me. As we left the trees behind, the whole of the Oberland became visible. The great range of peaks, Schwarzhorn, Finsteraarhorn, Wetterhorn, Eiger, Mönch and Jungfrau, marched away, their faces sheer rock cliffs. Two glaciers provided the only way of reaching the isolated patches of snow and rock at dizzy heights. 'The ramparts of heaven' as they were called – one sinner found them very frightening indeed.

At 2928 metres, the Schwarzhorn is a challenging hike, which is only suitable for sure-footed climbers accustomed to the mountains. Navigating the uppermost part of the very steep climb is tricky and the ridge becomes narrow and needs extreme caution. A typical climb takes between five and six hours.

The route up the Schwarzhorn.

The climb of the Schwarzhorn went as planned, although I took my time. I was surprised by the amount of snow and ice still here sitting openly in the summer sun, a reminder that there was a darker side to this paradise perhaps, and every time I heard an avalanche echo across the valley I flinched, reminded of the roar of bombers overhead or the barking of artillery guns. The higher I climbed the more incredible the view became, but my eyes kept being wrenched back across the valley to that incredible dark wall that I had come to conquer. As the last clouds dissipated, the whole panorama was revealed in brilliant light. Nothing could equal it for stark grandeur, extent or severity. Civilisation had disappeared completely, mankind's presence a sudden irrelevance. On the way down my thoughts were full of revised ideas – that I should ever stand on top of the Eiger seemed impossible. The day after climbing the Schwarzhorn, it seemed even more unlikely!

The immaculately tended streets of Grindelwald quickly gave way to rough tracks. The trees closed in, and the sound of gushing water was everywhere. A narrow wooden bridge appeared over a spouting torrent that steamed as if it were boiling in the cold air. On the other bank, only the slightest track began the steep climb through the woods. It was dark and oppressive and, once away from the stream, heavily silent. Since leaving the village, I had seen no one. Now I listened to the thudding of my heart as I plodded on through the gloom, until, quite suddenly, the trees stopped, and I stepped out onto the grass slopes of a 'Little Alp'. Little specs of colour burst from the green carpet, some of which I recognised. Primroses, crocuses, forget-me-nots and of course edelweiss were everywhere, as if the mountain itself were overcome with the joys of life. It saddens me to think how most people these days only visit the mountains in winter, when they are at their least interesting and attractive. They miss out on so much.

Only a few hundred metres further up that life cut out immediately as I reached what they call the 'snow line'. A faint drizzle was falling, my face was wet as I looked up at the great wall of rock that confronted me. This was the 'small rocky shoulder' that I had seen from the other side of the valley. Now it looked enormous. The way up offered no problems, however, and the route was easy to find, marked as it was by the passage of countless nailed boots. An hour's slog brought me to the summit and I looked out onto the glacier. It sloped steeply upwards between great shoulders of black rock and disappeared into the grey towering clouds above. Its surface had twisted and warped into very strange shapes and was cracked into great crevices into which little waterfalls of rainwater fell. A fierce bitter wind blew straight down from the clouds, across the ice, making movement difficult and chilling the very bones.

It was an awful place and I was in no fit state to tackle it, least of all alone. But it was what I had come to see, something that I must cross if I were to conquer the Eiger, so I endeavoured to work out a route to cross it and make the short descent to the ice itself. There was no use in hesitating, and no obvious alternative, so I took a running jump and landed in the glacier. It was as if I had landed in another world. In the Alps, distances and sizes can be deceptive and it was true here. Once on the ice, all but the most prominent features disappeared. The brain was unable to process the images received from the eyes. I have been brought up to hide my emotions and especially my fears. I was already frightened of what I was doing – no unusual thing in the mountains – now I was even more so. I was frightened of the crevices with their cold deathly depths; frightened that the ice might suddenly collapse beneath me, frightened even of the ghostly slabs of the ice through the mist that was now closing down around me.

I tried to focus on the technical details of my axe and where I placed my feet. Suddenly I came to a vast patch of smooth, unbroken ice which was totally unexpected. As I stopped in perplexity, the wind, now unhindered, screamed with renewed force. The clouds lifted, slightly revealing that great wall of ice towering above me, stretching up and up until it met them. What little spirit I had left, fled. I cowered down in the snow, overwhelmed by a fear greater than I had ever known, greater than any fear I had felt in the war, even when strafed by German bombers. I am not proud of this, but is it not strange? I knew that the ice stretched away for over two miles, that it was in fairly good condition and that I was in little physical danger. I was not lost and I was well-equipped for such an excursion, yet all of this counted for nothing at all. I had dragged my own fear with me, through the dark forest, up the grey rock and out onto the glacier, where it had bloomed into terrible life.

The Greeks, of course, had a word for it. They called it 'Panic', the fear of Pan. This is not the same as the word we use to describe a general sense of mindless fright, but their great minds defining a fear of wild open space – the domain of Pan himself. When one is most utterly alone, then one is in the presence of the gods. I am not a religious man, but I recognise the phenomena in the natural world that caused our ancestors to create them, and I respect the views of others, even if I consider them to be 'heritage mythologies' myself. The phenomena themselves have not changed over the years and, moments like this where one's true insignificance in the scheme of things is briefly understood, are humbling indeed.

My next recollection is of lying face down in the soaking grass of the 'Little Alp' at the foot of the rock, surrounded by those colourful celebrations of life and being inspected by an instinctively motherly Alpine cow. I must have climbed down by instinct, a very dangerous activity. Far more climbers are killed on the way down than the way up. When the tremors receded, I continued downwards at great speed – it was almost a rout – and did not stop again until I was safely behind a hot chocolate and, I'm not ashamed to say, a horseshoe pastry, in the hotel restaurant.

Two days later, in brilliant sunshine, I looked down on that very same glacier from the crest of the range, as I accompanied a German party of climbers towards the opposite summit. My university chums and army pals would have been proud of me, certainly the way I would tell the story to them, missing out the embarrassing bits. It looked as pretty and innocent as any Alpine calendar picture I had seen before I left England. It had not changed; it was I that had changed. Quite how I wasn't sure, but I was sure of it. I had finally met the real Alps.

The Eiger

My plan was to ascend the west flank, not quickly, but without stopping. Stamina was more important than speed, caution and respect the key rather than technical expertise. Perhaps I could not have done it if I hadn't scared myself so much on the glacier. The rock was loose underfoot and covered only in a couple of centimetres of dry and powdery snow. It was not as complex as expected, nor as interesting, just an arduous task that my little group had set itself. The Germans were reserved, as you would expect, and especially cautious around me. There were noticeably few men in their group and those that there were, were of too great an age to have performed meaningful military service. They were men that had spent a lifetime working outside, their gnarled and sinewy limbs turned brown by the sun. They were, of course, meticulously polite.

I was unsure what to say to them, but equally aware that to say nothing was rude. Worse, they seemed to want me to 'take charge' of the expedition. Who did they think I was? Here to tell them how to climb their mountain? We introduced ourselves simply, just first names. Our pasts were unimportant that day, it only mattered what each could bring to the group going forward.

'My name is Gordon. I've not climbed this mountain before.'

'My name is Joseph. I'm a butcher. I've not climbed this route before.'

'My name is Pietr. I'm a shepherd. I've climbed the Eiger many times…'

I tied us together with fifty-foot lengths of rope, using the butterfly coil method, checking for any signs of damage as I did so. The tragic story of the first ascent of the Eiger was fresh in my mind.

The party of seven had successfully reached the top, but, on the way down, one of them had stumbled, crashing into the others and sweeping four of them off the side of the mountain. The rope snapped, saving the remaining three, but leading to years of recriminations. If one of us fell, the other two would hold them, that was the theory anyway.

All of Europe had just been through six years of war, where both sides had done horrific things. There are good and bad people in every walk of life and we have to assume that people do the best they can in their circumstance, based on what they know at a specific time. It is not for me to judge people I don't know, on the basis of things I'm not entirely sure about. Had Pietr and Joseph been members of the Nazi party? Almost certainly. Were they still right-wing fanatics? It wasn't any of my business. For that day, they were my team and I treated them as equals.

I told Pietr to act as lead climber, as he knew the route best and it was a little unclear halfway up. I volunteered myself as the third-place follower, giving myself the task of unclipping the anchors and stopping Joseph if he fell. He didn't look too heavy, but muscle weighs more than fat so you can't tell.

We talked about the weather, as Englishmen and people everywhere do when they don't want to talk about other more meaningful things and started our ascent. Joseph tapped the ground with his axe as if testing its tenderness.

We stopped only when we got to the summit and looked back down the ridge. Below, far below and to the right, the Grindelwald valley was thick with cloud, grey and motionless, but beneath our feet. By some trick of the wind the Lauterbrunnen valley looked like some vast cauldron, throwing streams of cloud almost level with us. Interlaken itself and the Plain of Thun were lost under a great white blanket with their highest points in the sun. It was the first and only time that I have seen clouds beneath my feet. We laughed, slapped each other on the backs and shook hands. It was not awkward but instinctive and heartfelt. Perhaps it was because I was giddy with success, or perhaps simply with a lack of oxygen, but in that moment, looking down on the world, I felt that we could rebuild and reengineer a better Europe, if we worked together with our brothers. There were no words, in any language, to describe the feeling.

We were getting cold, so we did not linger, but pushed on down to the other side to get out of the wind. Descent, as I've said, was the most dangerous part. In those few yards we entered a different world. Gone were the neat busy valleys full of life, gone the scudding clouds and the cold wind. Before us lay range after range of peaks and, between them, stretching almost to infinity was the Great Aletsch Glacier. There was only rock, ice and sky. Nothing living was there, no movement save that of our own. There was no wind and the heat reflected from the ice kept all but a few wisps of cloud away. But what was most strange for me was the total and utter silence. So extreme was it that one's own voice sounded flat and lost. I was embarrassed to use it. I had read of this in various travel books, but in Britain, even in the most desolate of placcs, it is never met; there is always something in the wind, birds, the fall of water, the rustle of grass. Here, in this frozen landscape, was utter stillness.

It is, like everything, relative. Avalanches rumble in the distance, rocks crack and tumble, even the glacier itself moves and groans. But, in our own insignificant timescale, all was still. The Germans instinctively made the sign of the cross. I have no god to believe in but gave the sky a respectful nod and touched my metaphorical cap.

The Aletsch Glacier.

With an area of 66 square miles, the Aletsch Glacier is the longest and largest glacier in Europe. At its source it is about 3,000 feet thick, reducing to 500 feet in the Rhone valley into which it eventually drains. Like all glaciers in Europe, it is estimated that it will have lost 90% of its volume by 2100.

The light, that clear blue-white light, was intense. It was reflected by the snow and ice that coated everything, but it was effectively a desert out there and more deadly than anything we had faced so far. My skin began to tingle and I understood that the old joke about getting sunstroke and frostbite at the same time was perfectly true. Beneath the summit and slopes of rock, the glacier appeared smooth, but who knew what bodies and other things lay trapped in its terrible grip?

Two miles down, at the junction of two great ice streams, lay 'Konkordiaplatz', named after the great square in Paris. I knew that there was a mountain hut at the junction, but could not see it, even with binoculars. The mountain behind me was already forgotten. All I could see was that vast, vast expanse of ice and that immense, brilliant sky.

Pietr nodded and so I decided to take the lead, forging a path for the two old men through the knee-deep snow. They were grateful. Speed was not important, but consistency was and, when we stopped, it needed to be below the snow line.

As I ploughed ahead, I slowly became aware of a ghostly voice echoing in the wind, a harsh German nasal voice that I had heard on the radio and on newsreels. It chilled me as much as the wind itself.

'Eins, zwo, eins, zwo, links, rechts, links, rechts...' almost marching. Perhaps Joseph had been a concentration camp guard, perhaps he was still a Nazi, but most likely he was just motivating his friend.

We made it back, still one team roped together, walking in unison. I invited them to dinner at the hotel and was happy to pay, or at least for a beer, but, once back in the village, they no longer felt that it was appropriate. We solemnly shook hands and then they disappeared as shadows sulking off into the night. Germans to be seen, but not heard.

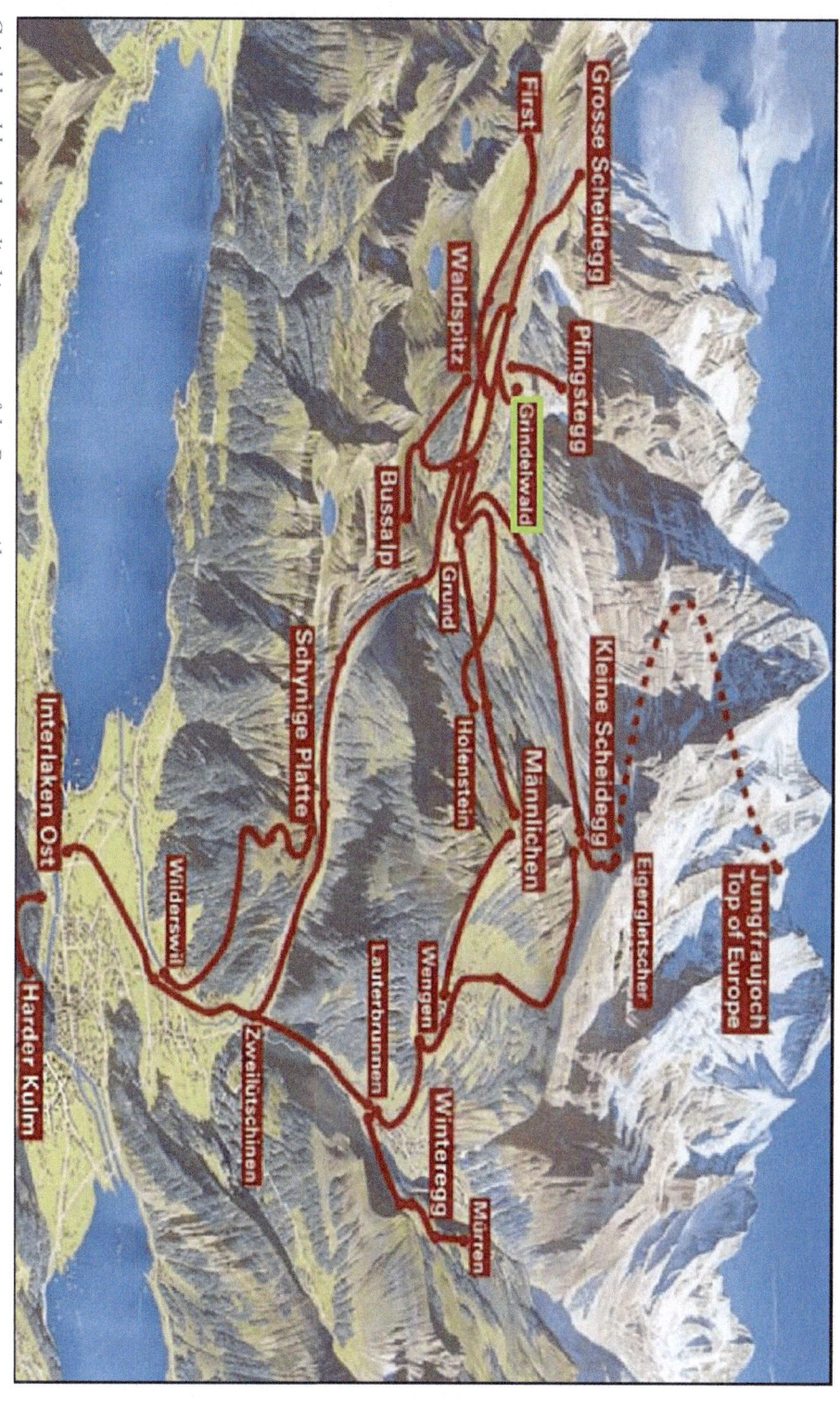

Grindelwald and the climbing routes of the Bernese Alps.

The fairy tale world that I encountered could not have been more different from war torn Bristol and I luxuriated in every moment. Every day I would get up early, keen not to waste any precious time here. Every day I would jealously eye up the outrageous selection of meat and cheeses at breakfast before helping myself to a modest bowl of porridge and heading out into the hills. Most of the peaks fell to me, the Mönch, the Grosse Scheidegg, the Augstmatthorn, Faulhorn etc., but, increasingly, I found myself hiking in the mountain air, in pastures above the treeline, filled with those wildflowers, rather than in the lifeless snow zone above it. It was more meaningful to be amongst the mountains, to be part of the scene, rather than on top of it looking down.

In the valleys, crystal clear streams bubbled from the ground and the gentle clanking of cow bells echoed off the rocks. They reminded me of my uncle's cows on his farm outside Bristol and, inevitably, I went over to talk to them.

Was there such a thing as Nazi cows or were cows just cows the world over? Hot breath gushed up my shirt sleeves and stiff whiskers scratched my palm. I had my answer. I scratched them behind the ears and handed over a piece of mint cake. I have always been a sucker for animals, we can learn a lot from them. And there, just like that, my desire to climb more mountains evaporated.

I suppose I had acquitted myself reasonably well for a first season, but I had originally drawn up a provisional list with a lot more targets for future years – the Matterhorn, Mont Blanc and many more. Perhaps I was content, perhaps I was too tired. Either way, I knew that I preferred to lie on my back in the field staring up at the mountain, mythological figures towering over me, to scrambling over rock. Being here was what I wanted. Not fighting it.

My money, and therefore my time here had virtually run out. It was time to go home but having suddenly lost my desire to conquer Europe's great peaks I was at a loss as to what I should plan for next. I brooded on this in the hotel grounds for a while. As always, I took my little Moka coffee pot and sat out in the sun to think. Switzerland had been like a dream, but it had also been a shock. The truth is, when faced with such an intensity of beauty, magnificence and scale of nature, we realise our own insignificance – and that is no bad thing. Indeed it is profoundly relaxing.

I realised that I was climbing mountains, not to be amongst them, or to witness their grandeur and scale, but simply as an intellectual and physical challenge. It had helped me to forget my friends from university, but my eyes had now been opened. Suddenly, nothing was more important than seeing Europe, being in places that I knew only intellectually, experiencing Europe for myself, understanding it. It was a continent that we had spent not just six years fighting over, but two thousand years at least. It was why I existed, it was who I was, but I knew hardly anything about it at all. I had to see it for myself, if anything was to make sense to me. Not just visiting the mountains, which I would do again in Austria, Spain and Germany, not just the lakes and the tourist spots kept clean by the wealthy, but all of it, or as much of it as a man of my limited means could manage to see in whatever time I had left to me.

With a heavy heart, I handed over most of my climbing gear to charity at the hotel and paid one final visit to the breakfast buffet. I am not ashamed to say that I veritably filled my pockets with a smorgasbord of meat and cheese for the long trip before boarding the train.

View-Master™ Reel (Switzerland)

HOLLAND

The Same as What You Had Before – But Better, 1954

My next venture was in every way a complete contrast to my first. While my trip to Switzerland had been more than a little extravagant, Holland was as prosaic as could be. I simply went to stay with an old army pal from the Signals Corps who had got a job with Philips and married a Dutch girl. At least that's how I explained it to my parents who disapproved of the notion of holidays having never really experienced them themselves. My chum had just moved into a new apartment on the outskirts of Rotterdam, which both he and his wife were fantastically proud of, Rotterdam in general being a fairly mundane place. You will laugh, I'm sure, but back then modern kitchen appliances like fridges, private bathrooms and indoor toilets were wonderous novelties. Their apartment was more like a luxury hotel suite than a working man's house and surely worth taking a short trip to see. I was happy for them.

The crossing from Harwich was one of the best bits of the expedition, such a marked contrast from the crossing from Dover to Boulogne a year before. The day was brilliant, the sea a flat calm and the ship, the Batavier 2, a Dutch vessel, was brand new. Lunch was served onboard the restaurant, an especially memorable East Indian service with delicious onion bhajis and pickles accompanying the main dish. Even the rice had a spicy tang about it and a colour that matched the sun. There was a massive, glorious salmon, too, and cucumber with a taste so strong and sweet that I wondered if it was another vegetable entirely. The passengers were so few in number that the whole thing seemed more like a luxury cruise than a channel crossing. I sat outside with the seagulls and watched the foaming ripples of our wake gently fold back on themselves into the cadmium green waters.

Despite the dangers, there is something deeply compelling about the sea. We are somehow incomplete without it as if our bodies remember something of their earlier forms. There is something primaeval about it that is hard-wired into us, a need for adventure, a source of food, a trade route, a common border, a village green of sorts between our homes. I cannot really imagine life without it. We are, of course, a maritime nation and the Dutch, perhaps, even more so than we.

They say that "God built the world, but the Dutch made Holland" and you can certainly see why. The Dutch are a tough seafaring nation and almost all of their flat featureless landscape has been reclaimed from the sea by them over the centuries. It must have been unimaginably hard physical work that undoubtedly required specialist skills and cost many lives. But the Dutch knuckled down to their seemingly impossible task, because they believed in a better future for their children. In the same way, the citizens of Rotterdam slowly got on with the huge task of rebuilding after the war. It seems a combination of behaviours central to a pragmatic Dutch way of thinking that I had to admire.

Ever since Bronze Age times, people have lived and hunted in the everchanging landscape of rivers and saltwater marshes of the Netherlands, but it was only with the Viking invasion of Britain that the North Sea became an inner communal sea with shared kingdoms on each side, and, therefore, only then that this coastline became a viable trading centre, a place where ports and cities would be built, collecting goods from Europe's rivers. In a way, the Viking Invasion of Britain caused Holland to be 'created'.

Holland itself appeared as a flat, grey smudge on the horizon and remained little more than that until we were almost in harbour. Such a contrast to the colourful mountainous landscape of Switzerland. I knew the land was 'flat' of course, and although I had no expectations, I confess I was a little disappointed. A motorway of sorts ran along the top of the breakwater, wide open and flat like the land behind it. Pools of muddy sand, full of twisted metal shards, accumulated on both sides. There were few structures of any sort to see breaking the monotonous and monochrome skyline, no church towers and hardly any trees. I wondered what kind of a wasteland it was that I was approaching.

Like Switzerland, Holland had declared itself neutral at the start of the war, but, unlike the sunny mountain playground, the Netherlands were strategically and industrially important to the Germans, so the neutrality had been distinctly one-sided. On the 14th May 1940, the city of Rotterdam was targeted by the Luftwaffe. Indiscriminate bombing by 90 Heinkel bombers caused significant damage to the city, which was made even worse by the fires that followed the initial attack. A strong wind caused them to spread to areas of the city that had not been directly hit. The docks and factories were ruined, over 25,000 houses were destroyed, and 638 acres of the city were left devastated. The Netherlands surrendered the next day. The threat of similar levels of devastation on other Dutch cities was the primary reason for the rapid capitulation. Nazi occupation until the end of the war in 1945 prevented any significant reconstruction.

Fourteen years after the Germans attempted to 'wipe it off the map', the Dutch were only beginning to rebuild the city, but instead of simply replacing what was there before or adapting old styles, they were bravely setting out down a modernist path, building with modern material and designs around planned civic principles with more open streets and open spaces. Rotterdam had been a busy mediaeval trading port, with winding lanes, ancient churches, warehouses and great buildings shaped like the ships that came and went. Its growth had been funded by spices from Indonesia, furs from Canada and the Baltic as well as the colonies in the New World. It had been the home of one of the most profitable overseas empires the world has ever seen. But all of that had gone. Now marram grass grew amongst piles of smoking rubble and sand blew over the surface of burnt cobbled streets, as large tracts of what had once been the old city centre became empty building land. The level of destruction was so great that the decision was taken to clear the city centre rather than rebuild the ruins that remained. I wonder if I would have been as bold or as pragmatic when making such a decision. I hope so; most likely the Dutch had no choice.

Central Rotterdam after the rubble was cleared. (1954)

There was little of architectural or cultural interest left of Rotterdam. I was keen to see Zadkine's evocative bronze statue of the 'Destroyed City', which had been recently unveiled. The large bronze statue is of a giant whose heart has been torn out, crying in pain. But for me it was thought provoking, rather than emotion provoking, and hard to connect to the visceral images of smouldering wreckage and terror that I had experienced in Bristol during the Blitz.

Zadkine's 'Destroyed City'

With no high art to distract me, I became fascinated by the details of the work going on all around me, the humdrum and the mundane. I was enthralled by the rapid engineering techniques being used to erect the steel frame and prefabricated buildings, such as my friend's apartment, that were going up all over the city. I understood the numbers and how weight was distributed through the structures, but, even so, the sheer speed of the build managed to surprise me. Suddenly I could see for myself how efficient modern property could be bulk manufactured in factories as an affordable commodity for the masses rather than impossibly expensive assets privately passed down through generations of the landed wealthy. It provided me with a vision for the future that was hugely exciting.

In the centre of the Hofplein a new railway station was being built, but, instead of taking up space in the centre of the city, the Dutch had decided to build it under the existing railway lines. As a result, the trains that continued to arrive were raised up on flimsy looking scaffolding and the passengers had to scramble up a series of temporary wooden steps and ladders from the subterranean station to reach them. It looked very Heath Robinson! The Dutch it seemed, were using the tragedy of the war as an opportunity to change things for the better. It sounds like an obvious thing to do, but it was almost the opposite of Britain's attitude at the time.

Right opposite the future station stood the new Lijnbaan, Europe's first pedestrian shopping precinct, which had just opened to much applause, and I decided to take a look at what was grandiosely described by architecture magazines everywhere as 'a living room for a city'. At the gate it was more modestly labelled by the Dutch themselves as: 'The same as what you had before but better!'. Despite having no interest in shopping, I wandered around there for some time comparing it with the Victorian era arcades and large department stores that I was more familiar with. It was a pleasant enough place to spend a few hours, clad in light coloured mosaics with bubbling fountains and young trees in earthenware pots; an Islamic courtyard for the modern era perhaps? Arcades like the one in Bath were designed in the nineteenth century to give women a safe place to spend the day shopping, taking tea and gossiping as they browsed the goods on display. The Lijnbaan, by contrast, was clearly intended for the entire family with rides and games for children built in. For me it could not compare to Bath's narrow lanes, but it was undoubtedly an efficient way of shopping, an oasis of calm and a safe space, full of people with young children, as everywhere in Holland seemed to be.

The newly opened Lijnbaan centre in 1954.

The Lijnbaan was built in the ruins of central Rotterdam after the total destruction of the old shopping district during the war. The car-free zone was felt to be a 'luxurious oasis for families built on an open wound'. Shopkeepers were sceptical that people would want to shop in an area that they couldn't reach by car, but shopkeepers were wrong…

A series of yellow and black buses were disgorging their confused and excited passengers out onto the pavement. They were parked nose to tail all along the Hofplein as if hogging the Lijnbaan for themselves, and left nowhere for the sleek new red trams to pull in. People came from all over the country, all of them dressed in their finest and all of them in family groups. Figures, dressed mostly in shades of brown, with long woollen coats and dark hats walked arm in arm through the precinct staring up in wonder at the mannequins guarding the brightly lit windows of the Filia fashion house. I was as surprised as any by Filia's colourful vision of the future, but I couldn't help feeling that for most of the amazed faces around me such a transformation would be as difficult a task as asking the Dutch countryside itself to look more   like Switzerland.

At the centre of the Lijnbaan was an exhibition showing how the Maas Tunnel, which connects both sides of the city, had been built under the river. It was not a topic I had any interest in, but anything can be made interesting with the help of an enthusiastic enough guide. My guide was a loudspeaker with a clipped British accent, whose received pronunciation crackled forth every time a lit button was pressed. I am unsure what I feel about out of work Thespians replacing local guides, but it is I am sure a typically sensible and commercially sound solution, doubtless as much a feature of the future as shopping precincts like the Lijnbaan. According to my tinny and slightly pompous guide, the soil, as with all soil in the Netherlands, was too waterlogged and sandy for any normal type of tunnel construction, so instead, the river had been diverted, a trench dug and the tunnel itself constructed on the surface and simply 'dropped' into place. It was a splendidly pragmatic and typically Dutch solution that must have sounded insane at the time. They got on with it anyway, as the Dutch do, and now it is here.

There were many plaques remembering the fallen members of the Dutch Resistance in the city, but they were all modest affairs, simple statements of fact, rather than great outpourings of grief. In Holland, the local Communist Party led the Resistance. Over one-hundred-and-fifty-thousand members of the 'Verzet', or 'Opposition' as they were called, were executed during the war. The Maas Tunnel had been packed with explosives by the Germans when they finally pulled out, but Rotterdam's citizens crawled through barbed wire and pools of water in pitch blackness to defuse the bombs. At the time of writing approximately seventy-five-thousand vehicles a day now use the tunnel, which on reflection is probably the most poignant and uniquely Dutch memorial of them all.

In the summer of nineteen-fifty-four, Rotterdam still lay in absolute ruins. I, who had lived through the Bristol Blitz, had never seen such devastation and imagined its residents would experience decades of grief and anguish. But as I walked reverently through the desolate remains of this once great city, I saw that that was not the case. Amongst the rubble and the marram grass it was very much "business as usual" for the formidable residents of this vibrant and uncrushable city. Somehow the Dutch had already moved on from the war in a way that we wouldn't for decades. They had fought off the North Sea and rebuilt their city numerous times, they would shake off the Germans like the droplets of rain that clung to their overcoats. Rotterdam had put the war behind it and was already getting on with the future in that typical Dutch no-nonsense way. It was both enlightening and inspiring to see.

A street sign in ruined Rotterdam.

I hope my host won't be offended if I tell you that breakfast was not up to the standard of the Hotel Bellevue. It consisted of slices of dry brown bread, a pot of jam and slices of a rubbery cheese. Lunch was a portable version of the same with the occasional addition of salted herring. The modest seafaring life was ingrained in their souls. Generations of Dutchmen had put to sea eating the same. It had been good enough for them to change the world, it was more than good enough for me!

Unlike Rotterdam, which was almost entirely destroyed in the war, the city of Delft had survived fairly intact, presenting the best of what any tourist would want from Holland – humpback bridges, peaceful, cobbled lanes and quiet canals. It looked like the world as painted by Vermeer.

The quiet canals of Delft unchanged since my father visited.

It is easy to think that the Holland of modern Rotterdam and old Delft are different places, that one is somehow 'right' or 'traditional' and that the other is 'wrong', even 'barbarous'. But you have to remember that Delft was a modern city once, too, its canals were not intended as the quiet setting for a peaceful café or a genteel bookshop; instead they were the highways of heavy industry, bringing coal and vital raw materials to the myriad workshops that lined its banks. The workshops have become houses and apartments, but the factories are still there although they are hidden away now.

Delft and neighbouring Leiden are famous for making precision lenses. The world's first microscope was made in the city four hundred years ago, the very first telescope in 1608, and binoculars made in their factories were extensively used by both the Allies and Axis powers during the war.

Schoolchildren in Dordrecht.

Dordrecht lies just off the Expressway between Amsterdam and Brussels. The new electric trains that scream through the countryside pass the little town by. You could easily not notice it at all. The great canal, that brought it so much trade before either the motorway or the rail network existed, was closed for major repair work, but here, behind the mountains of aggregate and piles of construction material the old quarter remained, almost untouched by the war. Here too were the famous vistas of merchant houses as painted by Vermeer, Vrel, Van Der Neer and many others. Here were the old markets with lace makers and pyramids of neatly stacked cheese. It appeared not to have changed at all in three-hundred years, and yet it was not stuck in the past. Once again, the cobbled streets were flooded with groups of young children. For the children, the canal was a playground, the building sites their home. A new generation of entrepreneurs and engineers was already growing up, with no personal memory of the war. For me, that was exciting. I was very keen to meet them.

While I was staying with my friends, I briefly visited other parts of Holland by bus or train. Tilburg, the wool capital of the world, with its twin spired Heuvelse Kirk that dominates the market and was funded by the multinational corporations of the seventeenth century. Industrial Eindhoven with its huge Philips factory that does exactly the same thing today. The Germans were said to have liked the work ethic of the Dutch. It didn't do them much good, but it's hard to disagree with their observations. I visited Haarlem with its incredible sunset over the empty grass dunes and the twin resorts of Scheveningen and Egmont, one big and sophisticated, the other small and quiet, but both sharing the same beach and the same bitter wind. Alkmaar turned out to be a delightful surprise with its cheerful cheese market that reminded me so much of Frome back in Somerset, where my uncles sold theirs. I wondered why, with so many excellent cheeses on sale, I had been eating such tasteless fare for breakfast and compensated for it by buying more goats' cheese than I could have eaten all week!

And so, to Amsterdam. I must be careful here. Everyone I met was friendly and helpful – a most unusual thing in a capital city – and I saw many glorious things, but, for some reason, I did not care for the overall result. It was probably because it seemed incredibly crowded, busy and noisy. Holland is the most densely populated country in Europe and Amsterdam is, of course, the most densely populated part of that. The city was never supposed to be historic or twee, it was, and still is, a major trading hub. Dirty, chaotic and loud, as, perhaps, it should be.

The Rijksmuseum had been top of my list of places to visit, an ugly word in Dutch for an ugly and very un-Dutch concept. The museum is the centre of Dutch art and culture, home to nearly eight thousand famous paintings. It should have been the highlight of my trip but for some reason my heart wasn't really in it; the paintings themselves I could see in a book and many of them I already had. The museum looked to me just like a London railway station and felt very much the same way too. Visitors marched grimly from gallery to gallery, finally coming to rest before the 'Night Watch', Rembrandt's colossal masterpiece. I was not impressed. What did it show with its empty imagery except the artist's mastery of light and his sponsor's face transposed onto a character from fiction? What was the message here? Really it was little better than billboard advertising. I found the 'Five Little Vermeers', tucked away in a small side gallery, much more satisfying.

Vermeer's 'Little Street'.

Vermeer's "Little Street" is a small painting, just 50cm by 40cm. The artist painted it in 1657 and it shows daily life in the area of Voldersgracht, where he grew up. It is one of the five scenes my father mentions above. The pictures are notable for their realism and they represent one of the first times that advanced perspective and lighting techniques were used in non-religious, non-sponsored art. Art for the common man, with the common man as the subject.

The only thing I really enjoyed in Amsterdam was a canal trip. Sleek, white, fibre-glass boats with panoramic glass roofs ran from the centre of the city, through the mediaeval part under incredibly low bridges. I instinctively ducked down each time we passed into the shadow. I confess the little boy in me wanted to shout out and listen to the echo. The mad chaos of people streaming around me on the street instantly dissipated. Something about being on the water felt inherently right. It felt somehow like home.

A modern canal tour of Amsterdam.

From this low angle, even the most familiar facades seemed strange and exciting. The boat dropped us off at the harbour where the great sides of ships from the Holland–America line, such as the HMS Oranje, towered high above us. It was a fitting reminder that it was upon international trade, economic cooperation, and water that Holland's past and future wealth would be built.

A mixture of boats and ships in Amsterdam's harbour (1954).

The early fifties were a time of mass emigration from Holland with high levels of unemployment and food shortages. With no money to support the colonies, the Dutch East Indies gained their independence in 1949, leaving more people to wander the streets looking for work. Large numbers of Netherlanders left for America in ships such as the Oranje from the port of Amsterdam.

On the way home I stopped off in The Hague. It was the part of Holland that I liked best of all. It somehow had the balance between Delft and Rotterdam right, between the pragmatic and the romantic. It was spacious and cheerful, with old and new mingled together in happy unity. It had the mediaeval Knights' Hall and crumbling old city walls mixed in with modernist shopping malls, quiet squares where bric-a-brac and books were set out on stalls and tree-lined avenues with the ubiquitous trams that simply didn't exist anymore in England. It also had the 'Mauritshuis', one of the loveliest art galleries I had ever visited.

The 'Mauritshuis' museum from the Hofvijer Lake.

I sat under the trees by the side of the Hofvijver lake, looking back at the reflections of the Dutch parliament buildings and the Mauritshuis, from which I had just come, in the water. It is extraordinary, even to an Englishman, to see how ingrained the water is in these people's lives.

Dutch children playing on the Amsterdam waterfront.

I was drinking coffee, which was unlike any 'coffee' that I had ever drunk in England. It was made in a large pot, like a samovar, that continuously made plopping sounds as it cycled nearly-boiling water through the coffee grounds. The Dutch have been importing coffee eleven thousand miles from Indonesia since the mid-eighteenth century. I can see why, but the logistics involved in the enterprise are mind-boggling. Unlike their British cousins, the Dutch never managed to convert their trading empire into a colonial Empire; their hearts were never truly in it. They are equally enthusiastic about the former and completely disinterested in the latter.

The Dutch transplanted coffee plant seedlings from Yemen to Jakarta in 1696, the Dutch East India Company first exporting coffee back to Europe in 1711. In the 18th century, coffee shipped from Jakarta sold for 3 guilders per kilogram in Amsterdam. This is equivalent to several hundred dollars per kilogram today.

You may think that having gushed over Switzerland and dismissed cities in the Netherlands in just a few words, that I did not enjoy my trip here as much. If so, then you'd be quite wrong. Switzerland was a fairy tale mountainous world, incomparable in almost every way to anywhere I'd been, with a lifestyle almost incomprehensible to someone from wartime Bristol. Holland was, by complete contrast flat, grey, ordinary, mundane, almost utilitarian, but it was easy for me to relate to, relevant to everyday life, in a way that the unreal, abstract beauty of Switzerland wasn't, and all the more inspiring for it.

The Dutch do not worry that their buildings sit, quite literally, in the water, below the level of the sea. They are not overcome by grief at the utter destruction of cities like Rotterdam or wedded to the idea that everything should be reconstructed as it was before. They have moved on in a way that we wouldn't do for decades. The desire to modestly knuckle down to work, make the best of a tough deal, to rebuild and move on is fundamental to who they are. Their goal, simply, is as the Lijnbaan so eloquently puts it, to give their citizens 'The same as what they had before, but better'. It is a noble thing that all of us should aim for.

The new generation of Netherlanders that fill the street with laughter have no comprehension of what war was like, but they already understand their mission and know that they must achieve it through international cooperation and hard work. It is lovely to see a nation so similar to ours, that is focused on the future rather than the past. We are lucky to have them in our great European family and we can learn a lot from them.

Learning from each other: Bath's original Southgate Centre.

View-Master™ Reel (Holland)

BELGIUM & WESTERN GERMANY

A Shared Loss, 1954

I left Amsterdam on one of the new express services to Brussels. It was a train unlike any other I had seen before and was known as a 'Dog's Head' due to the shape of its 'nose'.

Even though I understood perfectly well how the vehicle worked, it felt peculiar to be sitting in a space where I felt the engine should be and I worried if the motors attached to the axles really could have enough power to pull it. I need not have been concerned; the little dog sprinted all the way to Brussels in just two and a half hours. It all seemed centuries away from the filthy train I had caught from London to Dover, but I have said that I shall try and remain unpolitical in these notes.

An NS Mat '54 'Hondekop' TF2 Leaving Amsterdam in 1955.

I had a splendid dinner at the Atlanta Hotel, where scruffiness and luxury were curiously combined in a way that is a speciality of civil service departments the world over. Much to my shame, it was a combination that felt rather comfortable on me. I would perhaps have made a good back-office administrator in another life. This bureaucratic mix was something that I was to see as a trend for Brussels as a whole. I know that I enjoyed my stay, although few real memories come to mind. It was historic, but fashionable, mundane and bizarre, self-confident but not showy. It was somewhere to enjoy being in, rather than to visit.

The guildhalls of Grand Place in Brussels.

The Grand Palace stands out, as of course it must, with its superb old mansions in the town square as painted by Breugels. At night the whole facade glowed gold, more 'house of kings' than 'old bread house'! I tipped my cap to St. Nicholas, the patron saint of blacksmiths, armourers, gunsmiths, stonemasons and many more, at the wonderful guildhalls with their fine ionic columns and gilded windows. They hid the darker side of their history well. But there was no time to explore them as I had to press on to my main goal.

Germany

Europe means many things: the Romans, Christianity, the Renaissance etc., but absolutely central to the concept of Europe, arguably more than anything else, is the memory of the Holy Roman Empire and central to the idea of that, is the country that had dominated everything in Europe since 1939. Germany. There is no image of the concept of Europe that does not have Germany, or to be more accurate, Germans, at its very heart. Yet after two world wars, we had all had more than enough of it, and as I had seen in Switzerland, Germans were trying not to be seen. Both my uncles had been injured in the Great War and my father badly gassed. He remained ill for the rest of his life. In the second, I myself had been strafed by German bombers and had my city torn apart. So, Germany sat there in everyone's life, like a cancer, impossible to deal with, impossible to ignore. I was to tackle it head on, but had no idea what I would find, or how I would I react to whatever it was.

It was therefore with great trepidation that I crossed the frontier with Germany at Roermond in the early morning. It was pouring with rain which both my fellow travellers and I took as an omen. I was apprehensive, saturated by years of propaganda and mistrust. A red and white barrier blocked the way, tank traps beside the road. Long radio aerials flapped in the wind above concrete machine gun posts. A knot formed in the pit of my stomach as I spotted the angry muzzles of the Browning poking over the sandbags. Frontier guards with sub-machine guns immediately challenged my misconceptions, but, apart from the colour, their jackets and coal-scuttle helmets were unchanged from those worn during the war. It was difficult to stay open-minded. I forced a smile and handed my papers over. Soldiers like papers. The guard couldn't help clicking his heels, it was too ingrained, but much to my surprise, he smiled and took off his cap.

'Welcome to Germany,' he said enthusiastically. 'We are delighted that you visited. I hope your stay is satisfying. The weather makes you feel at home perhaps?' I couldn't help but laugh. It is interesting to see how for people everywhere the weather is a topic to fill gaps in conversation and I realised, that however awkward it was for me, it must have been much more so for him. I thanked him back and told him how pleased I was to have the opportunity to visit. I only realised after I said it that it was true.

The weather soon cleared, and the sun came out. I spent a curious day riding around the Eifel region, a strange area of small, wooded hills that were once volcanic. We crossed small rivers in steep, wooded valleys many times, discovering small country towns that clustered around their identical churches. Even the Germans admit that the area is somewhat wayward. Many of the little towns were unchanged from mediaeval times, a single, cobbled street that doubled as a marketplace, that could be closed off at either end by a fortified gate. Woodcutting factories with huge tree trunks stacked up outside invariably marked both ends of the conurbation. Villagers tended vines in the hills above. It was impossible to reconcile this gentle, still mediaeval, rural world with the screaming hyperbole of Hitler's speeches and the images of Panzer tanks and Heinkel bombers that sprang unbidden into my mind.

Monschau, a typical town in the Eifel.

The Eifel River is a tributary of the Mosel, which, in turn, is a tributary of the Rhine. Rivers have always formed the basis of

Europe's economy and it was along Germany's rivers that culture, laws and religions spread. We followed it too.

The rocking motion of the coach as it negotiated the twisted forest roads and zigzagged over little streams, combined with the small text of my 1926 Baedeker guide, was making me sleepy. One identical little town after another passed the window so when Bonn shattered the tranquility of the landscape, I was quite disconcerted.

Like Bath, Bonn is a Roman city. It was a sleepy rural backwater, but once it had housed the largest Roman garrison north of the Alps, commanding the river Rhine. It was the capital of Westphalia and seat of the Archdiocese of Cologne until the sixteenth century, after which Bonn's importance declined dramatically; something that spared it from Cologne's fate during the war.

Station Plaza, Bonn 1955.

The nineteenth century guesthouses surrounding the station had hastily been restored to a functional status, but in the main Bonn looked grey and tired, a hotchpotch of old and crumbling buildings, bombed-out ruins and new concrete structures with some, still to be defined, utilitarian purpose. It was yet to develop the suburban gardens and feeling of a political enclave that it acquired later. There were parks where people walked dogs, heads down against the wind, and where children could exercise, but they were not the sort of place you would want to linger or take in the views. Workmen in blue overalls were everywhere, grabbing a bite at the little wooden kiosks that lined the street, hot food with a high protein count but very little taste. A wide grey river, full of barges, crept past the otherwise nondescript town, passing under rain-soaked, concrete bridges with new steel spans in them. An American correspondent described Bonn as being 'half the size of a Chicago cemetery and twice as dead'. It was hard to believe that this almost forgotten, and quite ugly provincial place, had been made their new capital.

The locals were taking the job of making their town a capital city very seriously, as Germans everywhere tend to take most things. Despite that, there was none of the energy or enthusiasm that I had seen on the streets of Holland. No sense of excitement or building for the future.

Just as in Holland, young children were everywhere, but here they played quietly, seriously, as if being watched at all times. Like their Dutch siblings they had no memory of the war itself, but here they were being forced to learn about every terrible detail and Germany's guilt.

Children of the Rubble Women, Bonn 1954.

To the Allies, Bonn's position on the Rhine allowed military forces to penetrate deep into the German heartland; it gave the city a strategic importance that it simply did not have to the Germans. The Americans were determined to grab it and keep it as a method of controlling Germany after the war. They didn't just occupy the city when they got there, they took over running every aspect of it. Every factory was given new managers from the U.S., the police and judicial system were run by Americans, even schools and libraries had to have an auditor from the U.S. Coca-Cola, Lucky Strike cigarettes and American Pilsner were given away for free at US barracks. Hearts and minds were not just won here but overwhelmed. The American military became a surrogate father for the city and a generation of West Germans were actively Americanised, exaggerating, if not triggering, an equivalent reaction in East Germany.

The Germans have the word "Vergangenheits-bewältigung", which means something like "the struggle to deal with the past". Unlike the Dutch children happily growing up just over the border, the next generation of Germans were deliberately created with a crushing sense of guilt programmed into them. They were constantly lectured in the failings of their parents and gratuitously exposed to every crime. It was built into every aspect of the school curriculum from the age of five upwards and into many social and community events. Even the churches developed a particular form of atonement based on the need for continual repentance for wartime sins and dined out well on it. Post-War generations inherited a world where they were inherently both guilty, by association, and abandoned. The result was a terrible crippling neurosis, which doubtless achieved its purpose, but continues to cause significant problems internationally to this day. Seventy-five years later, Germany is still unsure what to do or how to behave on the world stage.

Beethoven's house is a small, rose-pink merchant's building in a narrow lane near the old town hall. It stands behind a small dark marketplace which was piled high with string bags of onions and cabbages. The home of the famous composer had been a museum since 1889, but there was nothing at all inside it when I visited. I got no sense of the man himself and could not see how such a dismal place had inspired anything except a trip somewhere else. With nothing to see in the rooms themselves I stared back at the sullen queues of women queuing silently with their ration cards for vegetables. The amount of calories a family was allocated was inversely proportional to their status under National Socialism. Victims received the most rations, ordinary families an acceptable amount, those in positions of responsibility or those identified as Nazis received less than the minimum needed to sustain life. It was understandable, but it also felt vindictive, and the wrong way to start building for the future. I felt sure that such policies could only encourage crime and black-market profiteering, especially with so many Americans washing about the place with so much. I left the town quickly.

Beethoven's house in Bonn.

Just across the river from Bonn sits Koenigswater, a nineteenth century summer resort famed for its walking routes through the Drachenfels hills. The names conjure images from ancient myths, but sadly the reality is that both the resort and the hills were named after Wagner's Ring Cycle in the last century, partly to increase tourism from England. Although I find Wagner's music to be exceptionally moving and his dramas unmatched, too much of it leaves me with the kind of indigestion I get from eating too much Black Forest Gateau. For me it also inevitably brings with it a slightly unpleasant aftertaste; something that my eldest son, a Wagner buff but not a fanatic, does not experience, unencumbered as he is by the 'cultural baggage' of my era.

Despite the heavy rain, I took the rack and pinion railway up the mountain to Castle Drachenburg, the Dragon's Castle; a much easier way of travelling than my trek up the Jungfrau the previous year. Remote and mysterious, the castle sat surrounded by mist, birds the only customers queuing up outside its empty café. I purchased something called currywurst more out of pity for the vendor than hunger, and instantly regretted it. A steamed pork sausage served with a spicy ketchup and chips. It was food invented by an enterprising housewife for occupying soldiers and every aspect of it was deeply unsatisfactory. I couldn't imagine a less German food. I walked over to the old castle that was neither old nor a castle, which had a large plaque on the door that I read, mistakenly thinking that it would be an informative note for tourists. Instead, it was a curt reminder that the Catholic Order of Christian brothers had been in constant conflict with the Nazi party, leading to the castle's closure in 1940. This was a statement that rang hollow, with me at any rate.

I sauntered back to the schnellimbiss stand to wait for the return train with my half-eaten currywurst in my hand. I stared out at the unbroken woods of the seven hills that disappeared off into the grey clouds. Beneath me great barges churned their way down the busy river as they had for hundreds of years. Perhaps some were headed towards Holland, perhaps some laden with goods bound for England. There was something curiously moving and deeply sad about the whole scene. Eighty-million people, three percent of the entire world's population, had died in the war; every single family had suffered horribly and for what? For nothing. To set the clock

59

back to how it was centuries before. We have to actively change the world for the better if such loss is to count towards anything. I was not sure that the quiet conversations that were happening behind Bonn's newly polished doors was the kind of change that Europe needed. I was thinking bigger.

As for the Germans themselves? A sorry lot they seemed so far. Quiet, sullen, overcome with both confusion and guilt, worn out, worn down, lost. I had seen nobody that even vaguely looked or acted like Aryans from a master race. Most were stocky round-faced peasants with brown or black hair, and I wondered how the Nazis ever thought their mythology would take root here. Should we let the behaviour of a military regime that governed, no, dictated, for only twelve years redefine the way we see a country with an established culture built up over two-thousand years? Did Bouhler wipe out Beethoven? Did Göring wipe out Goethe?

I was sure that science dictated that the answer was no, but it was too big an ask for me right then. Permission could be given with an open mind, tolerance and even trust could be a default, but forgiveness? That would take a significant period of time working together in partnership.

I felt sick, deeply sick, so I threw the currywurst in the bin, unbuttoned my jacket and started walking down the hill, letting the rain wash my thoughts and any residual anger away. I can't believe that Bonn will remain their capital for long. It's degrading, open to corruption and doesn't solve anything.

Just three hours march north from Bonn for a Roman Legion, lies the city of 'Colonia Agrippina', or Cologne as it is known today, named as it is after the wife of the emperor Claudius. It was, two-thousand years ago, the capital of 'Germania Inferior', a large and wealthy trading city, hence it was from here that many of the Roman forces that invaded Britain actually came. I am very fond of the Romans, as you will see, and in Bath you are constantly surrounded by them. You could argue that Bath owes its existence to the ancient soldiers of Cologne, another Roman spa town. It is a surprisingly small world.

Sustained allied bombing destroyed ninety percent of Cologne. Most of it was done by the RAF. It was never a particularly strategic target, and certainly not after the first few years of flattening its factories and railyards. British actions here are officially listed as a war crime, but who these days is keeping score? A city of over eight-hundred-thousand people was reduced to just ten thousand. More than five thousand residents died in the attack on just the night of 30th May 1942 alone. It was not by any means our finest hour. I cannot help but feel that the British in particular have no right to judge others on their behaviour in any war, or to ever take the moral high ground.

The shocking ruins of Cologne following British bombing (1946).

Nine years on, huge sections of its steel railway bridge still lay in the water, derelict buildings stood everywhere, often with makeshift stalls set out in their burnt-out interiors. It reminded me of Bristol after the Blitz and was far worse than Rotterdam. The pungent stench of powdered brick and plaster, leaking gas mains and scorched wood was everywhere as if the disease of war was barely being treated, let alone recovery underway. New buildings were going up and the sky was full of yellow cranes, but very few of the tower blocks had been completed. The roads had been levelled, but what may have been left of the pavements were buried beneath the heaps of rubble that had simply been pushed to the sides. Above the endless scenes of devastation rose, gaunt and black, the cathedral itself. Its two great spires were chipped and cracked, but still intact, the chancel untouched. The nave was roofless but otherwise sound. It was impossible not to take it as some kind of divine comment, but saying what exactly? It could easily have been as satanic as heavenly. I didn't know, but I found myself wanting to somehow keep the cathedral as it was in that very instant, a memorial to the horror of war. My mind suddenly filled with exotic concepts such as invisible support buttresses, plastic cladding and glass roofs. Wouldn't that be so much better than Zadkine's bronze statue in Rotterdam? A monument of a fitting scale for such a scale of destruction. There are lessons that we must learn about the destructiveness of war, and it seems to me that the perfect restoration of ancient buildings largely ignores it. It is simply too easy a way out.

One of the British bombs that rained from the sky on that night in May 1942 exploded in the cellar of a large house opposite the cathedral. It killed the human occupants who were sheltering in the basement but, in doing so, uncovered the remains of an ancient villa. In addition to a large amount of Roman glassware, jewellery and pottery, one of the most glorious mosaic floors outside of Italy was literally brought to the surface. It was this and the associated collection at the Wallraf-Richartz Museum that I had ostensibly come all this way to see. The museum contained a large number of magnificent works of art as well as a hoard of Roman items. Gothic and Renaissance art from Italy, Baroque works by the Dutch masters and Impressionist paintings from France. It was a timely reminder that for two thousand years this was an international city at the heart of an integrated European community.

What I saw in Bonn and Cologne was repeated throughout the Ruhr valley at Moenchengladbach, Essen, Dortmund, Mulheim etc. A string of dreary, barren cities, with no money or resources to rebuild. The industrial reconstruction that was soon to dominate Europe was taking place behind the scenes, but I could see none of it from the tourist bus. The phrase 'They that sow the wind shall reap the whirlwind' was often heard, an understandable, if historically incorrect sentiment. I had stood in my own city and smelt the same acrid smell of burnt buildings drifting like the homeless through ruined streets, but I felt no exultation, no sense of revenge. There was only blackness inside and out. The knowledge that we had ruined this land deliberately was horrifying. American B-52s had bombed strategic targets during the day, but squadrons of British Lancaster bombers had carpet bombed all of them during the night. Weather conditions, flaky equipment and lack of information meant that whatever the people back home had been told, precision bombing was out of the question. It was simple unregulated, bitter violence as I knew from first-hand experience. Kill or be killed was the only instruction given and most likely both were the outcome. I was appalled, but this was really why I had come. Not for the art. What could I say to my friendly German border guard? Was I satisfied? No, I felt sick.

The so called 'Trümmerfrau' or 'Rubble Women' of Germany.

It seemed patronising, almost voyeuristic for me to be sat raised up in a nice warm coach with a packed lunch on my knee, as I stared out through the thick safety glass at the starving old women sifting through the rubble, as they tried to get some semblance of normal life back together. It is true that I had done my fair share of digging through the ruins of Bristol's bomb-damaged streets looking for survivors and was involved in projects to help the homeless, but that had been the war. This, this was the infinitely bleak aftermath for millions.

I saw no enemies on the streets of Germany, just fellow brothers and sisters who desperately needed help, now as perhaps we should have helped twenty years before in order to have prevented the Nazis rising to power and avoided any of this happening. Extremism is always the result of desperation, and desperation is equally often the result of neglect.

I returned to Belgium quickly, by train, where I made my way to Bruges which was the next place on the return leg of my journey. What is there one can say about a perfectly preserved mediaeval city? Belgium is in fact, not one country but two (Flanders and Walloon). Whereas Brussels is clearly part of the old French-speaking, industrialised country in the south, Bruges is equally obviously part of the outwardly looking and entrepreneurial Dutch dominated region of Flanders. The two could not be more different.

Bruges seen from the canal 1954.

Bruges is a mediaeval city, but it is not a fortress like so many others of its time; it was built as a commercial hub and a financial powerhouse. The Genoan navy arrived in the thirteenth century bringing trade goods from the Mediterranean and spices from the Levant. Wool arrived here to be processed and resold, and then goods from all over the Hanseatic League. Although to us it looks beautiful, almost quaint, everything here was optimised for trade.

The first stock exchange in the world opened here in 1309 in what is now the Frietmuseum, and countries opened their own embassies here. For hundreds of years, German, Spanish and Italian were heard daily on its streets. Perhaps it is not too much to say that it was the New York of its day.

I was keen to put the blackness of the war behind me, there were still enough reminders of that back home in Bristol, and at every turn Bruges delights. Cobbled streets, narrow alleyways, little bridges, towers and palaces appeared in turn, all pleasing to the eye, all causing little sparks of joy in the warm sun, that had come out from behind a cloud.

Michelangelo's 'Madonna', housed in the Saint Salvator cathedral, actually designed by an Englishman, was unmoving as a piece of sculpture, but brought to mind the children I had seen everywhere in Holland and the Dutch's attachment to them. I preferred the little Renaissance paintings of Van Eyck and Van der Weyden in the Chapel of the Holy Blood, all of which served to act as reminders of how wealthy Bruges was before the river silted up, and Antwerp became the main port on the coast.

The roar of international trade has long since died away. There are no street signs and no advertisements here now, cars are not permitted into the centre and grass literally grows in the streets. The twentieth century intrudes in only the smallest manner. Now half-blind ladies sit in a circle in quiet courtyards making the lace that their city is now famous for, while waiters stand quietly in the shade of their restaurants' awnings, indicating a menu of chocolate-covered treats. As the golden sun slowly sank behind the rose-coloured bricks of the Belfry, I decided to join the old lace makers, clutching a half pint of the local beer and a greasy packet of what the Belgians call 'Bintje Frieten' but the French, who stole the idea from them during the Napoleon invasion, call something else entirely!

My father had a very sweet tooth and is missing the purchase of a few souvenirs out of his travelogue. Amongst his most sacred possessions were his socially acceptable Dutch coffee percolator which sat on the sideboard in the dining room and a rather chunky Belgian waffle maker which was not deemed to be so acceptable by Bath high society, so languished in a cardboard box in the attic. He mentions here the packet of fries, which he always thereafter ate with mayonnaise not ketchup, but strangely he does not mention the large packet of sugar mice that he has in his pocket. He talked of Bruges' sugar mice being the size of rats, their hand-painted, sugary bodies large enough to fill the palm of his hand, their pink, beady eyes begging for attention. I do not like sugar mice, but solemnly eat one for him whenever I visit Bruges.

Ghent, another mediaeval Flemish powerhouse, but one that has aged less well than Bruges. Tall three masted ships from around the world once graced the silent crumbling quays of what, for a time, was the largest city in Europe north of the Alps. Now only a series of dirty factories and dilapidated historic buildings serve to remind us that three times this city became the centre of Europe's textile industry, in the thirteenth, fifteenth and eighteenth centuries. Standing on Saint Michael's Bridge, three great towers rose above the tangle of tram wires, the Belfort, St. Baaf's cathedral and of course, St. Niklaas. I left the traffic to roar around the castle of the Spanish Knights and found myself drawn to a very efficiently-run restaurant – it could almost have been Swiss – in the crypt of the lovely Town Hall with a tankard of a local brown Gruut beer.

The Old Post Office & St. Michael's Bridge, Ghent.

Few trades have shaped England as much as the mediaeval wool trade, a major driver of enclosure and the rural revolution and sponsor of large churches and cathedrals throughout East Anglia. Wool was sourced in a raw form from England and exported to the emergent centres of cloth production in the Low Countries where innovations such as the pedal-driven loom and spinning wheel were prominent. English wool processed in this way was sold at the 'Champagne Fairs' all around the Mediterranean, the finest cloth being reserved for the merchants of Florence. It was this trade that gave rise in turn to the Italian financial industry that funded the Reformation and the building of these cities.

Zomerverblijf van de Koninklijke Belgische Familie.
Summer residence of the Belgian royal family.

We tend to think of Ostend mostly as a ferry terminal nowadays, Dover's main connection to the European rail network, but before the war it was one of the main holiday resorts on Europe's northern coast. British and Belgian aristocracy descended on it in the nineteenth century creating a sea front filled with exotic hotels. Yachting events and polo followed. In 1920 it hosted the Olympics and suddenly people from all over the continent were flocking to its brand-new yacht basin, enormous beaches and sporting facilities. Guesthouses, Bed & Breakfasts and cheap hostels sprung up to accommodate them.

Sending factory workers on package holidays to spas and beach resorts where they took part in organised physical activities was a fundamental part of all Socialist movements at the time. In other countries commercial organisations like Butlins sprung up to address the leisure needs of working-class families.

Ostend was still extremely pleasant when I visited. The Mercator sat elegantly in the harbour, its fifteen white sails catching the sun, a flotilla of little boats surrounding it. To the right, a delightful old town with meticulous flower displays hid behind a city wall. For those seeking sun and sand, it provides everything from cheap, backstreet doss houses to modern luxurious hotels on the seafront. But many other activities are accommodated here too, some of which the militia have to turn a blind eye to.

It was all lovely, but my mind was still back in Germany, back amongst the rubble of the Ruhr valley and the crime that was the destruction of Cologne. The Wall Street crash of 1929 had an horrific effect in Germany. Food shortages and disease followed on its heels. By the early thirties people had resorted to eating grass and plants, cats and dogs had disappeared entirely from the streets of Munich. Popular protests were not listened to but rather put down with guns.

If only the people I had seen in the towns of the Rhineland could come here for a vacation as easily as I had, but for them it was generations, not decades away. I suddenly wanted to take the people of Europe and mix them up, like the Romans had done millennia before, sending auxiliaries from one region to live in another. I wanted everyone to have to take state organised annual holidays, both to relax in places like this and for educational and cultural reasons. If we wanted to avoid war again, we needed to be more radical in our approach.

In deference I avoided the expensive hotels and sought out something more modest, a simple 'Bed and Breakfast'. I chose to spend the final evening of my holiday sitting on a deckchair eating a very English-like packet of fish and chips, sand swirling in the wind around me. It seemed to me that the narrow channel in front of me did more to unite than divide us.

View-Master™ Reel (Belgium)

THE PYRENEES

Bigger Than Us, 1955

Emboldened by the success of previous journeys and having been handsomely compensated for a piece of work I'd done earlier in the year, I planned a holiday with a difference; not just a holiday, but a grand tour, travelling along the French/Spanish border in a large arc from the Atlantic to the Mediterranean. On reflection, it was too long a journey and makes for difficult reading. For that, I apologise in advance. It was partially Miss Seawright's fault. She wanted me to join her in Biarritz where she was staying for some Admiralty conference, but more about her later. I, on the other hand, was still trying to get away from the austerity of post-war Britain, somewhere bright, warm, happy even, with just a touch of the magic that I'd glimpsed in Switzerland. Mountains were the starting point, but it was no longer my intention to climb them. It was enough to be amongst them for now. I would start with a leisurely journey through the rocky Pyrenees, visiting the various spa towns like my own city of Bath, spot the occasional mediaeval castle and then follow in the footsteps of the great artists as they reflected on the art, architecture and history of southern France. Looking back on it now, none of these things is what I remember about this trip. It is often this way with travel. Whilst it is intellectual thinking that prompts a journey abroad, it is the cultural and sociological aspects that bring the greatest pleasure and form the most lasting impressions in my mind. I had spent months researching every detail of my tour before nervously handing my plans to Thomas Cook with a mixture of excitement and trepidation. I need not have worried as they carried everything out impeccably.

I travelled up from Bath the day before and spent the night in the Grosvenor. You will see in this journal that I have a bit of a thing for hotels. I think that they are fabulous institutions and I'm not sure why we don't all live in them. They do work out cheaper than purchasing a house if you actually do the sums, and I've always felt that the concept of owning property was morally wrong. Anyway, the Grosvenor was an exotic choice, but it was not actually mine. Miss Seawright insisted, and Miss Seawright was a fearsome woman that was not to be crossed. She had paid for it, too, as well as my train fare to Biarritz, so I could not complain. There was no buffet enticingly laid out at breakfast, instead a quiet waiter in gloves and a complicated menu of eggs and tea. I do not recall what form of either I had, suggesting that the hotel's reputation is a little over-blown. Then my case and I were transported to a reserved seat on the 'Golden Arrow', a luxury boat train, linking London and Paris. Unlike the train I had taken two years before, where I had had to disembark and sit on the deck, this time the carriage I was aboard would be loaded onto the ferry itself after which it would be taken to Paris by SNCF. I didn't need to move an inch! Quite why we are deliberately running down our railway infrastructure, when every other country in Europe is investing in theirs, is beyond me. We are already being left behind in the post-war world, but it was a political question that I didn't wish to ponder on my way to Paris.

One of Monet's eight paintings of the Gare Saint Lazare (1877).

The Gare Saint Lazare was far busier than in Monet's paintings, but fortunately also far less smoky. Monet, who rented a studio near the station, made seven famous paintings of it and many less famous studies and sketches. Whilst I would not call myself an artist of any sort, I do try and do a bit of painting every so often and I could instantly see the appeal in capturing the scene: the dramatic scenery of the steam, rising up past those soaring columns to the huge glass roof, the vibrating energy of the engines themselves and the emotions of those meeting or leaving friends, waiting tediously on the platform with their worldly belongings or simply trudging off to work. It was the city itself encapsulated.

'Mr. Nicholas? Your taxi is waiting, sir!'

I have never felt comfortable with this common English form of address. It is a contraction of the word 'Sire', which has a legal definition connecting it since the Middle Ages to land holding knights and a subsequent legacy of being used by people for those of higher social standing. Neither could be further from how I see myself, the humble son of a shopkeeper from one of the poorer districts in Bristol. However, I am inherently English and terrified at the idea of causing others offence.

'My name is Nicholas. Pleased to meet you!' I replied in French and followed him to the cab. On discovering that this was my first time in Paris, the driver took me on a tour of the main sites before depositing me at the Gare Austerlitz. I had, of course, seen innumerable pictures of them all, but no photograph can convey the sense of the traffic swarming around the Arc de Triomphe or the burst of excitement at seeing the Eiffel Tower appear from the buildings that it had been hiding behind, only to dwarf them seconds later. It is true that such buildings, such as Notre Dame, are architectural gems, well worth travelling to see in their own right, but how much more marvellous is it that they are part of a city that interacts with them in a thousand ways, some respectful, others less so, every day. I went everywhere with the window wound down, breathing it all in, anxious not to miss a second of it. Cars are just 'tin boxes on wheels' to me and I couldn't care less about them, but I have always loved taxis. They are the best way to see a city.

As there was plenty of time before my train's departure, I crossed the road to a restaurant called the 'Jardin des Routes'. The garden itself was full of exotic plants and tall pine trees. An oasis of calm in the middle of a bustling city. Monkeys leapt from branch to branch joyously while little furry faces peeked out from carefully concealed cages. From this patch in an imaginary forest no part of the city could be seen, save for the minaret of a mosque which added its own esoteric note. Even the noise of the traffic on the Boulevard de l'Hôpital was muted. I bought an orange drink and sat and watched two old men playing chess on a path with large concrete pieces, moving each one with a wooden stick. Twilight fell upon the garden, bringing with it a quality of life suspended that is a common feature of many Dutch paintings, such as those by Van Hoek, Mauve and van Gogh. Only the lengthening shadows and the slanting rays of the sun told me that it was just an illusion. My train beckoned.

An SNCF 2D2 9100 class en route from Paris to Biarritz in 1955.

The station was clean and strangely quiet. Steam engines had been banned from the station several years before; everything was now electric. I found my bunk and fell asleep with a small glass of brandy, remembering as I did my last night ride to Switzerland. There was no comparison. I didn't even feel it leave the station! I woke up fully refreshed, to a breakfast of pastries, bread, yoghurt and fruit, as we swept through Rion-des-Landes and Dax. It was all washed down with a cup of tarlike French espresso, mercifully accompanied by a glass of water. The French have certainly got the hang of breakfast, but they need to speak to the Dutch or the Swiss about their coffee.

We pulled into the station at 9:00 a.m. precisely.

Biarritz

I had expected Biarritz to be hideous, but it wasn't anywhere near as bad as I'd feared. I love the sea, but I've never been a beach person. I feel no inclination to strip off and dive in amongst the waves or sun myself on the sand, so instead I walked along the promenade dressed in a suit and tie, with a good book. Victor Hugo said that he had not met any place more perfect in the world, with its cheerful white houses, large dunes, proud sea and fine sand, but he was worried that it would lose its honesty and turn money hungry. He was right, at least in part. Grand hotels from the Belle Époque lined the seafront, the air was full of a sense of gentility and hydrangeas were being cultivated everywhere.

This was the playground of Europe's aristocracy and Hollywood stars in the twenties and thirties. It was no longer a place for ordinary people. But the Atlantic still rolled in against the rocks, wind still echoed through caves in the hills and, in the distance, thunder grumbled in the foothills of the Pyrenees mountains. The U.S. military had taken over many of the hotels and American servicemen were everywhere. They lounged outside bars and ran through the surf, but their presence, peculiar though it was, did much to offset the stuffiness of the place that would have been insufferable otherwise.

Biarritz's most famous hotel is the Hotel du Palais, which was built by Napoleon as his holiday home in the middle of kilometres of dunes that he had purchased. Hemingway, Chaplin, Mansfield and Sinatra stayed here, as did the German Wehrmacht during the war. After the fall of the imperial family in the 1870s, it fell into disrepair and was closed for renovation when my father visited.

Hotel du Palais.

I was staying at a modest guesthouse on the suburbs. It had a hard bed and a bathroom at the end of a corridor, but pretty roses in the courtyard. Miss Seawright by contrast was staying at the 'Le Regina', one of Biarritz's fanciest hotels, where I was to join her for afternoon tea. As both my employer and the person who had paid for my night at the Grosvenor and my train ticket, I could not refuse. Le Regina sat like a bloated palace overlooking the seafront promenade, fancy cars and doormen in tailcoats lining up outside. Tea was taken in a huge atrium with a glass ceiling and panoramic views over the bay. I scanned the room critically taking in the art deco cornices, the marble columns and the large terracotta pots spouting greenery. The war had toned everything down, but it was still easy to see how the other half had liked to live. I felt that it would have made a nice public library.

Miss Seawright was sitting, or rather had positioned herself in the way that grand ladies do, on one end of a green Louis XVI antique sofa, a cup of tea in her lap. She was ordering men in uniform around as if she were back in Bath hosting one of her infamous garden parties, that I was so often reluctantly roped in to helping her with. 'Gordon, get the admiral a pink gin when you've finished setting up the projector'. She has been fundamental in shaping my entire life so I will now take a moment to briefly introduce you to her here.

Miss Seawright was an effusive woman, and on the surface a thoroughly obnoxious one, but she was also an incredible lady, of the type that you simply don't see any more, and unquestionably deserved respect. The daughter of a ship's captain and a second-generation immigrant, she had fought her way up the social ladder and married cleverly. In the 1920s, when other women were campaigning for the vote, she was already leading expeditions across Arabia and into Tibet. She had known Howard Carter and could read hieroglyphs as well as speak numerous foreign languages. Her husband, a commander in British Naval Intelligence, had done the decent thing and died during the war leaving her with a significant fortune, social status, a large house, and, of course, the bookshop in Bath. She was, so she said, always on the lookout for a replacement for him but was far too crafty and independent to settle on any man in particular. Somehow, she juggled them all. She definitely did like a man in uniform, though, and there were plenty of them here.

She came only infrequently to the bookshop. But despite owning it, she cared not a jot for how it was run and never bothered looking over the books. She'd march down Milsom Street like a brass band, dishing out regal smiles and handshakes to Bath society, before ducking, seemingly reluctantly, into the bookshop. Her visits were invariably to give me some type of briefing: 'I have scheduled you to give a talk at the Guildhall', 'I need you to accompany me to RAF Upper Heyford', or worst of all, an instruction to accompany some admiral's daughter to a ball. It was odd to bump into her here, and yet she seemed completely at home in these decadent surroundings.

Miss Seawright was apparently on her way to 'observe' a Coal and Steel Conference in Messina, where plans for a new European Customs Union were being drawn up. I have no idea what 'observing' involved, but it was the kind of thing that she did for her friends in the Admiralty all the time. I had images of black-faced miners from South Wales and steel workers from 'Up North', in thick overalls sitting around a table looking slightly confused. But the Americans were seriously concerned about it. She dismissed the U.S. colonel with whom she had been flirting. Three silver stars on his epaulets, a lieutenant general no less, and yet she'd already bent him to her will and got him carrying trays of sandwiches as if he were just another waiter. He seemed to think that he was doing her a favour. Miss Seawright could do that to people, however important they were.

With a wave of her gloved hand, she bade me sit down. I eyed the dainty morsels on the three-tier tray and grabbed a sandwich, biting into it eagerly like a hungry child without asking. She raised a disapproving eyebrow but said nothing. I assumed she was criticising my manners, but perhaps she was also silently warning me. The sandwiches were insipid, the cake was rather dry, and the tea was so over-brewed that I sent it back and ordered black tea with lemon instead. I felt no guilt at all.

Just a couple of kilometres along the windswept coast from Biarritz lies St. Jean de Luz, a pleasant, more natural place free from the pretensions of Biarritz. It was a historic fishing harbour such as Victor Hugo would have recognised but was now increasingly giving over its waterfront to pleasure yachts. I strolled along the jetties munching a crepe and listening to the calls of the gulls and the incessant pinging of cables against masts. I watched a man in a little boat tacking against the wind and felt a certain empathy with him. As he disappeared against the brilliant blue sky, I considered the similarities with mountain climbing, a lone man's struggle against mother nature and I wondered if it was something that I might like to try at some point, if I never managed to overcome the Alps. Boats were not seen as expensive luxuries back then and there were even kits one could send off for, to build one for yourself. I was often tempted but unsure of my woodworking skills. It would have been a good group project for me to attempt with my university chums. Standing in the fresh Atlantic wind, I realised that I was still missing them, which is an odd thing for a loner like me to say. The coach turned inland following the River Nive and climbed slowly up into the limestone foothills of the Pyrenees. Cambo-les-Bains was our next stop, a spa town, as the name suggests, and the home of the French author, Edmond Rostand, who wrote silly romantic plays about salon life. Parisian society obviously disliked being parodied which is why he was exiled here. It was the first of many resorts to spring up in the valley, with promoted health benefits and an equally promoted licensed casino. The comparisons with Bath were obvious, its mineral waters pulled people to the city, its roulette tables keeping them there. Whereas in both Georgian and Roman times

Bath had been a playground for the rich and famous to recuperate during the day and spend their money at night, it had always been a real city where people lived and worked too. But here there were nothing but saunas, grand villas and hotels. It was not a real place and felt even more unsatisfying than Biarritz. I started to worry that I should not have spent my money this way. I turned the pages of S.G.P Ward's guide to the Peninsular War rapidly...

The trees soon dropped away revealing a barren and empty landscape of plunging valleys and brown snow dusted peaks. Thousand-year-old monasteries slumbered amongst the mountains as did numerous ancient forts. The whole area had been fought over during the closing stages of the Peninsular War and reminders of that conflict were everywhere. Gun emplacements and redoubts poked out of the craggy hillsides, as did several well-tended cemeteries. What on earth were the British doing fighting here in the mountains of Spain?

It is easy for us in Britain to think of the Napoleonic Wars being all about the Battles of Trafalgar and Waterloo, or for the Russians to only recall Borodino, but the fight against Napoleon's empire was a world war, fought all over the globe. The conflict between France and Spain started when Napoleon invaded Portugal, a country that Britain and Spain were fighting over at the time. It rapidly escalated into a major conflict with Napoleon finally installing his older brother as King of Spain. It was a war of attrition that hastened the end of the Spanish Empire, causing it to lose many of her overseas colonies, and whilst France dominated the battlefield, it eventually capitulated, exhausted by skirmishes with the British in the mountains and its parallel invasion of Russia. It was a loss all round, as most wars are, leaving the countryside littered with its scars. One long-term effect of the Peninsular War was that Spain could no longer afford to police her colonies, so they began to govern themselves, giving rise to the Libertadores movement and, ultimately, to the independence of South America.

We came down from the rocky, sun-blasted hills into the little town of St.-Jean-Pied-de-Port, standing, as the name says, at the foot of the pass. It was a quiet place these days but had once been an important stop on the pilgrim route to Santiago. Here the long, weary caravans rested before facing the crossing of the mountains.

On the hill above the town Vauban had built one of his forts, but to no avail. It fell to Wellington in less than twenty-four hours. The road, now lined with hostels, ran past it and down to the River Nive. The old town, a warren of little alleys, still displayed many of the trade signs of the many small craftsmen who once repaired the ravages of the long journey for those pilgrims who could afford it. One, a bakery, still showed the price of wheat in 1789, doubtless shockingly expensive at the time! We headed out into the brown rocky wilderness again, to where the fourteenth century church of Notre-Dame du Bout du Pont stands beside the Porte d'Espagne. The backs of the houses slope straight into the water, their roofs pulled low over their faces shyly. It was not a place on the tourist trail and barely a place at all. I sat on the little footbridge eating a memorable plate of ham, truffles and peppers with a deliciously ripe slice of Roquefort. Woodsmoke hung in the evening air and drifted slowly towards the distant mountains, their steep sides covered in pine trees, their peaks shrouded in clouds.

The Bridge at the Porte d'Espagne. Unchanged since my father visited.

As I ate, I realised that this was the only place on the trip so far that I had actually enjoyed being in. There was absolutely nothing here to see or to do, but it was an honest and unpretentious place, simple but beautiful. I felt supremely comfortable here, lucky to be here and I was reluctant to leave. No doubt the ham and cheese played some part in this.

We crossed into Spain at Henday, almost as slowly as the pilgrims did. There was a long queue at the international bridge, where soldiers were checking papers. Not with any effectiveness from a security perspective, but as a means of eliciting bribes and gifts from travellers. Bandits effectively. I held the guard's eye coldly as I offered my passport and dared him to try anything.

There was little enough to see after the brightness of the French coastal towns. Scruffy villages and dusty conurbations passed by slowly until we reached Donostia-San Sebastian. I took an instant dislike to the place for reasons that I did not understand at the time or really with the benefit of hindsight. Superficially some of its lanes and passageways reminded me of Bath and perhaps I held that against it. Perhaps it wasn't foreign enough or different enough for me, but more likely it was its attitude. It was a rather grandiose place built in the Victorian era and far too commercial. It was being rapidly expanded by the addition of new concrete towers with faux historic facades which I found slightly gauche. The feeling of artificiality stayed with me and despite the gay beachside areas it seemed rather gloomy and soulless. The sun shone, the water sparkled, but there was no gaiety here; the trees were planted too close to each other and enormous buildings, such as Stalin might have demanded, towered over us.

New apartment blocks going up in Donostia-San Sebastian.

Tolosa, just a few miles down the road, was, however, a complete contrast to San Sebastian. It was an ancient provincial town dating from the Iron Age and flourished as a trading centre under the Romans and into the mediaeval period. Churches, crumbling brick palaces and a baroque town hall all bore testament to its former wealth. At its centre lay the bustling Zerkausi market overlooked by large town houses with colourful balconies. Tables groaned under the weight of bowls of black beans, chillies and olives and the smell of charred steak drifted on the air. I instantly felt hungry.

In the shade of an arcade on one side of the market was a 'sidrerías', a restaurant selling cider, and, being from Somerset, I had to give it a try. A pale honey coloured liquid, a little too watery for my taste, but perfect for sipping in the sun, was decanted from a giant wooden barrel and was served with a small side plate of walnuts, quince chutney and various local cheeses. Yes, Tolosa I liked very much.

The town bridge in Tolsa with St. Mary's Basilica in the background.

The Gorrotxategi family has been making sweets in the town since 1680, adding cake, pastries and chocolates to its portfolio as fashion demanded. When I visited their little shop and museum in the marketplace, cigarettes were all the rage. I carry them as a universal form of currency, but don't smoke myself, and it was chocolate cigarillos and sugar cigarettes that were boxed up on the counter that day. I wondered what my old university chums, always trying to cadge a smoke from me, would have thought of them and so I bought a small box for no one in particular. I tried to suck it casually as you might a filter tip, but my jaw instantly rebelled and crunched down joyously on the sugar crystals. The rest of the packet disappeared quickly, they would have melted in the hot sun and spoiled, as I'm sure you'll understand.

As I wandered the dusty narrow lanes munching on the remains of a sugary cigarillo, I saw the exuberant spirit of the Basque people pouring out of every crooked window and dark doorway. You could see it in the way they babbled so energetically in a tongue that was neither Spanish nor French, in the way they almost danced as they walked along, in their smiles and in their ubiquitous red berets. There was something delightfully straightforward and down to earth about them which I liked a lot. What they made of me in my dark suit and silk tie I couldn't tell, but they had seen the likes of me off the premises many times before so did not appear bothered by my presence.

Pamplona, my next stop, was a fairly homogenous blend of buildings new and old. It was once the capital of the region of Navarre, an unlikely fact reflected only in its cathedral and the grand churches of San Lorenzo, Saturnio and San Nicolás. The older narrow lanes were a solid mass of people, the wider new ones a swirling mass of red berets and men and women dancing impromptu to the tune of fife and drum. Groups spontaneously formed and linked arms, before breaking apart moments later. A reflection of our lives and friendships condensed into mere seconds perhaps? The harsh sounds of a brass band echoed off the sand-coloured walls and the sharp tang of cordite tweaked my nostrils. A twenty-foot-high version of Saint Fermin, the city's mythical first bishop, appeared around the corner of the town hall, accompanied by saints, kings, queens and moors, all of whom were gyrating slightly and jigging their way towards the cathedral, chivvied along by fake monks. It is said that he baptised forty thousand pagans in just three days, kings and peasants alike, but the legend gives us no insight into how he accomplished this great feat. One solemnly dunked in a font every six seconds seems unlikely, and my mind instantly imagined a series of giant rotating hamster wheels suspended over the Arga river.

Also baptising the masses was Federico Sánchez, writer, politician and organiser of the now banned Spanish Communist Party. He was using the cover of the festival to drum up anti-Franco sentiment in the north, which appeared to be an easy task. Quite who had gathered to hear him speak and who was there to see the bulls run, was impossible to say, but there was clasping of hands and back slapping everywhere.

The Basques are a crafty lot; they enjoy their lives, living life in the moment and show little respect for their overlords. I heartily approve. The Pyrenees form a natural barrier between France and Spain, and that area belongs to neither of those countries despite what lines are drawn on maps. Here is a region with its own clear history, industry and culture, its own language even, that has no use for terms like 'kingdom', 'nationality' or 'state'. The area is what it is. I felt this sentiment should be supported rather than forced into some artificial political construct, even if I disagreed with their later extreme methods. Nationality seemed to me to be little more than an answer to a question in a passport, as alterable as a name for a bit of cash under the counter, as changeable as one's overcoat. Meaningless.

The Basque will play his part as required. If the running of the bulls is an occasion for bravery, then the Basque will play the craven coward and the magnificent hero alternately. The bulls, no real danger in fact, run their appointed course. A direct parallel of the Spanish Communist Party leader's life, or of Basque history itself, as the people of the region bowed first to one monarch and then another, letting both French and Spanish soldiers wash through their streets like water off a duck's back.

They hammed it up for the crowds of tourists and the women waving red neckerchiefs from balconies overhead, until the savage heat of the mid-afternoon sun caused a lull in the proceedings. The delicious peppery smell of a spicy lamb soup wafted down the street and bottles of rich bodied wine tasting of cinnamon and violets started to appear. The famous Antonio Ordonez was fighting in the ring. Now there was a man that the women would vote for! The balconies were hung with banners, various amateur bands competed simultaneously and the church tower, visible above the ring, was black with the bodies of watching priests. The men stopped raking the sand, a trumpet sounded and then the "Passo" began. Two "bailiffs" dressed in black galloped across the ring to the Resident's Box where the keys were symbolically thrown and caught in a great hat. The matadors, right below me, carefully folded their ceremonial capes and proceeded with the prosaic preparation of their craft, scuffing up the sand, drawing their swords, testing the weight and speed of the cape and rinsing their mouths.

Bull running in Pamplona (1955).

The trumpet sounded again, the gates opened and the bull was there, and what a magnificent creature he was, so big, so black, so very, very fast. There was a deep grunt, the harsh sound of his hooves and the almost total silence, the crash of his horns onto the wooden 'bararrera'. Green and white ribbons fluttered from his back symbolising strength and fertility. I have no idea whether he was a good bull or not, or whether the matador was doing all the work and putting on a good show for his audience in the way that I would now expect any Basque to do. Either way, I was fascinated, for this was no struggle of wily hero against wild beast, this was a game in which both players played their part and knew the rules, the bull almost as well-trained as the matador himself. There was a structure to the fight, a prelude, opening act, intermezzo and, of course, a finale. There were march pasts, flashing armour, ducks and feints where the matador didn't even reach for his sword. He ran with the bull in great swerving circles, teasing, encouraging, playing with him even, his thin yellow pompom hat bouncing as he went, and then there was the sudden anticlimactic death, a single strike and a look of grudging acceptance when done well. I began to see how something seeming so shocking actually included elements of grace and beauty, of physiological and psychological knowledge and even caring. It was operatic.

So it went; one matador tossed aside but otherwise unhurt, one bull jumping over the railings completely to land in the laps of panicked policemen and aficionados, much to the delight of the Basque audience and one terribly botched killing that got its perpetrator such howls of abuse that I'm sure he never returned. The sinking sun threw a great crescent of shadow over the ring as Ordonez waited for the last bull. He was tall and slender, his 'suit of lights' a simple black and white outfit in contrast to the colour of his colleagues but embroidered with fine lace that would have made the old women of Bruges applaud. He stood frozen still as the bull entered, watching carefully, immune to the crowd. To me the bull seemed no different from the others, but it was not so for the matador. Ordonez had already played his part; he had supported the earlier matadors in their fights and taken the bull from the man thrown earlier, but for some reason this pairing was a special one.

I am told that bulls cannot see the colour red. Everything instead is about the movement and stance. Ordonez locked eyes with the bull and never once looked away. With his cape folded neatly over his arm he stood there calmly, feet neatly together staring at the bull. The bull shook his head in confusion, finding himself in new surroundings. Ordonez took a single step nearer making it clear who the challenger was. The bull responded as bulls do, scraping his hooves in the sand and snorting heavily. Ordonez copied him exactly, kicking up the dust and shaking his brimmed hat. The bull sneered and lunged at him, charging in a straight line. Ordonez did not leap, or jump aside, he simply took one carefully calculated step and twirled the corner of his cape like a giant marigold flower gently brushing a fly from the beast's nose. Olé! The bull, having almost as little idea what had happened as I had, tried again, but without the run up this time. Again and again, the same thing happened like a scene from Don Quixote, Ordonez letting out more of the cape each time until the bull was almost wearing it as a headscarf. The plucky Basque had outwitted and exhausted the thuggery of his greater opponent. It was a rather pleasing spectacle. Then to my utter astonishment, Ordonez, who had not even acknowledged the presence of the crowd, took his hat off and simply walked away, turning his back on the frustrated bull. He sauntered casually around the edge of the ring, searching for a pretty woman to throw his hat to and receiving the adulation of the crowd in return. He knew full well where the bull was and led it in ever widening circles into the sun. Ordonez picked his spot well and turned, but this time the bull was not going to let the one who had embarrassed him get away. It did not run at him as it had before but came forward one step at a time moving left or right as Ordonez did, until it was but six feet away and Ordonez's back was against the barrier in the zone of death. He did not need to run or use his horns; one thousand kilograms of weight would be enough.

'No! No!' the crowd gasped, but Ordonez could fight as well as run. He showed the bull his sword, dazzling it with the light of the sun on its blade. Nobody saw what happened next. There was a brief flash of the muleta and the crash of horns crunching into wood. The giant bull tore himself free only to find his opponent standing beside him, almost patting him on the back mopping his brow with his cape. Ordonez was covered in blood, but the golden hilt of a sword was buried deep in the bull's back. Slowly it turned to face its conqueror. There was no look of malice in the animal's eyes as it gently knelt down in the dust and died, only acknowledgement. I wondered if Napoleon had felt the same way…

They carried Ordonez on their shoulders back to his hotel cheering him all the way. I had seen what I came to see, but what I saw was not what I had expected. Until that evening the thought of killing defenceless animals in such a way seemed barbaric. It probably still was. But I found that my loyalties lay not with the bull, who had barged his way into the proverbial tea shop, not with the thuggish brutes with their superior firepower that thought that they could dominate this place. No, instead, my loyalty lay with the underdog, the cunning Basques, who played one side off against the other and neatly sidestepped their invaders' ambitions. They ducked into the shelters of doorways as the herds gushed through the streets, but after the bulls had gone, they were still here, not French, not Spanish or British even, just their own selves, being cheerful and doing their own thing in the sun.

Backstreets of Pamplona, 1955.

Antonio Ordonez had a long and successful career, only retiring in 1988. He died of liver cancer ten years later on his bull stud farm. For thousands of years, imperial powers had fought over theoretical lines drawn over piles of rock in the Pyrenees. All parties benefited from hundreds of years of trading, knowledge transfer and transport with a clearly homogenous independent culture. The Basque separatist movement was formed four years after my father's visit, and conducted a series of terrorist campaigns, mostly against Spain for the next fifty years, resulting in the deaths of over a thousand people. Despite being recognised as a protected region by the European Union, and overwhelmingly voted for in every election, neither France nor Spain agreed to the creation of such an autonomous region. The Basque separatists have now laid down their weapons, but they may not have lost the war. As the economy of Spain struggles with current problems, cities such as Valencia and Santander have once again started voting for independence and the government of Galicia, which supplies a disproportionate percentage of Spain's revenue, continues to challenge central government.

I probably should have ended this chapter there, with my clear statement of support for the cheerful folk of the Basque region sticking it to the evil imperialists, and comments about how ridiculous it is when countries meddle in affairs so far from home. But my journey was not like that, there was no specific point at which the simple bit ended, no point at which the Spanish Pyrenees became French and, according to my schedule, the best was yet to come. So, I press on here, as I did back then.

We crossed back into what was officially France, like mediaeval monks on a pilgrimage to Le Puy, in pitch darkness guided through the mountain passes only by a man on a donkey, a single candle flickering in the darkness in his lantern. We emerged in a world of greyness and rain. Not exactly the backdrop I had been expecting.

We arrived, with several thousand others, at Lourdes. What can I say? A filthy, tawdry, commercial little town without a single redeeming feature. It is a fairground of religion without anything honest or passionate about it at all. I was disgusted and unsure why I had made the mistake of putting it on my itinerary, but the truth was that it was there, blocking the route into France. Whatever your beliefs, its vulgarity and culpability reduced religion to its lowest level, the exploitation of the sick and needy. Yet still the visitors flocked there in their thousands. I did not understand why, even if you were a Christian. How could such sincerity of belief combine with such vile cynicism and exploitation? I felt a strange anger growing inside me, not an emotion that I normally feel.

Until February 1858, Lourdes was a sleepy market town theoretically under British control since the Hundred Years' War. Wellington had kept a garrison here for a while before deserting the place, leaving behind a dilapidated old villa. Then a fourteen-year-old girl with cholera, who was living in the basement of the old jail, had a series of visions when out gathering wood. It's strange how often teenagers faint when given physical tasks to do, isn't it? Less than four years later, the chapel of the Sanctuary of Our Lady of Lourdes was built in the grotto and, just fourteen years after that, an entire purpose-built, architecturally vacant cathedral was created on the site, a Disneyland for believers. The girl died anyway, which somewhat calls into question the healing powers of the water, and was hastily made a saint. Perhaps the Vatican found the reality of the real girl an inconvenience. Whatever, eight other churches now surround the purpose-built assembly square and grand avenue.

Every day, at half-past-four, thousands of pilgrims, poor people mostly, many of them in wheelchairs, gather at the Lourdes grotto hoping for a miraculous cure for their ills, and the world is full of ills, especially if you're poor. The water here is said to be holy, certainly by those that sell it, and there is no lack of opportunity to try it for oneself, for a fee. Not working yet? Then you'd better buy a bit more…

There are nine 'stations of the cross' where believers are invited to wash or drink, while they contemplate passages from the Bible, nine chances to buy, not just water, but additional services and plenty of other opportunities to pick up a souvenir on your way out. The only exits are through the gift shops. The nuns, dressed in black, give the place a solemnity that it does not deserve, their medical accoutrements and mannerisms giving a false impression of science, and, unqualified though I am to judge, a false impression of godliness, too. There is no God here, Christian or otherwise, but I could feel Satan's breath.

A variety of Vatican owned hotels now surround the site welcoming guests from around the world. Their prices range from the "Hôtel Croix des Nordistes" at a "modest" €109 per night to the Ligne St. Barth at a luxurious €662 per night. But those too poor or too sick to travel will be relieved to know that they can buy Lourdes Holy Water online and have it delivered to their door. It currently costs $5.00 for a 300ml bottle of water onsite at the Basilica, but water can fortunately be purchased form Lourdes online in 1.5L and 5L canisters for £60 and £150 respectively.

The Rosary Basilica at Lourdes did not appeal to my father.

Hot spring water has been gushing from the rocks in Bath for over two thousand years, curing many diseases and lessening the effects of others. The scientific effect of the water and the minerals within it are well-documented. The benefit comes largely from the heat of course; the water emerges from the rocks at forty-six degrees centigrade, but the salt minerals it contains also make it particularly good at helping the body purge toxins, such as lead, and with dealing with skin diseases. Several hospitals and scientific institutions have been built on those springs, including the Royal Mineral Hospital, and the baths have been used by the National Health Service for over thirty years. But there is none of that clinical rigour here in Lourdes, no attempt to make a process, no attempt at credulity, no obvious attempt to ease the suffering of the sick or even to appear to care. You must want God to heal you, then you must deserve it; you can't demand that God does so, and yet you must show your devotion by paying. I am told that three hundred and fifty thousand people visit the site each year, burning eight hundred tonnes of wax. Lourdes receives nearly eighteen million dollars a year in donations, a truly sickening figure.

Twilight fell and I was glad to leave, but, as I gratefully climbed onto the coach, I saw something that I had previously seen but not understood. Darkness did its best to hide the gauche spires of the basilica and its gaudy cousins and my eye was instead drawn to the 'Rosary of Light'. Thousands of candles carried in procession down the long avenue, a great flood of humanity walking behind their banners with the endless monotonous chant of 'Ave Maria'.

'Ave Maria, Gratia plena… Hail Mary, Full of Grace, Hail the Lord, the Lord is with thee. Blessed are you amongst women, blessed is the fruit of thy womb'. Schubert's 'Ave Maria' is one of the wonders of classical music and has been recorded by all the great opera singers, male and female. But Schubert never wrote it for the Catholic Church. The tune was originally called 'Ellen's Third Song' and was written as a lullaby. Misguided or not, there was something powerful in the simple faith and unity of mind of the masses at Lourdes, something ancient that the church didn't own. I wished that those modern-day pilgrims were marching for a better purpose and to a call on an organisation that would better care for their needs. We need more faith in the world, we really do, but organised religion is not the answer, and the Church is not the instrument to dispense it. I wished them well, nonetheless.

I was still angry the next day and not enjoying the scenery that passed the window. Why had I gone to Lourdes when I could have spent the day hiking in the Pyrenees? I was angry at the Catholic Church, but only on the surface; they were just a capitalist organisation doing their best to make a quick buck and doing that job well. No, I was more angry at the world for exploiting such people and for there not being a sensible alternative for them, a government department or town hall for them to turn to instead. If nations were going to fight over this rocky land, then they should make an effort to look after the people that lived there when they won it! That was all very easy to say, but what was I doing to make the world a better place? If I felt that way, shouldn't I be rolling up my sleeves and out there healing the sick as my mother had done? Or leading a charge of soldiers over the top like my father? What was I doing sitting on a coach being chauffeured around the countryside? Perhaps I was angry at myself. Lourdes should not have come as a surprise.

Anyone who knows me would say that I am a calm and quiet man, thoughtful and keen to avoid conflict, but that is just the outside shell, a lifetime of discipline and laziness. On the inside I am often angry and passionate, a hopeless romantic, yet desperate to fight for some cause. Lourdes had caused the 'Red Mist' to come down and none of the reading material Miss Seawright had given me was any help. When the coach stopped at Luz-Saint-Sauveur, I had no idea where I was or why I was there. It was not in my notebook, a stop on the itinerary, nor was it obvious why we were stopping. Had the coach broken down?

'Luz' as it is known, was a modest and instantly likeable place. It was almost as if the driver, sensing my mood, had sought out an antidote to my anger. Luz was hardly a village let alone a town. It smelt of dust and straw and consisted of little more than a single church, high up on a rocky crag, but it was a church unlike most others I had seen. It had none of the usual features, no spire, no cross, no stained glass. There was none of the trappings of the religion I had seen at Lourdes. Instead of decoration, the old church had thick crenelated walls and arrow slits along the clerestory. It was a fortified temple built in the twelfth century in the most pragmatic way, able to protect all of the citizens of the hamlet when needed. And yet its tough dark grey walls were covered in roses, like some forgotten fairy tale scene, every one of them from shades of coral through to magenta, shining almost luminescent in the afternoon light. The contrast of colour and shade, and of fortification and flower could not have been more extreme or more delightful, and the suddenness of this random discovery simply added to my delight. These are the experiences that travel really is about. The Mary that waited in the cool darkness behind the altar was not one who was full of grace, she was not surrounded by sheep and angels or holding her palms out in welcome. She wore a dark travelling cloak, a stern expression and clenched in her fist were snapped arrows. This was the tough Byzantine version of Mary protecting Christ's followers as she was before she was morphed into leading the late mediaeval cult of motherhood in the fifteenth century. She was a woman that I could believe in, offering the sick and needy a fortified castle rather than overpriced water.

Outside a row of horses waited, lined up in single file in the shade where the old mediaeval houses extended out over the cobbled street. It was a scene where any sense of the twentieth century had been erased, nothing had changed here in centuries; it didn't need to. They had nothing and everything in equal measure. One of the locals sauntered over towards me, chewing a piece of straw just like his horses and I remembered why we were here, only here wasn't where or even when I had thought it was.

Mine turned out to be an evil-eyed, hard-mouthed animal. Our dislike was instantaneous and mutual. The only other 'foreigner' accompanying me up the mountain was a doctor on leave from the Congo, who had no English, and my grasp of French, though workable, did not extend to 'Les Matters Mulet'. Nevertheless, we looked out for each other, observing each other's progress and taking riding tips. We soon left the valley path and began to climb. If the journey was uncomfortable when on flat ground, it was far worse now. I was thrown around like grain in a flour mill. Despite the sun, water poured down from rain clouds that had been hiding in the shadows of mountain passes. Every turn seemed to bring new weather and new pain. The ground dropped away sharply on my right-hand side, from this angle, a seeming waterfall of brown rocks on whose backs sun and shade seemed to fall alternatingly. How different it was from the Swiss Alps. Whereas they had curving green pastures that rolled over one another like waves, here in the Pyrenees, it was almost as if the rock had been chiselled away from the earth in slabs. Still, we climbed upwards. Walking would surely have been more comfortable?

We emerged, eventually, on a small flat shelf, where there was a shallow pool and small, stunted trees. The donkeys drank and rested, while the 'Doctor' and I gave each other a nod of acknowledgement on a tough job well done. The still snow covered peaks of Gavarnie now loomed over us very closely and I watched them change colour as the sun climbed over a crest. It was a glorious moment. I was surprised to find that I felt no great compulsion to climb them, just to be there with them was enough.

Only when I turned round did I see what we had come to see, the 'Breche du Roland'.

If I had seen a painting of it, I would have said it was science fiction, something from another planet. Mars perhaps. The mind struggles to comprehend what it cannot measure relatively. Three great terraces of stone surrounded me, carved by the glacier from the mountain in one vast, sheer arc, two miles in diameter, two thousand feet high, and, in the middle, perfectly placed architecturally, Roland's neat 'cut-out' doorway. I could not see a single sign of life growing on its rocky slopes and it was easy to imagine rockets parked within its sheltering arms. The sun made no attempt to climb it either, instead choosing to hover over the horizon like an exotic bloated star.

The 'Breche du Roland' at Luz-Saint-Sauveur.

A single silver thread of a waterfall fell across the rock into a small lake at its feet. The air was still, the clouds moving slowly over the rock. The only sound was the faint splashing of the water. There

95

was no one else at all. My companion had disappeared and left me sitting on a rock. I tried to absorb every atom of the scene into my body, as if burning the experience into the silver halide crystals on a film. Here was raw nature, almost untouched by tourism. No ski-lifts, no hotels. No Hemingways, European aristocrats or Hollywood starlets. It was as if I had discovered a new part of the world for myself. I could have stayed forever in that timeless moment. If God existed anywhere, it was here, not at Lourdes.

The horses seemed to resent the return leg of the journey even more than the way up. Perhaps they too had enjoyed the view. Is it impossible that when an animal gazes out at such a view they are awed by the beauty and the scale as we are? How can that not be so? Still, I doubted that my horse felt that way. When the path was narrow, the evil beast would throw itself against a rock, hoping to catch a leg and pretending to stumble in a vain attempt to throw me off. While Exmoor is nothing like the Pyrenees, horses are horses everywhere, and I had enough riding experience to know what to do. Once he realised this, my mule did not put a foot wrong, which was just as well as the return journey was vertiginous in the extreme. I saw little of the landscape on the way down, reins, saddle and rocks were my only reality.

I searched for somewhere to buy a souvenir once back in the village, something to remind me of that wondrous experience, but there was nowhere, for this was not a tourist place. I felt compelled to buy something, anything, not so much for me but for them, to give something back, but even the shop was closed. So, I left with nothing, except that wondrous memory. Over forty years later I still feel the desire to go back and pay back my debt to Luz.

The commune of Luz-Saint-Sauveur has not changed much since my father's day, except that canoeing has replaced mule-trekking as the main activity for tourists. When I visited I bought the generic postcards, fridge magnets and overpaid for fizzy drink, as one does, and when it came to pay for the car park, I handed over an obscene amount of money, not with gritted teeth but in thanks for that old debt.

River sparkling at the foot of the mountains.

We zigzagged for days from one side of the mountains to the other, passing small towns, often spas, along the foot of the mountains, the sunlight glinting on the occasional river dazzling me and causing my eyes to close. I remember a particularly magnificent lunch of Cocotte oeuf, foie gras and Magret de canard at Bagnéres-de-Luchon, perhaps that should have been 'Bagnéres-de-Luncheon', before Foix with its fairy tale castle appeared floating on a hill as if in a dream.

Christianity came late to the inaccessible Basque region and Islam made little impact on it at all when it swept through. There are few towers or spires to be seen once outside the large towns. The people already have their gods all around them in the form of those Pyrenean peeks and the mountain birds that circle them. But, when Christianity did arrive from Byzantium, it took on a peculiar form that was not seen elsewhere.

Perhaps there was something about the Pyrenean landscape that inspired its dualism and fatalism. I remember the Pyrenees as a harsh but honest land, with high contrasts of light and colour. I remember the brownness of the rock and its gaunt mountain passes. I remember how death was every-where, from dehydration, from war, from falling rocks or being tipped over the edge of a single lane road into a plunging gorge, and yet I remember it as an area that is full of bright colours, wildflowers and passion. Perhaps that is why the Cathars found their stronghold here in this region. It made sense in a practical way to the people who lived here. The Cathars were Christians, but they believed in two Gods, one good, one bad, and that we, as the spirits of angels, flitted between the two. I have to say that it makes far more sense to me than the confused mix of Jesus, Mary and the Holy Spirit that Catholics have to contend with, but what do I know? Still, almost four million others seem to have agreed with me, especially women. The 'Perfecti', the Cathar clergy, which included women in all its ranks, worked hands on in the communities they served and, unlike the Catholics, didn't impose taxes, charge for indulgences or take collections. They were hugely popular, but as a result, there was little money to spend on great monuments to what was a terrifying form of religion for the Pope.

In the early Middle Ages, France was a much smaller country than now; the area that is France today was then a hotchpotch of kingdoms, duchies and counties, some with allegiance to the French crown, others with different loyalties. 'Languedoc' was the generic name given to the southern half of the country, where they did not speak French at all, but a family of languages between French and Spanish known as 'les langues d'oc', or 'Occitanian'. Instead of holding mass in Latin, Catharism was preached in the language of the locals. It became so popular here that in 1208 Pope Innocent III, already at war with the Muslims in the Holy Land, launched a crusade against the 'heretical' Cathars. Cathar country's strongholds, such as the castle at Foix, predate the Pope's Albigensian Crusade, but many of them were strengthened during the twenty years of the conflict, as local lords resisted the incursion of 'foreign' French barons such as Simon de Montfort and Italian cardinals. Half a million people are estimated to have been killed in what is the first documented case of genocide in Europe, committed solely by the Catholic Church, directly on the Pope's orders. One has to assume that God was not involved and was unamused…

Worryingly, Pope Innocent III is one of two popes among the 23 historical figures depicted in marble relief portraits above the gallery doors of the U.S. House of Representatives in honour of their influence on the development of American law.

'Old ducks' with new ducks. Foix 1955.

Imagine my surprise when, the next morning, after days of dusty hillsides and rocky crags, the coach pulled up in the shade of an old oak tree, beside an immaculately manicured lawn. It had neatly trimmed hedges and a white picket fence. A neat gravel path edged with white stones and bordered with flowers led towards a rocky outcrop. Nothing could have looked more like an English garden. There was no building to be seen, instead a small hut guarded the entrance to a cleft in the rock barely big enough for me to enter. We stepped inside the cave and there, swirling silently before us, was an underground river. At Wookey Hole in Somerset, one is aware that one is approaching both a cave and a river, all is wild, dark and damp, and the rock closes in. Here the flat prettiness gave absolutely no hint and so the impact was enormous.

We sat in flat-bottomed punts and were poled efficiently along. The excited chatter died away and we drifted in silence and almost total darkness. Gradually light glowed ahead. Groups of stalactites hung down to the water and were reflected in the smooth surface. Cunning lighting picked them out on both sides of the river and they shone with a thousand faces as we drifted through this stone forest. On we went until we came to a flat, stony shore just above the main river level. There, on the smooth rock wall, were images drawn by the people who had found these caves, speaking across centuries to me. Wall followed wall of cave painting. Pictures of hunting and other rituals. Image superimposed on image of deer, bison, bears, all running. In one niche, alone, a carefully modelled group of bison, crude but clearly recognisable, covered by calcium.

Images of running bison and other animals visible on the walls.

I have talked about the sense of being dwarfed by scale when it comes to mountains or scenery, but it is also possible to feel dwarfed by the enormity of time. It was extraordinary, nay impossible, to comprehend that humanity had inhabited these caves so long ago. A time five times longer than the ancient Greeks are to us. To think that such magnificent cathedrals as the 'Salon-Noir' were constructed from droplets of calcium carbonite built up over that time is humbling. We are truly nothing in the presence of nature.

Roaring waterfall in the cavern.

We drifted past vista after vista, until the river began to narrow, and the current became fierce. The lights showed not only the art but swirling angry whirlpools. A dull roar became noticeable, and we came out into a bright cavern. Before us a waterfall spouted out of the wall and crashed down into the basin. It was not very high, about fifteen feet, but the roar in the confined space was tremendous. It was a coup de théâtre indeed.

As we drove further east, the country began to change. The mountains receded yet the ground was covered with huge boulders. The locals called it 'Desolation' and I could see why. Spanish influence began to appear again as the paper border ebbed and flowed in real life. The layout and structure of the villages and towns changed, the food changed noticeably, and Romano-Catalonian paintings appeared in the churches. Villagers flash grotty passports at sleeping border guards as they push carts between their houses in one country and their gardens in another. The paperwork is clearly a nonsense. The town of Llivia, is literally a little Spanish enclave in France as well as a cultural one. It was left out of the boundary treaty because the wording was 'villages' and Llivia counted as a town. And then there was Latour-de-Carol, a name famous in railway history. The great expresses once bore the legend 'Paris–Latour-de-Carol–Madrid'. It was where the gauges changed before France and Spain standardised their rail network. Today it is little more than a dusty siding where shingle is loaded into wagons as the international express trains speed by.

Up into the mountains again and on to Andorra, a misty and rain-swept ski resort, that glimmered golden pink in the evening sun. The rain, warm as it was, was a welcome change from the heat of the valleys below. Font Romeu, so I was told, has the most consistent temperature year-round of anywhere in Europe. What a peculiar claim to fame! I wondered who discovered that and why. It seemed rather chilly to me.

A single-track road crossed the plateaux and plunged over the edge down through the Gorges de St. George and Pierre-Lys, with no safety barriers, and finally arrived in the town of Quillan. It was to be the last of many such hair-raising descents. The Pyrenees were finally behind us and the country became gentle. Vineyards clothed the rolling hills.

Cyclist and cavalcade in the Tour de France.

The temperature began to climb. Somewhere along the road we met up with the Tour de France and its travelling circus. Small villages were decorated with the ubiquitous red, white and blue. Cars were piled high with everything but bicycles – advertising drinks and, back then, camel cigarettes. Police escorts wailed noisily through the mountain passes, but, out in the middle of nowhere, a group of cyclists were locked in a quiet world of their own.

Eventually the whole cavalcade left us, and there, sitting quietly above the rolling lilac-coated hills of the valley, were the towers and walls of Carcassonne, the most famous of the Cathar strongholds. It appeared so suddenly after the harsh modernity of the Tour de France, and was so perfectly complete, that it seemed quite unreal. It was a page from the Duc du Berry left over into this century, an illusion that was difficult to dispel. As a citizen of Bath, I know well the arguments about restoration and the debates as to what lengths it should go. I can see immediately that the Viollet-le-Duc, the famous French architect who restored Carcassonne in the middle of the previous century, had made a mistake in using the wrong tiles on the roofs, making them look more like the Châteaux of Normandy, but I still feel that this was but a small wrong considering all that he did that was right. Such a place had to be preserved and preserving is not to deal with something as a dead object, but as a living organism.

The 'living organism' and Viollet-le-Duc's rooftiles seen from afar.

Being from Bath, I know quite a bit about restoration and conservation. Restoring a building is not about simply maintaining it, repairing it or remaking it as it once was, assuming of course that you know which version of how it was that you want to restore, for living buildings do not stay the same. No, restoration is about re-establishing it in a complete state which possibly may never have existed at any one given historical moment. Four conditions should be considered. First, the 're-establishment' has to be consistent with plans and photographs which guarantee work in keeping with the given style. Second, the restoration has to involve not just the appearance of the building, but also its structure; it has to use the most efficient means to assure the long life of the building, including using more solid materials, used more wisely. Third, it has to exclude any modification contrary to obvious evidence, but the structure can and should be adapted to conform to more modern or rational uses and practices, which means alterations to the original plan. Last, the restoration should preserve older modifications made to the building, excepting those which compromised its stability or its conservation, or those which gravely violated the value of its historical presence. There's a lot for an architect to consider.

Carcassonne is a fortified mediaeval town and a town that is still lived in. Its origin is Roman, having for centuries guarded the main route between the Languedoc coast to the southeast, and the plains of Gascony to the west. But as the border of France changed and grew, so the strategic importance of Carcassonne declined. When I visited it had about eight hundred inhabitants, many slopes, churches, a cathedral and a large castle. We entered through a narrow, well-fortified main gate and came into a warren of tiny, cobbled streets, all full of people. It is lined with souvenir shops, but why not? Towns like this always had tourists buying souvenirs. The walls protected the markets and were often paid for by the money raised by monks selling indulgences. It would be hypocritical to abandon the practice now and the revenue is doubtless needed more than ever. I bought an ice-cream and tried to eat it before the hot sun caused it to melt and I dropped it on the floor. It does not matter too much how the money is raised, within boundaries, no? What is important is that the revenue is used to help the town and that the work is centrally coordinated in a longer-term holistic plan.

Everywhere I looked I saw parallels with my adopted home city of Bath. The whole effect is of an enclosed but safe way of life within the mighty walls. The castle in the centre dominating all, as it always did. Many people have inhabited the hill of Carcassonne; the different types of stone, the different ways they were cut can show these changes as strata in the walls. Viollet simply levelled them up with his own last layer of blocks. The effect is splendid. Everywhere one goes there are views down alleys, over flights of steps, along the ramparts, all diverse, yet bonded together into a single artistic unity. There is nothing quite like it – it had to be done.

Carcassonne at night, floodlit.

At night, floodlit, seen from across the river, the unreality increased as the walled city seemed to float in the darkness. As the 'Son et Lumiere' ended, clouds of coloured smoke billowed up from the ramparts, the pinnacles shining above them.

The light slowly faded, and the vision of Carcassonne was gone. It could easily have been a dream.

PROVENCE

Land of Light and Lavender, 1955

The bus drove through Narbonne along a wonderful, deserted coast; the Etang on one side, the sea on the other. After spending so long in the mountains, it was good to see the sea again, even this mild-mannered version of it. I wondered how my Dutch seafaring friends would have coped with the long absence.

Avignon, showing the famous bridge.

I arrived in Avignon, that most famous of places, the capital of the papacy throughout the fourteenth century, the playground of kings. These days it is a UNESCO World Heritage site, like Bath. It should have been fabulous; perhaps I expected too much. The Palace of the Popes was an empty shell, so often altered and rebuilt that it had no atmosphere left at all. As for the town? Petrarch, the great mediaeval poet and wit, called it 'dirty, windy and cold'. Cold it wasn't, but the rest had clearly not changed in six hundred years. The Garden of the Rock lies in an abandoned fort above the city. It hides a reservoir which supplies the town with fresh water, but somehow the garden itself was parched and dried out. The view from it, however, was magnificent with Mont Ventoux, the Rhone River, Barthelasse Island and the Saint-Andre fort laid out below me. I was awestruck by the immense power of the river Rhone, the size of it, and its obvious strength and speed. Beneath me, too, was the bridge of Saint Benedict, the one made peculiarly famous by the song.

> Sur le Pont d'Avignon
> L'on y danse, l'on y danse
> Sur le Pont d'Avignon
> L'on y danse tous en rond.

The bridge was clearly a beautiful, delicate structure, built on the site of an old Roman bridge. In the thirteenth century, its twenty-two arches were the only river crossing between Lyon and the sea. But clearly too many fine lords and ladies had 'dansé' on the bridge, or perhaps those portly musicians from the fourth verse 'comme ça', because all but four of those magnificent, curved arches had collapsed or been swept away by the mighty river. It was a glorious bridge to nowhere, a not unfitting symbol of the city itself.

Speaking of the Dutch, about twelve miles north of Avignon, glowing like its name in the morning sun, lies a small town called Orange. It's a strange place to give its name to the line of kings who went on to rule over the Netherlands, places as far away as Indonesia and, of course, England itself. It is, like so many of the places in this journal, a Roman city, and the Second Legion's Triumphal Arch and magnificent theatre still lie, completely intact, at its centre. Military insignia and weapons cover one side, along with plenty of earthy Roman graffiti. The other side is worn smooth by the abrasive wind.

The theatre itself contains the biggest free-standing Roman wall in existence, towering four storeys high, containing within it a statue of Augustus. I sat high in the steep arc of seats and ate my packed lunch of salted bread, eggs, salad meat and cheese, very much as Roman theatregoers would have done two thousand years before.

The Roman Theatre at Orange.

The Roman province surrounding the town of Orange prospered so much so that it was turned into a fiefdom of the Holy Roman Empire in the "Golden Bull" of 1356 which attempted to fix the boundaries of Christianity. "William the Silent" inherited this principality in 1544 along with the Spanish colony of Nassau and land near Delft in Holland, which was then a possession of the Spanish crown. This created the House of Nassau-Orange. During the "Wars of Religion" and the following "Eighty Years' War" the strategic position of the principality was used by France to inflict significant losses on Spain, leading to Dutch independence, which the Catholic French ironically thought was a good thing, and the Princes of Orange-Nassau becoming the de-facto royal family of Holland, and ultimately to William III being crowned King of England. The actual process by which William would seize the crown was plotted in the city of Bath. Everything is somehow interconnected.

As a Bathonian, I was delighted to be briefly reunited with my Roman friends whilst on holiday. They are everywhere, all the time in my own town, a people who are curiously ancient and modern in equal measure. Grabbing a caffeine fix on the way to work, a quick sandwich midday and a takeaway in the evening were everyday activities to them. Using concrete to build or anaesthetic in medicine was just standard practice and yet they fervently believed in their panoply of gods and thought nothing of buying or murdering slaves. Their economy was essentially based on socialist principles with central planning and pricing, yet they were entrepreneurs and capitalists to a man. Tricky fellows and brutal pragmatists, they are our shared ancestors and I have always felt strangely proud of them. Having bumped into them once here, they were suddenly everywhere, as if they, too, were on holiday in the sun.

Nimes is as brisk and bustling a modern city as you could get, full of wide boulevards, cars and shops. It lies on the old Via Domitia, the first Roman road built in Gaul, where its creators have left behind an impressive array of remains. The Roman Gardens, the Temple of Diane, the Augustine Tower, and the most beautiful of all, a supreme jewel of Graeco-Roman art, the 'Maison Carrée', which sat in the middle of the town centre square. The temple is a stunning piece of Vitruvian architecture and is almost unparalleled for its completeness. It was originally dedicated by the Emperor Augustus, who we met at the theatre just down the road, to his two grandsons, Gaius and Lucius, who both sadly died in childhood. Since then, it has been used as a granary, a church and a tomb for the sixteenth century Duke of Uzès, all helping to keep this magnificent building in one piece.

The Maison Carrée (Nimes).

Despite their beauty, these buildings now seemed set aside, removed from the communities that they were supposed to serve. Relics perhaps, both sacred and otherwise, but leftovers nonetheless. There was no sense of continuity in the city at all. But less than four hundred yards away, in amongst a maze of narrow lanes and cafes, stood the Roman Arena. Unlike its famous cousin in Rome, it is only two storeys high, so it is still shaded by the poplars and sycamore trees that surround it, helping it blend into its surroundings, and unlike the Colosseum, it is completely intact. This is no ruin or restoration, but a fully functional Roman building still effectively performing its job after two thousand years. The arena, I was told, holds over twenty thousand people, and its stairwells and exits are so well built and so well configured, that it passes all modern safety regulations comfortably. As a result, it is still used regularly as both a concert venue, and of course, this still very much being Basque territory, for bull fights. Indeed, you can make out the sculpted heads of bulls just above the upper tier of arches.

Unlike the incredibly beautiful but lonely Maison Carrée, 'Les Arènes' is a hugely successful building that still belongs to the town and the people of Nimes. I raised a glass of local wine to it at the 'Brasserie des Antonins' opposite. Long may its success continue!

Les Arènes (Nimes).

Arles, just down the road from Nimes, was once the capital of Roman Gaul. Two thousand years ago it had a population of over a hundred thousand people, far more than it does today, but, without a huge cloth manufacturing industry to sustain it, it had become a sleepy little town of narrow lanes beside the river Rhone, dust covered in the summer, rather shut down in the winter.

Although they were crumbling ruins, its theatre and arena were still very much in use, part of both its past and present. There was a certain charm about the place and light that had inspired numerous artists. Van Gogh spent a manically productive fifteen months here, painting more than two hundred works, in his 'Yellow House' on the Place Lamartine, while Picasso painted his wife, Jacqueline, in numerous Arlesian costumes here. Here is the 'Allee Champs' with its sarcophagi lying under the fragrant lilac trees that Gaugin said he could rest a canvas on top of quite comfortably. Nothing of it was architecturally exceptional, but it was a lovely, ordinary place, every spot full of light and colour, worthy as a painting in its own right. The cathedral was a modest affair, the exact opposite of what I'd seen in Avignon. It was a simple Romanesque church from the outside, made from mud brick and bits of stone, but inside its walls were covered in superb carvings. Its cloisters were long and cool, with lilac trees intertwined with Corinthian columns. I would recommend it to travellers over either Nimes or Avignon, but perhaps I was overly influenced by a superb tartine – foie gras and onion jam – at the restaurant L'Ouvre Boite! I felt myself becoming a little bourgeois!

The Pont du Gard stood livid against a thunderous sky. Waves of purple clouds had swallowed up the sun and the first lightning was flickering in the sky by the time I had climbed up through the surrounding woods.

By the time I had reached the top it was pouring. It had been such a glorious morning when I had caught the bus, that I had left with no equipment other than something to eat in my haversack. I was absolutely alone so I stripped off everything but trousers and shoes, stuffing my suit jacket, shirt and tie into my bag. Then I started walking across the Pont. It was one of the bravest and also the most foolish things I have ever done. The bridge is about a hundred and fifty feet high. The top is covered with great slabs of slippery stone, at most three feet wide. There is no parapet, safety rail or rope. I had no crampons, ropes or carabiners with me, and my leather-soled shoes were slippery even on the cobbled streets.

111

The Pont du Gard.

I cannot say why I did it other than the sheer compulsion to explore the thing and be at one with it. I had the overwhelming sense that every bolt of lightning was aimed directly at me and either the shock of the explosions taking place above my head, or the sheer force of the rain would push me over the edge. I was frightened in a way that I had not been since being alone on that glacier in the Swiss mountains. But I was not alone with the gods, for the Pont itself seemed to hold that terrible sky back. Eventually I made it to the other side and clambered thankfully down to the road. There was still no one around, except for a small Fiat 500 that seemed to have been abandoned (see page 7), but I could not have cared if there were thousands. I stripped off once again, rubbed myself dry with a sweater and changed into my semi-dry suit. The bus shelter was hollowed out of the rock, so I stood at the mouth of the cave looking up at that vast satisfying structure until the bus came to take me back to Tarascon where I was staying. The bridge is, of course, not a bridge but an aqueduct, built in the first century AD by our mutual friends, to bring water from fifty miles away in Uzès. It is an amazing structure with three tiers of arches, the lower row being seventy-five feet high. My Roman friends used no cement or mortar in its construction, instead cutting each stone to a mathematically perfect size. The stones were brought to the site by barge and holes and protruding stones for the wooden scaffolding could still be seen in its side. Despite my soaking, I could have stared at it for hours, there was nothing about it that wasn't awe-inspiring or strangely beautiful. The owner of the Fiat 500 seemed less impressed.

The bus ground up the twisting, ever-steepening road. Gigantic boulders lay upon the side of the hill in such profusion that I felt that the whole range of small mountains was nothing but a pile of stones. Below me the cliffs descended past a pocket of small houses and ruined buildings, towards a quarry. It was not possible to see where man's handiwork ended and Mother Nature's began, so did one merge with the other. Van Gogh and Cézanne found their inspiration on this beautiful, wild outcrop, most famously seen in Cézanne's painting of the limestone quarries (carrières).

Cézanne's 'La Carrière de Bibémus'

A final savage bend and a rise to a hilltop isolated from the rest and we had arrived at that most fantastic place, Les Baux. The castle that stood on top of the rock, was built in the tenth century and, for the next five hundred years, it stood firm whilst savage conflict swept through Provence. It was at Les Baux that the famous minstrels and troubadours of the day sang songs of courtly love to queens and princesses.

The Provençal writer, Frédéric Mistral, described the owners of the old castle as a 'Race of Eagles', but the 'Eagles' had long since flown the nest when I arrived. When the city turned to Protestantism in 1633, which partly evolved out of Catharism, it was razed to the ground by Cardinal Richelieu. I stared over the edge of the precipitous cliff drinking it all in and then down into the 'Val d'Enfer', said to be the inspiration for Dante's 'Inferno', where locals believe a fairy guards an immense treasure of gold. Today there is just a small village of dusty narrow lanes there and one of the greatest hotels in France, the Baumanière, but neither are easy to spot amongst the olive tree groves and the steep rocks. For an Englishman from a world of grey smoke and the Bristol channel, the intense colours and strong light of the south were a revelation. Under the blue sky, the orange, yellow and red splashes of the flowers took on an amazing brilliance. After five hundred years of violence, there was an atmosphere of peace in the languid air and, for that moment, time stood still.

The remains of Castle Les Baux.

I was a little nervous, or rather uncomfortable, at staying in the Baumanière. It felt inherently wrong that I should seek out such luxury. I was, in my own mind at least, a fairly down-to-earth and humble chap and certainly not a wealthy one, but Thomas Cook had insisted that it was the only 'approved' facility in the area. I could see why, and it was only for one night after all. It was not what I had expected, it was not like the fancy 'Le Regina' with its gold-plated walls and armies of frock coated servants, and that was entirely a good thing. It was quiet, almost deserted, and fairly plain. A two-storey seventeenth century coach house covered in ivy, stood in a well-kept garden with small, deep, green ponds. Ochre plastered walls, from which green shutters peered out, soaked up the sun. Pots of conifers and bays stood on the patio where white cloth tables had been laid out for dinner. The occasional tinkle of glass and the gentle sound of pétanque balls clicking in the sand could be heard, but I saw nobody. The rooms were in the old premises, large, plain but strangely luxurious.

The luxurious Baumanière Hotel.

French windows opened out on a pool the same colour as the sky which it eventually meets. There was a small library tucked away in a nook full of art books, which I was happy to supplement with those that I had brought with me. I swept up an armful of them and went to sit in the garden with a glass of lemon tea, trying, and failing, not to get too comfortable in such luxurious surroundings.

St. Remy sits on a shelf of rock high on a small pass. Here stood a triumphal arch and an extremely fine mausoleum with an ornate columned lantern. They seemed strange, standing all alone in the olive trees. But not far away, excavations had discovered a 'lost city' and I was allowed to see it. Students from the University of Provence were working everywhere and there was a real sense of excitement as gradually the paved streets, markets and houses of ancient Glanum appeared out of the earth and a few of the ornate stone columns were returned to an upright position. Now the dig is complete, the whole site has been cleaned up and, in the cold light of day, its streets seem as dead as a dinosaur's skeleton, just another academic ruin. But it had been a strange and moving experience to see an ancient town reborn and I was glad to have been a part of it.

Alphonse Daudet's Windmill.

Other isolated places float into the mind as I remember that long trip. Montemayor, the fortified abbey with its great under croft and its lovely cloisters. The Chapel of the Cross, plain and austere, and a woman's voice, splendidly true soaring up to echo and re-echo around the barren walls. Châteauneuf-du-Pape, the great turrets looking across the river to Avignon, the pebbles round the vines and the endless glasses of dark red wine flashing in the hot sun. I still like to drink a bottle of it on my birthday. Then the home of Mistral – Daudet's windmill (opposite) – Aix-en-Provence, with its dried roads all part of the general impression of Provence, the county and the brilliance of the light.

Mostly I remember Provence as a palette of emotions rather than places, small hilltop villages with yellow houses and egg blue shutters, bustling markets, cobbled streets and narrow lanes, stark red cliffs and dramatic canyons and of course its famous lilac-coloured fields of lavender.

Finally, my long journey led me to the Riviera. I was not impressed and won't lengthen this already overly long section by describing it. True the views along the coast were splendid and I suppose that the great villas were indeed magnificent in their way. Fréjus was not too bad, nor I suppose St. Juan-les-Pais. Cannes I found shabby with a faded gentility that had none of the vulgarity of Nice. It had not yet become the home of the celebrity film festival. Villefranche too must once have been a nice place, but Menton was too English by far with its 'Eat your picnic here' signs. Monte Carlo however impressed me least of all. Why anyone should want to stay crammed in among all those tower blocks of flats and offices or to moor up in that solid mass of shipping in the harbour I do not know. I was glad to have seen it, but no, the Riviera was not for me.

I popped over the border into Italy for my last night partly to cheer myself up, as Italy, which I had briefly visited on my way back from Switzerland in 1953, had been such a happy memory for me. San Remo had a touch of Monte Carlo about it, but the old town was likeable, a warren of a place with gardens tumbling down into the sea. I ate a humble but splendid fish supper on the harbour wall, before the long train journey back from Nice to Boulogne. Italy, which again has to wait for its own chapter, had come to the rescue once more.

I had seen and done too much on such a long holiday and, reading back over this account, when combined with the section from the Pyrenees, it seems like more of a shopping list rather than an

117

adventure. I had enjoyed everything of course, but I realised that many of the things that I had expected to be highlights of the trip, had actually left me cold. I had enjoyed Carcassonne, of course, and being where the famous artists had got their inspiration. It was wonderful to see the Maison Carrée and to sit in the great theatre of Orange, but it had been so much better to walk across the Pont du Gard in the pouring rain, to stare at the desolate 'Breach of Roland' at Luz, and nothing had topped the highlight of my holiday sitting on the little bridge in Porte d'Espagne munching my lunch. The beach resorts were all pleasant enough, the sleepy towns of Provence were delightful, but they all paled into insignificance beside the vivid world of the colourful Basque people, their passionate politics and the bulls running chaotically, or perhaps not, in the streets of Pamplona. Twenty years later, their warmth still radiates stronger than the Spanish sun.

For the English in particular, Provence has acquired an air of middle-class gentility, a place for the wealthy to retire to over the summer, a place of deckchairs where armchair detective novels are set. We can picture ourselves outside some gite sipping a glass of cold white Châteauneuf-du-Pape (which I prefer to the heavy reds) or enjoying coffee and croissants with a morning paper. But Provence isn't what it appears to be and should not be trivialised in such a way. Beneath the Mediterranean brightness is something dark and mystical, something that the Cathars understood and tapped into with their unique brand of Christianity. Dig under a mediaeval church and you'll find a pagan temple. Sip too much wine and you might catch a glimpse of the mythical "Tarasque" of Tarascon, a scaly, spike-backed demon with a serpent's tail and a lion's head, or the Drac de Beaucaire, a dragon that lives in the Rhone and feeds on maidens and children. Provence is full of dark myths as is the Pyrenees as a whole. Even the benevolent climate has a dark side. It often changes without warning, turning from mild sunshine to bone-bleaching white heat or gothic thunderstorms. Film stars, celebrities and resorts come and go, but this area remains a region of great drama in all senses.

PARIS & THE ÎLE DE FRANCE

La Ville Lumière – City of Lights, 1956

I knew that I had to go back and see Paris 'properly'; it would have been wrong, impolite even, to have dismissed the city of love and the home of the Enlightenment after spending so short a time there the previous year, but I do not know whether my return was a success or not. I have a strange relationship with Paris. My previous journeys highlighted how different the reality of the place was from the intellectual idea of it. It highlighted that the things that stand out are not always what you had expected. Grubby and yet refined, chaotic but still serene, rigid but liberated, and so it was with Paris.

From the Arc de Triomphe to the Eiffel Tower (Lee Miller 1954).

I have visited the city seven times and still, I cannot make my mind up about it. There is more than one Paris to see, of course; the mediaeval town, the religious centre, the industrial slums and the majestic boulevards of the belle epoque all mixed in amongst each other and, to a certain extent, you see what you expect. Rome is, of course, beautiful and Amsterdam is friendly, but there is a coldness about Paris, an air of indifference about it that sits ill even with other Frenchmen. It wears its pride on its sleeve, the pride of an ancient land of God-Kings, the pride of being the home of enlightenment and culture and the bitter pride of an imperial capital occupied and reduced to ruin. Now it is forced to share its remaining funds with people, servants, slaves from its former colonies. It is noble, aristocratic and unhappy.

The city is attractive enough in parts, stunning even in places when the light is right, and the buildings have been cleaned, but the untainted areas were few and far between and in nineteen-fifty-six much of the city still lay in the shadow of the war. The Île de la Cité, the St. Louis, the views across the river from the tree-lined 'quais' are well photographed. To walk through the Tuileries, over the Pont des Arts to the flower market behind Notre Dame is a very pleasant thing to do in the early morning. So too is the ascent, at least once, if you can afford it, of the Eiffel Tower. The view from the top really does make the experience of getting there worthwhile. But the city is dirty, tired and broken.

The Louvre was overwhelming. There were simply too many treasures to see, and they tended to cancel each other out – the mind can only take so much. The Mona Lisa, recently returned from exile on the Loire, had no effect on me at all, but neither did any other painting stand out in my mind. The good lady herself was clearly in on the joke, but I did not understand it. What is the point of a painting with no message or a message not on the canvas? Perhaps if Leonardo had painted it just once, instead of tinkering with it his entire life, the silk merchant's wife would seem more endearing, more real and less like an academic exercise.

Only two pieces of sculpture made any impact on me: one, the enormous Egyptian sphinx mooching about in the crypt and two, the Winged Victory of Samothrace at the head of the stairs. Instinctively I hunched my shoulders against the wind tearing at her vestments. On the other hand, the impressionist paintings in the Jeu du Paume museum exuded their quiet beauty around that lovely little gallery, a constant source of joy and refreshment.

The 'Field of Mars' in 1956.

I queued to get into the Sainte Chapelle, which lies buried in a part of Paris more reminiscent of Whitehall. It was the quintessence of high Gothic and its design a tour de force. The entrance to the dark crypt, the narrow twisting stairway and suddenly the blaze of glass, the sweep of the stone mullions rising higher and higher to the dizzy roof. Everything about it was exquisite. But it was the glass that was the chapel's most exotic treasure. The colour of the glass, dancing over the floor, over people's upturned faces, drenching everywhere in a glorious living light that changed as the sun moved. The real genius of the building is in how the master builder has disguised the thickness of the columns between the windows. Each one is, in fact, seven separate columns of which we only see the edge of one, lit by the light from the windows on either side. Two others are diagonally in the shadow, which is lost to us as perspective, with three much larger ones outside the structure. The curved angle of the walls means not only that the gap between the windows is narrower inside than out, but also gathers the light and channels it into the building. Gaudy it is, but technically brilliant, too!

Versailles left me completely untouched. The mind registered the effort but was unmoved. It was little more than a three-dimensional drawing, repetitive, irrelevant and completely detached from its surroundings. The interior made me feel queasy. It was too ornate, too vulgar. Gauche. As an Australian in our party said: 'There's a pub in Sydney that looks like this'. I laughed, how harsh for the French to be culturally criticised by an Australian! Harsh, but eminently fair. My sympathies lay with the Revolutionaries, and I would happily have burnt the place down. Only the little chapel had anything to say at all and I only lingered to look at the great waterwheel that lifted water to the palace, impressed by its mechanics and sheer physical size.

Fontainebleau was much more 'real' and a very attractive building. It was florid and decadent, of course, but in the Napoleonic context, entirely fitting. How odd to stand on that great staircase that I had seen in so many historic paintings and drawings, its steps worn down by famous boots and feel that I, too, was part of that shared history. Better than the palace by far, however, was a painter's studio in the woods nearby, the centre of the Barbizon School of Art. The glorious landscape paintings, each meticulously capturing the fall of the light on the leaves of the trees, sat unframed upon their easels, Millet and Rousseau's accoutrements lying just where they had left them.

Far nicer than either of the main palaces was Josephine's 'Malmaison', a real house rather than a showy, administrative palace. It was easy to believe that she and Napoleon actually lived there as a family and really used the furniture and china. I wondered what the bold general liked to eat for dinner and how often he cheated at cards. Where had he sat when he planned his invasion of Spain, on which tables had the cutlery been cleared to make room for the maps of Switzerland, Italy and Russia? Every scraped plate and saggy-bottomed chair had somehow played a part in Europe's great story.

Chartres, too, was lovely. The cathedral towers, first seen from afar across the plain, then and best of all, the great green roof capping not only the church but the entire town as it struggled up the hill, binding the two together. The town itself was a fitting setting for the cathedral. From the joyous bridge jumping over the little river, a winding road made a stiff climb up to our destination, giving me the odd glimpses of a tower, a buttress or an ancient door. Only ten years before, Nazi collaborators had been hounded through these narrow lanes, beaten with sticks, and led to the cathedral to have their heads shaved and their souls purged. The odd, asymmetrical towers take a little getting used to, but the tension between them is not unpleasing and they are clearly brothers, which gives the whole building an informal, homely feel that most grand cathedrals lack. As I walked from the south porch to the north, the figures high on the walls illustrated the entire development of the mediaeval stone community. It was a delightful experience.

A view towards Chartres Cathedral, 1956.

Another mediaeval gem was the Musée Cluny, tucked away down a side street in Paris, hard to find, surrounded as it was by great commercial buildings, but well worth the effort. The building itself is an old mediaeval hall and contains glorious tapestries, domestic artefacts and a kitchen garden. Like the Malmaison, it was easy to imagine travellers like myself, ordinary people on a pilgrimage, staying here and telling stories by the fire. I sat, exhausted, on a stone bench in the little garden, the smell of parsley filling the warm evening air. I had walked too far and seen too many things in too short a time and things had begun to blur together in my mind. Old Paris, mediaeval, pre-empire Paris I decided that I liked, as I liked much of the surrounding towns and countryside, but the mix of royalty, imperialism and religion gave the more famous version of the city a bad taste in my mouth. It was an act that the battered reality of the place couldn't pull off in those days. It was time for me to leave.

The two faces of Paris.

The Paris my father visited in 1956 was very different from the city we know today. The country's economy was in tatters after the war and nearly three million inhabitants from the former colonies had flocked to a city that had seen no new housing created in half a century. Close to one hundred thousand buildings had been declared uninhabitable but were nonetheless crammed full. One in five apartments had no running water, two thirds had no toilet and three quarters no bathing facilities.

Paris was a city where those pretending to be something that they weren't had to make do with what they had, maintaining the impression on the outside that things were better than they were. There existed a separation between its private and public face accompanied by an increasing build-up of anger and resentment on all sides.

Street corner exemplifying the secular and religious, the medieval and the modern, 1956.

View-Master™ Reel (Paris)

CAIRO

City of a Thousand Minarets, 1956

I have to be honest, I didn't want to go. What with the heat and the politics; besides it wasn't even Europe. But those who knew more about the world situation than I did told me that it would be alright, and those who knew me well knew that I would cope with anything Egypt would throw at me. Surely, I was not going to turn down the opportunity to visit the home of civilisation, where it all began. A chance to see the famous images of the Pyramids that we know so well from books for myself! And in the end, I was glad I went; what a sight they are. But what a change from a cool and damp Paris.

On paper it was a ten-hour flight from Paris Orly airport to Cairo. Direct with no stopover, but in practice it took a lot longer. I believe it was a Lockheed Constellation, a large plane with four propeller engines and three tails. It did have beds in first class, as I understand that they do now, ones that folded down from the overhead lockers like on trains. But that was only for fancy folk and ordinary types like me had to make do with a thin blanket, trying to ignore the endless drone of the turboprop engines. I curled up with an ancient guidebook and a pocketbook of handy Arabic phrases. Marhaba, Kaeef halak and most importantly of all Asef – I'm sorry, especially important if you are British.

We flew directly over the Alps, which was an amazing experience. It was fascinating to see the same mountains that I had tried to climb a few years before, but from above, the spikey carpet hurling the sunlight back at clouds. From there we followed the Italian coast, the wide beaches and Rome quite visible from this height. Then we turned out over the blue. We flew south for a long time and the quality of the light slowly changed. Egypt is instantly recognisable from the air, a crumpled yellow blanket with a thin green thread sewn through it. The land is completely barren apart from this long, thin strip and I was immediately struck by how fragile the whole situation seemed. It made me wonder why people had settled in such an area and how such an exotic civilisation had grown from it.

Egypt then was not the country that you would recognise today. It has changed, and many would say not for the better, but freedom often comes at a cost. Back then it was a colony of the western powers, with western mannerisms. It was a Muslim country, but not in a radical way: women wore skirts and had their hair and faces uncovered, even in formal situations. They were free to drive around the streets of Cairo on scooters or sunbathe on the beach. Since the end of the nineteenth century, there had been a considerable amount of investment in the city, by all sides, not least the British and French, given its strategic location and the canal. Back then all traffic to India passed through the Suez Canal and two-thirds of the British Empire's oil, like grain flowing back to Rome in ancient times. The British, like Mark Antony, were here to ensure nothing disrupted that flow.

I was met off the plane by a disreputable-looking man in a thin, grey suit and what appeared to be an almost coral, open-necked shirt. He looked more like a back street hustler than an official. A funny little car was waiting for us, and my driver seemed very excited about it. It was a dusty cream colour and looked like a square biscuit tin. Apparently, it was made in Egypt, in a new factory built by the Russians on the edge of town and was named optimistically after their greatest pharaoh Ramses. It whistled and rattled oddly as we went along, and my driver was quick to open the window. 'It's ok. German parts!' he was keen to point out.

Apart from any new Russian factories, time seemed to have stood still. All along the river men in loincloths ladled buckets of water from ancient water pumps to irrigate the muddy fields, ploughed by bored-looking ox or donkeys while women harvested reeds.

Cairo, even then, was a huge conurbation twisting its way around ancient holy sites, medieval citadels and the Nile, but at its heart it was very much a colonial town, and it was extremely easy to like. The similarity with Paris was immediately obvious, wide straight boulevards, lined with white-fronted tenement buildings three or four storeys high, ornate iron balconies, bedecked in scarlet bougainvillea flowers jutting out over the pavements. It reminded me, too, of the seafront in Brighton or Hove where the middle lane is used for trams on the main roads and for parking in the side roads. Cafés and bars were everywhere. I had expected the city to be dirty and dusted in sand, but neither was the case; it was immaculate. Policemen, and women, in crisp white uniforms stood in the shade of their little booths, guiding the traffic and overseeing proceedings. Sculpted art deco shops and cinemas swept by with names like 'Diana' and 'Raviolo' in lights, and grand, open squares with huge, circular fountains. I wondered how so much water was available and at what cost to the labourers in the fields, but Cairo was confident all was well.

Traffic police on duty in 1950s colonial Cairo.

We parked up in Ramses Street, named slightly unimaginatively, as was our car, after the pharaoh. I was told that the street used to be named after King Farouk's wife, but it was one of the first things Nasser had changed. This was to be a recurring theme. My driver led me to Cafe Groppi, a high-class tearoom and patisserie that looked out onto a busy junction. Vespa scooters and red and cream buses swept past constantly. Groppi was an exotic affair, marble columns, high ceilings, a slowly spinning fan and pot plants in copper pots. The sound of foaming milk, excited chatter and the clink of cups against saucers filled the air. Men in wicker chairs smoked giant cigars and tutted over the newspapers, while women with beehive hairdos and polka dot dresses exchanged news. The glass counters were full of a bewildering display of ice cream and pastries. The rep feared the ice cream would be a disappointment and steered me instead to the baklava – flaky pastry, pecans, grated pistachio and icing sugar, on a bronze platter. It was truly extraordinary. Rommel had publicly promised that he'd dine at Groppi. He never made it, but I discovered, much to my surprise, that they serve a drink here in his honour all the same. Order a 'Rommel' and they cheerfully bring you an empty cup.

The entrance to Cairo's historic Café Groppi.

After an initial spin round the city to orientate me, he dropped me at the Windsor Hotel. I was greeted by a gated porch, like a prison cell, but full of books and pot plants. It allowed the air to circulate but kept anyone from wandering in off the street. I scanned the titles as a dark beady eye inspected me from behind a slot in the wall. Rommel's book was not there.

The Windsor was dark but cool inside. Heavy mahogany furniture and deep red carpets filled rooms with tobacco-stained walls. There was a long-polished bar with chairs shaped like beer barrels. The air was heavy with the smell of stale beer and sticky port. It had been, perhaps still was, a British military officers' club. If they thought I'd fit in here they were dead wrong. Still, it was convenient for a number of sites including the Egyptian museum, the Khanel-Kahlili bazaar and the opera house.

I was keen to explore for myself and, having checked in and deposited my few possessions, I ventured out onto the streets once more. The sunset over the Nile is fantastic, a colour palette almost entirely of orange, brown and green. I have never seen anything like it, before or since. The sun grows as it nears the horizon and bubbles like molten iron in a foundry. Its glow bleeds out across the entire sky and spills over the glittering surface of the Nile. Palms and reeds are thrown into stark silhouette and, in the dusty distance, the instantly recognisable forms of the pyramids appear, as if levitating in the air. Horses stand shoulder deep in the river to be washed, while ancient figures with strong arms hurl their nets out across the water. This was real Egypt.

Darkness fell quickly, but after dark was when Cairo was most alive. I sat outside in a small restaurant and ate a plate of grilled kebabs with splendid black olives as I soaked up the atmosphere, listening to the eerie call to prayer echo off the rooftops. A line of donkeys was being guided through the darkness by a policeman with a red lantern. Reluctantly I returned to the Windsor Hotel with its gaudy, red neon sign.

I was up early, but already the day was hot. The occasional breeze did nothing to help, coming as it did from the Sahara. I looked out for more funny little Egyptian cars, but I don't recall seeing another one at all. There were, however, a surprising number of bicycles and scooters about and the streets were full of noise. The mosques of mediaeval Cairo lurk in shade behind the twentieth century apartment blocks that soak up all the sun. They are, by and large, dark and plain buildings, especially compared to the cathedrals of England, but the two are not analogous. Rows of shoes are dutifully piled up at their door. At the highest point in Cairo, dominating the hill, sits Saladin's Citadel built in the twelfth century. Its giant canon-topped walls look out over the city, private wells as well as the old Roman aqueduct supplying it with water. It has never fallen to its enemies and was still an active military base for Nasser's forces, so only the gardens were open.

The Grand Mosque of Mohammed Ali was open however, and, although it is a youngster by comparison to many of the ones in town, I was keen to see it. The large, alabaster-covered courtyard immediately reminds you that this is, first and foremost, a university, a place to study, a role that English cathedrals never had. It was, after all, in the mosques of the Middle East that the knowledge of the classical world was kept safe until the Enlightenment.

Cairo's Grand Mosque of Mohammed Ali.

There are innumerable places to sit and read or debate by the water as the burning sun passes overhead. It is calming and the acoustics dampen any noise. Inside it is far more ornate than I had expected, with paintings and mosaics covering the cupola. Huge chandeliers hang from the ceiling, the domes pierced by over one hundred and thirty-six stained glass windows, flooding its gilded surfaces with light. It is decorated in an Ottoman style rather than a Mamaluk one on the direct instructions of Mohammed Ali Pasha, whose tomb lies at one end. I'm not sure that I appreciate the difference between the two styles, but he can rest satisfied with the end result. It is fabulous.

They say that only 'Mad dogs and Englishmen go out in the midday sun'. They are probably right. It was so hot that even I took off my suit jacket and loosened my tie. I wandered back slowly through the narrow lanes and small courtyards. People congregate around water sources, a single tap in a garden, often in the shade of a jacaranda tree. The appeal and practicality of these small spaces is obvious. White eyes peer out behind doors and windows, cats congregate under cars. A flash of black fabric, like a wraith, appears briefly behind me and vanishes silently. I decided to walk through an indoor souk to cool off. After the bright sun outside it was like entering a cave. There was an overpowering smell of rotten fruit. Slowly my eyes made out toothless beggars sitting on grotty carpets, their tatty wares spread out in front of them. They were all glaring at me silently. Why was I there? I was clearly not welcome. But I am not the ruthless colonist that they think I am. A legless cripple, still wearing his military uniform, hobbled towards me on his crutches, a negotiator. I wonder how much of the money spent downtown in places like Groppi ever reaches these people. The soldier spoke English, so I addressed him by rank and tasked him with distributing the small sum of funds that I had with me amongst them fairly, as he saw fit. Suddenly he was the centre of attention rather than me, a man with a civic mission, while I was free to go. I heard more cries for help behind me, but nobody attempted to get in my way. By the time I got back to my hotel I had developed a thumping headache. My stomach was disagreeing with me, too.

I ordered room service, including a tomato juice and a large jug of boiled water. Shukran! The water from the taps was as brown as the Nile.

Noise and music in the street disturbed my sleep that night. The haunting off-key melodies, non-harmony, quarter notes and an incessant rhythm.

I vowed to pace myself better the next day, heading out for the Egyptian Museum before queues got too long. The great red brick building that houses it was itself a monument to colonialism, built by the French in the French Empire style. It could easily be mistaken for a train station and was just as busy. There were far too many exhibits to take it all in and I quickly became quite blasé. Although the first of the mummies is fascinating, after a while they all become the same and you run from one to another looking for names you recognise. I can think of no other instance in life where non-medical personnel look down at semi-decomposed dead bodies. It is incredible how preserved they are, flesh, hair and skin intact, expressions of pain and anguish on their faces as well as peaceful rest. Their sarcophagi, beautifully decorated with scripts from the Book of the Dead on the inside, are huge and I wondered how they were ever placed inside the pyramids by workmen. I smiled at the idea. 'Left a bit… right…' etc. All accompanied by much stopping for tea.

The treasure of Tutankhamun is, of course, indeed incredible, not just the death mask itself, but the quality of the grave goods that he was buried with. Miss Seawright says that Howard Carter took at least half of it for himself, and she actually knew the man, but even so, what a haul! This, for a fairly unpopular minor king, whose reign was cut short and who died before preparations were ready. The chariot, his throne. Such amazing work. It makes you wonder what treasure the famous namesake of the funny little car was buried with. The mask itself is beautiful, but enormous and more like a diving helmet. I let others crowd around the case and went off to find other things that I found more moving, including the stunning granite statue of Khafre. Three other statues stick in my mind as being particularly memorable. A small statue of the King, Mentuhotep, who stands in what seems like a red fez hat, a bored look on his face, like an old grouch at a New Year's party. A statue of the dwarf Seneb and his family, his wife's arms lovingly wrapped around him, and an amazingly lifelike sculpture in wood of a clerk called Ka-aper. One wonders about the story of such a modest person being so honoured.

The museum had by then become quite overrun with children and tourists, so I headed back to the hotel to avoid the worst of the heat but took a route that went via the market so I could fill up once again on those magnificent pastries and sweets. The sharp smell of citrus mingled joyously with almonds and the sharp scent of mint cut through the dry and dusty air. I followed my nose back into the old mediaeval town, barricaded in behind its high white walls like a Sultan's daughter.

The Khan el-Khalili bazaar was clearly a tourist trap, but it lay close enough to my hotel to be worth a visit. Hundreds of stalls are crammed in under the arches of this ancient market. Alcoves are piled high with metalware, lamps, slippers, furniture, carpets and crockery. There were bowls piled high with spices and buckets full of beads and coloured stones. There was little that took my fancy, but I did stop for a delicious thimble of that tar-like coffee and some pistachio nougat.

An outer section of the Khan el-Kahlili bazaar.

A cruise along the Nile is a must for any visitor and so the following afternoon I found myself aboard the 'Khartoum', a splendid paddle steamer built back in the twenties and unchanged in any way since. Sun loungers and wicker chairs were arranged on deck, while the restaurant was full of white tablecloths, cut glass and square cushions. Men with fezzes and waistcoats brought up trays of drinks attending to everyone's needs. I found a spot under a canvas awning and got out my book. The heat of the day had already broken by the time we cast off and the horizon was beginning to turn to haze. Just

135

before we left the quay however a group of English ladies in grey tweed uniforms, looking very much like vintage governesses, were escorted hastily aboard accompanied by the sound of hearty laughter. I gave it no further thought.

Ripples soon lapped along the hull as the paddles slapped the water. A faint breeze rustled the reeds that grew on the banks. I had scarcely read a chapter when, to my surprise, a gong sounded, announcing tea. At the back of the boat tables groaned with cucumber sandwiches and scones. I took a black tea with lemon only to get a very curious look from the waiter, but I didn't fancy the idea of milk having spent however long in the hot sun. Numerous submerged temples passed by, but there were also crocodiles in the green water. At the bow a couple of men in crisp linen suits played with a carbine rifle. The crocodiles liked to sun themselves on the sandy banks of the little islands dotted along the river. Some they have to themselves, others appeared to be populated entirely by goats. I wondered if they had some agreement between themselves or if it was a case of never the twain shall meet.

After an hour or so we pulled into a quay at the bottom of a formal garden. It was like the garden of an English country house with roses and clipped hedges everywhere. At the other end of the garden an old palace sat glimmering in the sun like a slightly tipsy hostess. It was now a Swiss-owned hotel and a popular spot to eat ice cream and watch the sun set. I did both happily until I saw the bill! The ice cream wasn't particularly good, my driver had been right.

For the return leg of the journey, the Khartoum had been decked out in strings of coloured lights with hurricane lamps on every table. Arabic music swelled up from the loudspeakers and a series of exotic dancers with tambourines appeared to 'entertain' us, amongst whom I recognised, much to my surprise, at least some of the prim ladies that I'd seen boarding the boat earlier.

I chomped through my dish of boiled beef and carrots, watching as a series of intoxicated elderly businessmen clapped their whisky tumblers enthusiastically in time to the beat trying to out smoke the Khartoum. A trip on the Nile should have been a perfect experience. I had been looking forward to it, but instead it had simply reminded me that this was an artificial world, a bubble of entertainment for the colonists, the latest wave of foreigners that had marched in to run something that they didn't understand. There were no real Egyptians here and no real Egypt. I vowed to try and see where real people lived and worked before I left. Perhaps even to see where our funny little car was made.

The rep visibly recoiled at the idea of driving out to the suburbs. He was clear that there was a packed itinerary planned for the day and we had no time for such things. He pulled in by the side of the road at a dingy cafe and made a call from a phone behind the bar, smoking nervously all the while. I did not offer him any of my cigarettes as I was annoyed with him. I do not smoke myself, but I find it useful to carry a pack. I drank a glass of mint tea while I waited. The liquid was almost as muddy as the Nile itself and the bunch of mint stuck in the top was almost as big as the palm trees that grew among the rushes. The tea needed sugar, lots of it. I looked around for a waiter or waitress, but all I saw was men in grubby kaftans chewing menacingly or coughing over their backgammon boards.

Sunset over the Nile and the Great Pyramid.

Giza, what can I say? Wherever you are in Cairo, the Pyramids are somehow lingering on the horizon in the dust and the bubbling sun. How far away they are it is impossible to say, but they are forever present. So, it's curious that when you actually go to see them, they completely disappear. We were driving down a typical tarmacked road down which girls and boys in smart blue and white uniforms were skipping to school, books tied to their backs, when we turned left past a little shop, into a yard that was half-filled with sand. 'Little Ramses', as I had taken to calling the car, stuttered to a halt, seemingly terrified of a group of camels sat in the shade.

For nearly a thousand years the pharaohs of the second millennium B.C., used the plateau at Giza as their Royal Necropolis. As a result, it contains hundreds of tombs and temples scattered in the sand as well as the main buildings. There are three major Pyramids, the 'Great Pyramid', the 'Pyramid of Kafre', who if you remember had very much impressed me at the museum, and the 'Pyramid of Menkaure'. There are also a number of smaller, supporting pyramids, those of various queens, two major graveyards, temples and a workers' village. Plus, of course, the Sphinx. The pyramids are all perfectly aligned with the north star and laid out in the form of Orion. Although they are not particularly high, compared to say a mountain, they are unquestionably huge, and obviously man-made. Each layer of stones is half the height of the average man, and I was instantly appalled by the sheer amount of effort it must have taken to create this literal mountain. The power a king or president wields these days is fortunately fairly esoteric but looking up at those huge silhouettes from the sand there was no mistaking the unbelievable life and death authority that those dead kings held over millions of subjects.

Today the pyramids are yellow sandstone with steep, stepped edges, but originally, they were clad in polished, white limestone and had smooth sides, still visible at the top of the Great Pyramid itself. The tips were apparently also painted gold to catch the sun, which must have been dazzling, but even as they were, they were stunning to behold, a statement of godliness which I found curiously difficult to disagree with. Inside there is nothing to see; a steep ramp down to some small rooms which might have held grain, a tight turn then a long climb up a steep slope with a ladder laid on the floor and a rope as a banister. The grand gallery is a long, thin slice cut into the interior of this man-made mountain, as clean-cut and as beautifully polished as the lines of the fanciest new cinema in the heart of town. It is incredible and I couldn't help but be filled with anticipation. At the end lies the King's chamber, devoid of decoration or hieroglyphics, completely empty except for the broken stone case. An anti-climax, possibly, but it is still an incredibly peaceful and regal environment. In the opposite wall a small hole, the size of a single normal brick, allows the King's soul to ascend to the heavens. It points, at an impossibly accurate angle, directly at the north star on his birthday.

For me, the quality of engineering seen here is far more magical than any ancient tale of Egypt's mythical kings and gods, and unlike them, the reality is here to see and test. It is surely impossible that such accuracy could be achieved with unwilling slave labour. This was the work of experts, possibly ones that I could relate to. I was intrigued by what I would find in the workers' village.

The workers' village lies just south of the pyramids and consists of small huts and shed-like stone tombs buried in the sand. 'Village' is of course not the right term, hundreds of thousands of seasonal workers lived here in a tented complex that spread far out into the desert. Unlike the tombs of their employers, theirs are decorated with everyday scenes from their lives. The colours are faded, but many are still visible thousands of years later. There are scenes showing brewers, bakers, brick kilns and restaurants with fish and food in clay pots. Cats are immortalised in the act of stealing food and dogs loll in the sun. There are paintings of foremen with clipboards, clerks getting their sums wrong and quartermasters wagging their tongues. It is all very down to earth and accessible, which only serves to make the surrounding Pyramids themselves even more shocking.

Slightly to the west, aloof as cats are, sits the Sphinx. With no frame of reference, it seems both bigger and smaller than I'd expected. Somehow it is more alien than even the pyramids. Its paws are twice the height of myself and as long as a bus. Its eyes follow you around the plain; it is like being a mouse played with by a cat. 'Sphinx' is a Greek word describing an animal with the head of a human and the body of a cat, but the word was invented two-thousand-years after this was built. There are apparently no references to it or pictures of it in Egyptian writing. It is a mystery. Its purpose remains unclear and somehow that seems right. It doesn't need to explain itself to us. We aren't worthy. I wonder how

Napoleon felt when he stared up into that godlike face. It is neither caring nor dispassionate. Small and irrelevant I am sure, even if he did not admit it.

Memphis

Little Ramses headed bravely off down the road following the Nile. The city soon dropped away leaving us in a strange world of skeletons of buildings and a forest of cranes. New homes were being created in the desert, factories too. Great sheets of corrugated iron were lifted over our heads. Soon this, too, disappeared and sand started blowing freely across the road. I began to feel a little nervous. What if the car ran out of fuel or the engine overheated? Who would find us if we were out here? But my driver was not worried. Little Ramses was prepared for anything. There were cans of water and fuel in the boot and an old field telephone kicking about on the back seat. I noted the long aerial on the car and prayed he was right. Long aerials with black and red pennants were up ahead, too, and, out of the desert haze, bubbled a line of T-54 tanks. We had reached the edge of the Cairo bubble. The checkpoint was highly efficient. Our papers were studied and stamped and we were let through without ceremony. It was a timely reminder of how serious the situation was in Egypt; war was just around the corner.

Memphis, the original capital of Egypt, sat in a floodplain with a long thin river port. An oasis of green in the desert. Tall brown statues of our little car's namesake grew like trees in the swamp. The stumps of columns and ruins of temples and buildings poked out of the ground and converged on the royal palace. The forecourt and approach paths lay like washing on the ground drying in the sun, but they serve to frame majestically both what is and isn't physically there. Little remains of the buildings themselves, as the city was plundered heavily in the Middle Ages to build Cairo, but the business of it, the sheer number of fragments of statues, leaves the impression of a busy city. Although only ruins, the sheer size of the immense columns and capitals, metres in diameter, tell of how big they were. It is from here that the colossal statue of Ramses the

Second, that stands in front of the station in Ramses Square, comes. It is a staggering eleven metres high. I wandered happily around the gardens studying the sculptures of the Temple of Ptah and discovering lots of small, friendly versions of the Sphinx lying among the long grass. Another lunch of boiled beef and carrots, this time stewed in a pot, eaten under the shade of canvas awning, spoiled slightly by cheerful touts wandering between the tables with their squeaky reed instruments and tambourine bashing. Mysterious men in linen suits and sunglasses smoked anxiously before returning to their tinted glass Mercedes, parked all along one side of the gardens.

Saqqara

Too much to remember. The 'bent' pyramid, the 'red' pyramid, the original stepped 'Pyramid of Djoser'. On the north side there were a series of tombs with colourful reliefs far more interesting than the pyramids themselves. Particularly memorable was the tomb of Mereuka – an absolute riot of colour! Impossibly, after five thousand years incredible bright red and blue paint leapt out of the walls, as brightly as the day it was painted. It made me wonder what the dusty halls out in the desert had really been like.

The tomb of Mereuka at Saqqara.

Finally, the 'Serepheam', a series of underground stables carved out of the rock, where the sacred oxen were kept. Alcoves, still smelling of animals, contain beautiful statues of the great beasts, every bit as skilfully carved as the statues of the pharaohs.

We returned safely to Cairo, the car whistling and clanking, to see a flock of pink flamingos descending from an equally pink sky. The burning, red sun was reflected in the sparkling water casting a strange crowd of people into silhouette. They appeared to be walking along the bank accompanying a series of boats that were proceeding slowly through the water. They were walking alongside the boats, moving in parallel slowly down the river. A pale, white arm could be seen ploughing through the green water. Hearty calls of 'Come on girl, you can do it!' rang out from the crowd of obnoxious, moustachioed gentlemen. The British champion, the appropriately named Brenda Fisher, didn't seem to be bothered by the competition or by the crocodiles that I had seen in the same spot only the day before. She went on to win the Women's Nile Swimming Championship easily. I do wonder, however, who exactly was competing in such a competition. I can't imagine too many local women were signing up. Mad dogs and Englishmen, eh? As we made a circuit of Ramses Square, I looked up at the face of the great King and wondered what he would have made of modern Cairo with its colonial buildings and its strange social cliques. I rather feel that he would have been on Nasser's side, and rightly so.

My driver had agreed to take me out into the suburbs, but only on the condition that I accompany him to an Um Kolthoum concert, reportedly the finest example of Egyptian music living. I readily agreed, assuming that I could do a little research first. This proved to be a lot easier than expected, as there was no shortage of assistance from bar and kitchen staff at the Windsor Hotel when I mentioned her name. My driver arrived sheepishly in Little Ramses, as requested, but I couldn't help noticing the slim black form of Comrade Tokarev's pistol hiding beneath his crumpled jacket. 'We should be fine,' he said, catching my eye. 'It is the British and the French that they do not like...' 'Well, that's alright then,' I sighed. I hoped that he didn't want me to try and converse in Arabic. I could have got by in German, but given Herr Rommel's experience, I didn't think that was a good idea either. I was glad that I had my

Arabic phrasebook with me. So, we drove off, Madam Kolthoum's music wailing from the little car's radio. He asked if I liked it and in truth, I did not know what to say.

I have no idea where we went, but it was a very different city from the one that we left behind. It was almost like another planet, entirely brown, buildings, people and fabrics all the same colour as the dusty earth. The streets were narrow and full of people, sexless figures in white and black hijabs the only break from the monochrome background. Panoramic balconies hung off every building and canvas awnings were extended so far out into the street that there was no room for traffic. We continued on foot. Every inch of shade was packed with people, Jew and Arab mixing freely together. Everywhere skeletal donkeys were either pulling carts or loaded directly with poles across their backs, children packed tightly in amongst the vegetables. Dark-robed women darted about, tugging their shawls over their faces when they saw me, or anyone. Everywhere people seemed to be shouting, tradesmen haggling with thin air. Great mountains of oranges were piled up on makeshift boxes and their smell was so acute it stung my nose. No one made any attempt to stop the flies from feasting on them. A young man on a bicycle crashed through, handing out pamphlets for the Revolutionary Council. An old man sat cross-legged in the sun and chanted prayers. A policeman spotted my suit amongst the crowd and was dispatched to find out what I was doing here. I told him it was none of his business, but he didn't understand. Suddenly we were back at the car and he was giving my driver a stern lecture. I took out my notebook and very clearly wrote down the number on his uniform. He decided to let us go. It was too damned hot to fight. We followed an ancient bus that was covered in men in kaftans clinging to the outside and sitting on the roof. Some fell off as it bounced along, but it was driving so slowly that they simply got up, dusted themselves off and ran alongside and jumped back on again. I could smell the burning fuel, even above the smell of excrement and the dust. We passed an area where the whole ground seemed to be on fire and men poked the skulls of long-dead cattle with long sticks. Further out and I see makeshift garages dug into the mounds of rubbish that surround the city, where ancient wrecks were being torn apart for scrap metal, people stripped naked to the waist cooking on barrel fires while they worked. Behind them I saw great rolls of barbed wire stretched out across the ground, beyond which men in army fatigues with large guns I did not recognise patrolled. There was a sound of metal wire tapping against flagpoles and then a line of Egyptian and Soviet flags fluttering proudly in front of a complex of white concrete buildings. Change is coming to Egypt.

Little Ramses is apparently already obsolete. I don't have the heart to tell my driver. I'll store that gem away just in case the concert is dreadful.

My driver appeared on time, although for a moment I didn't recognise him. Gone was the thin suit and stained coral shirt, gone was Little Ramses. Instead, he had found from somewhere, what passed for a dinner jacket and black tie. It was, apparently, what he had got married in many years before. This was clearly a special occasion. The restaurant was within easy walking distance and there was, of course, no fear of rain, so we arrived ten minutes later, looking to all the world like a couple of undercover policemen trying to blend in at a society event. The immaculate tables, each with a lantern, were neatly arranged around an illuminated pool. A long, thin bar ran along the entire length of the building, black and white portraits of Egyptian intelligentsia hung between polished wooden beams reminding guests of its historic past. On a raised platform, behind the pool, stood a well-built woman with a dark, beehive hairdo bright lemon dress. Behind her a small orchestra.

Um Koulthoum and her orchestra in Cairo, 1956.

Although I do not play – why try when there are those who do it so much better? – I recognised instantly the familiar faces of the band. The broke clarinettist, the lovesick oboe player, the tired and hungover cellist, the percussionist with loose morals, the trombonist who deals on the black market. I thought I knew their music. But there are many different types of music in the world. Western music is based on a limited set of tones and harmonized scales and comes in forms that we are familiar with. Arabic music is different. It uses quarter tones which to us sound 'off', but it is the structure and presentation that makes it so different and so hard for us to understand. We expect one instrument to hold a melody and others to harmonise, whereas in Arabic music, the melody skips across the group and is thrown back and forth, more like jazz, while other instruments contrast or echo as much as harmonise. Arabic music is a little like poetry. As well as notes and refrains, there are groups of notes like words that invoke reaction and tell a story. The tempo of a piece collapses and expands with the emotion of the tale and does not follow a fixed beat or a set shape. For a westerner it is hard to follow. Um Kolthoum hardly moved from her spot, but she did her best to convey to me her happiness, curiosity, pain and grief. Just when I least expected it, long after I had forgotten how her story started, even my dull ear recognised the leitmotif returning to where it had begun, bringing with it a sense of calm and closure.

I wanted to like it, I certainly respected it, and I had begun to understand it, but it was simply too different from everything I had ever known for me to say that I liked it. Not yet anyway. How does one begin to change all you have ever known? Cairo was about to find out. Soon all of this colonial nonsense would be gone.

On the 26th July 1956, just three months after my father visited Cairo, President Nasser nationalised the Suez Canal, taking it out of British control. Instead of removing her troops in line with international peace treaties and United Nations requests, Britain increased the number of troops on the ground and sent her navies to blockade the canal. However, the threat of American sanctions prevented Britain, still very heavily in debt to the U.S. and reliant on Marshall Aid funding, from invading. On the 29th October Israel invaded Egypt instead. Seven days later Britain decided to take 'defensive' action and followed Israel in.

A moment from what proved to be the end of the colonial era.

The operation went badly from the start. America, keen to diminish Britain's role on the world stage, forced a withdrawal, causing British Prime Minister Anthony Eden to resign. However, America's failure to act as an international peacekeeper emboldened the Soviet Union, who had lost millions in the whole affair, to intervene in Hungary. Nasser's grip on power was substantially strengthened and, almost overnight, Westerners became unwelcome on the streets of Cairo, ending, the colonial era that my father witnessed.

View-Master™ Reel (Cairo)

THE TREATY OF ROME

A Treaty for the European Community, 1957

Miss Seawright had seen it coming, she had been there, at that peculiar coal & steel conference in Messina if you remember, when the plans had started coming together, and now we all knew why. On the 25th March 1957, despite the best efforts of the Americans, who were justifiably terrified of the whole idea, the Treaty of Rome was signed in the Palazzo dei Conservatori on the Capitoline Hill. It was a fitting location. For the Romans the hill had been sacred, representing eternity. Roman temples had been replaced by mediaeval churches, and during the Renaissance Michelangelo himself brought order to the chaos, by laying out a new ordered plan for what was then the seat of the government of Rome. The Emperor Marcus Aurelius himself looked over the paperwork as six countries: Belgium, France, Italy, Luxembourg, the Netherlands and West Germany signed the EEC into existence. It proposed to create a single market for goods, labour, services, and capital across member states. It also proposed a Common Agriculture Policy, a Common Transport Policy, and a European Social Fund establishing the European Commission. Proposed for the future were European Defence and Political Communities, part of a longer-term plan for a 'United States of Europe'.

By and large the treaty was more of a framework for the future than a legal change at the time, although it did set up the European Court of Justice to which national courts were able to submit cases for final arbitration.

It goes without saying that Miss Seawright was there at the meeting, 'observing' once again for the British government, whatever that meant. Ballgowns and cocktails certainly. I am genuinely excited about it. It represents real progress towards a safer, better future, a return to how things were for hundreds, if not thousands of years. The numbers will undoubtedly speak for themselves and other states, including even Britain, will surely join.

Britain applied for EEC membership under both Labour and Conservative governments, its application being rejected by France in 1961, 1963 and 1967. France approved Britain's application in 1973. The British public voted comprehensively (67.2%) in favour of EEC membership in a referendum held in June 1975. The treaty was extended in 1985 and 1990 as Conservative party election promises approved by the voting public.

ROME

The Eternal City, 1957

Rome. The city that spawned the Empire that was Europe's ancestor, the city from which the popes ruled, holding Christianity and Europe together, the centre of international trade and finance through the Middle Ages, the home of the Enlightenment and the Renaissance. The place where the new European Community was legally brought into being. I had to go…

I imagined myself as a citizen of that ancient Empire, an inhabitant of the town of Aquae Sulis in the Provincia Britannia travelling for the first time, two thousand years ago, to the Imperial capital. With over a million residents at the time of the Roman invasion of Britain, Rome was by far the largest city on earth until the late industrial age. The Aurelian Wall, built in the second century around the ancient city centre, is itself twelve miles long, encompassing over three thousand acres of high-rise apartments. But even then, the suburbs stretched beyond the walls in every direction for miles on end. It must have been verging on impossible to comprehend.

I had bought tickets for the cheaper night flight and the plane, a forty-seater, Vickers Viscount 700, was nearly empty. There were a few simple formalities and then the lights of London dropped away. The stewardess came round with blankets and I ordered a cup of hot cocoa as the Viscount's gleaming aluminium wings stretched heroically upward towards the stars.

Dijon glittered like a sequined purse and the first dawn came up as we crossed the Alps. Clouds hung over the Po Valley, but cleared shortly before we came into Rome. The white mass of the Vittoriano and the egg cup shape of the Colosseum were easily recognisable as we circled the city before landing at the little airport of Ciampino in early morning sun.

A typical Vickers Viscount in 1950s BAE livery.

Rome was different from the start. As I waited for the bus from the airport, I could see the almost undamaged arches of the Claudian Aqueduct stretching across the grassy plain like a ghost from the past. It was one of four aqueducts that supplied the city with water from the distant mountains, over five hundred gallons of it per second. Tunnelling through hills with a drop of just one foot per mile, it would be quite a feat of engineering even today with modern equipment. How they managed to build it two thousand years ago, I can only speculate.

Towering over it was the neon-lit, ultra-modern office of 'Cinema City'. For me, the juxtaposition of the ancient and modern was a shock, but not for those that called the city home. Two nuns rode past on a motorbike beeping furiously at a farmer with a donkey and cart. For the natives all around me, this was just part of normal everyday life. Here it all was, the Roman, the religious, the industrial and the modern all mixed together, not as exhibits in some confused museum of different ages, but in the present tense as an exotic, but somehow cohesive cosmopolitan living city.

My hotel was a typical example of this interaction. It was located in part of a Renaissance era palace that had been damaged in the war and rebuilt on one side with concrete and steel. But it was built on an older Roman villa. Whereas we might have been inclined to stick a blue plaque on it and wrap it in aspic, the locals had decided that such a heritage site could still be put to good use and pay its way. An ancient mosaic was embossed in my marble bedroom floor, chipped and wonky, but still colourful. It disappeared under the wall that had obviously been added much later and reappeared in the bathroom, where one could sit in state regarded with disdain by a two-thousand-year-old yellow lion. Such an extraordinary mindset. I loved everything about it.

I couldn't possibly list all the things that I saw, not least because so many of them weren't labelled. A sculpted column in the middle of a playpark, a Roman villa in the centre of a roundabout, a marble bust in the graveyard of a tumbled down church. I made what I was beginning to realise was a mistake, dashing around looking at as many sites as I could, rather than attempting to digest Rome as a whole, at leisure. My excuse is that I thought I'd never get to go there again, let alone three more times. Everything in Rome was exciting, even a tram ride, in a way that Paris never was. Whereas the Parisians were cold and unfriendly, the excitement of Rome was reflected in its people, talking quickly, voices raised, passionate kisses, blaring horns and frantic gestures. Perhaps they were simply drinking too much caffeine. It was easy to do.

I had secretly been hoping for a Moka pot, like I had in Switzerland; they were an Italian invention after all. What arrived instead was a silver tray with a thimble full of a dark foaming liquid, almost like the tar-like substance I'd drunk in Egypt, and a glass of water. All around me men were smoking. They took a sip from the tiny cup and then washed it down with a glug of cold water. A peculiar ritual. I followed suit, but without the cigarette. The flavour of the coffee was all in the 'crema', the hot liquid slipping easily down my throat, instantly soothing the dusty, smoky air that I had been breathing. Then the caffeine hit me like a punch in the chest. I blinked in surprise, suddenly desperate for a glass of water. How bizarre that drinking coffee should be so completely different in Switzerland, Holland, France and Italy, each one so perfectly customised to its own situation. I took another cautious sip and was overcome by the desire to crack on with the day, to see everything and to join in. It was the hot passionate spirit of Italy.

Rome is a bubbling cauldron of frenetic activity from when the vendors first crowd into the tiny cobbled markets at dawn until the last party goers stagger home nearly twenty-fours later. People rush about grabbing food and an aperitivo on the go, shouting over each other as motor scooters, bright colours and a scent of oregano spirals on the hot air. Even the terracotta tiled roofs of the ancient city seem to be trying to outdo each other, like the Renaissance popes who shaped its skyline. Rome is exhausting just to listen to, so I wonder where in this chaos my reserved and refined father got to.

The hero & heroine of the film 'La Dolce Vita' dance in the Trevi Fountain.

Throughout the 1950s and early '60s, Rome was considered by many to be the coolest city on earth, synonymous with fashion, style, design, glamour, and of course the movies. It had a vibrant, if sometimes disreputable nightlife, the epicentre of which was a 200-yard street named 'Via Veneto'. But espresso coffee or not my father would not be here.

Three minutes stroll from the Tiber across the old Ponte Sisto footbridge is the district of Trastevere, whose labyrinthine passages are filled with crumbling buildings, faded paintings and tiny shops or cafes, many no larger than a fold-up table. Plants and religious shrines stretch between the walls that have become co-dependent on each other, strings of washing hang overhead drying while priests in long black flowing robes sweep silently along through the shadows.

There is a little old man with trousers hiked halfway up his chest by his braces selling old books from a suitcase. A pomegranate and an olive tree seem to be fighting over an old, rusted bicycle, and in the darkness under a collapsed cupola can be seen the golden flashes of cats' eyes as they fight over some leftover pasta.

The delicious smell of roasted aubergine and artichoke dipped in garlic butter wafts from the slats of the faded green shutters of a trattoria opposite. Yes, this is where my father will be, but I am half a century too late.

Seventeenth-century townhouses of the Trastevere lanes.

Roman Rome was of course top of my list to see and their reassuringly familiar style, which I had seen throughout France, Spain and England, too, was everywhere, not just in the form of the ancient ruins that lay scattered at every corner, but in the form of the frame that held the rest of Rome together, the canvas on which the Renaissance had been painted. It was extraordinary to think after years of war destroyed our continent, that two thousand years before we had all been part of one great family, with common architecture, common languages, common currency and free trade.

How had we lost our way so badly and what could we have achieved if Rome had not fallen? The Roman engineer, Vitruvius, writing in 15 B.C., described the working model of a steam engine and how it could be used to propel boats when there was no wind. His famous book, 'De Architura', illustrates a version of his boiler moving a cart along a series of parallel tracks. Only fifteen hundred semi-wasted years later did da Vinci try building it.

As I visited the great sites, each one reminded me of an example from elsewhere. The Colosseum, the Baths of Caracus, the Triumphal Arch. I had seen their smaller brothers all over the empire already and every schoolchild was familiar with their form. It was not these, wonderous that they are, that impressed me. Instead, I was struck by how very like us the ancient Romans were: the little shops in Trajan's forum, the fast-food takeaway with stones stained by coins, graffiti in the barracks. 'Remember Victuix who is poor and bloody cold'. 'All the way from Gaul and straight on night duty!'. These were people we could understand and sympathise with, people we all knew, people who would be right at home in the Rome of today. It left me scratching my head and wondering why then did it end, where did the Romans go?

My father's Roman forum, digitally remembered.

I pondered this question further as I ate a picnic lunch on the Palatine Hill, under the shade of a great tree, looking down into the forum, as busy now as it was two thousand years before. How peculiar and yet satisfying that our modern cars have exactly the same wheel and axle size of the carts the Romans designed the forum around. It was the Romans who invented taxis, too; a fixed gearing mechanism attached to the wheel automatically calculating journey cost. The taxis were still here circling the outside. On the hill the sound of the traffic was muted to a quiet rumble, while birds hopped the stones where the emperors once stood. I rested in the sun, brooding on the temporary nature of life and power and cracked my hard-boiled egg on the imperial door lintel.

Then there was Christian Rome. The Vatican, the excessive richness of St. Peter's and the barely more palatable St. Maria Maggiore, St. John's, St. Peter in Chains, and hundreds of other churches, where gold leaf was plastered over the top of marble. It was an orgy of excess that made me think about the machinery of an international organisation that gathered funds every week from ordinary people and channelled it here for hundreds of years. They certainly knew how to spend it too. Never have I seen so many shops advertising priestly garments and heavenly accessories. It was laughable really, but sweet in equal measure to see clerics from the Vatican seminaries, draped in fine lace and velvet tassels discussing the latest episcopal eggcup or whatever it was on the way to prayers.

Renaissance Rome and the Rome of the Medici was also on my list of things to see. Seven hundred years ago, English lords were hiring Italian contractors to build their castles and train their men. They borrowed money from Italian banks to do it and mortgaged their estates across England. Wool from the sheep in the fields of Hereford, Gloucestershire, Oxfordshire and Norfolk made its way slowly to Rome, where it was converted into the most expensive cloth reserved for princes, cardinals and the popes themselves.

I looked for the Rome of great names such as Michelangelo, Bernini, Raphael etc. and I saw much of their work, but what impressed me was not any one individual piece, but the realisation of what an explosion of energy, creativity and thinking happened here. The dawning realisation that the Renaissance didn't mean books in a library or paintings in a gallery, but street after street of workshops filled with the noise of hammers, smoke drifting from fires and ordinary workers shouting at the top of their voices.

An audience with Pope Pius sounded not dissimilar I suspect. The square was full of priests and nuns all shouting at the top of their voices. A young couple with a small baby had shared the long wait with us. Eventually, the lights came on and the Pope began the long procession up the nave, enthroned above the people. The noise of cheers was deafening.

The young man by my side lifted his baby up in the air and shouted 'Papa, Papa' at the top of his lungs. At least a hundred people did the same. The great head swung round, the eyes blinked, perhaps in recognition, perhaps in understanding and a smile appeared on that cold grey face. The hand was extended in blessing leaving the parents in tears of joy. He could not have seen the child or distinguished one of the white blobs from another at such a distance, but each adult left convinced that the Pontiff's greeting had been reserved exclusively for them.

An audience waiting for a 'Blessing' in St. Peter's Square.

The Alban Hills were pleasant after the heat of the plain. No wonder the Pope goes to Castle Gandolfo in the summer. The sun is so hot, but the air is beautifully fresh and the wide-open views are a glorious change after the crowded streets of Rome. The perfect circle of Lake Nemi, an ancient volcanic crater, looked cool and inviting under the spruce trees, reflecting the moon like a mirror. The smell of wild strawberries drifted on the air. It was a holy site for the Romans to reconnect with nature and even a cynic like me could see why. 'Diana Nemorensis' they called it and built the little temple of 'Diana of the Woods' here. Goethe and Lord Byron were inspired by it too. But the gorgeous frescos on the ceilings paled into insignificance compared to the view from the cardinal's window. It had me reaching for a paintbrush. St. Peter's had nothing on the natural majesty of this place, nor could Christianity promise us anything more heavenly.

The view from the Cardinal's terrace at the Villa d'Este.

I visited Frascati with its ice-cold wine and rude biscuits, Tivoli with the great Villa d'Este and its garden of a hundred fountains terraced down the hillside. What a feat of engineering again, this time not Roman, and mathematics. Someone had, at some point, carefully calculated water pressure at points all over the hillside and adjusted layout and pipe width accordingly. Everywhere water flowed, gently, musically or with a great roar like the sea. It was an idyllic haven for wealthy cardinals hiding from the summer heat. I ambled along the terrace and purchased a tub of 'gelato' with a scoop of lemon sorbet. Italian ice cream is a little different from other types; it is denser, more strongly flavoured and slightly chewy. I don't really like it. The sorbet was, however, perfect.

The Romans, of course, had access to ice cream, too, or at least sorbet. Women brought blocks of ice down from the mountains in carts, mixing it with sugar syrup and milk. Gelato in its modern form, however, is credited to the Italian chef, Francesco Procopio dei Coltelli, who used buttermilk and sugar syrups to prolong the life of the product, sufficient to get it to the table at least. In the late 1600s, he opened his café in Paris, where his ice-cream was very popular with Robespierre, Danton, Voltaire and many others. He not only obtained French citizenship, but an exclusive royal licence issued by King Louis XIV, at the time making him the sole producer of the frozen dessert in the kingdom and, until his son-in-law stole his recipe, the richest businessman in Europe.

The circular dining room in Hadrian's Villa, Tivoli.

The emperor Hadrian's villa, by contrast, was enormous, more like a small town than a summer getaway. I felt naturally drawn to this modest bearded emperor who had invested heavily in Britain and was keen to see what had been his personal house. There were suites of rooms decorated in the national styles of the countries he reigned over, suggesting at least an active interest in his overseas possessions. I particularly liked the circular dining room with a moat of water around it for coolness. In fact, three circular things stood out from the holiday as a whole: the dining room at Hadrian's villa; the temple of Venus by the side of the Tiber; and Bramante's Tempietto, a jewel of a temple on the Janiculum hill, marking the spot where St. Peter was supposedly crucified. Scarcely large enough to hold the priest and his assistants, it suffers a little from being cramped into a narrow courtyard but is perfect in its proportions and its modest but beautiful marble floors.

My trip to Rome was over far too soon. I had only begun to scratch the surface of what was here and had barely grasped the need to soak it up as an entirety rather than studying specific things. I would need to come back.

On the last night, I found myself sat outside a trattoria in a small square, a triangle, in fact, where a narrow mediaeval lane passed the delightful little church of St. Ivo. Clouds of pinewood smoke, scented with rosemary and paraffin, floated through the alley over the dark forms of the men that had packed themselves into the small space.

A small shrine was built into the wall and next to it, a man who was sweating profusely was preaching at the crowd, waving a pamphlet like a conductor. His voice burst forth in violent waves like machine gun fire, echoing off the crumbling walls. Every volley stirred rumblings of angry agreement. It had been ten years since the ancient tenement buildings by the river had been pulled down and still there were no replacements. The suburbs were expanding without planning control yet there was still no affordable accommodation. The iron and steel industries had not recovered, there were food shortages, and the sewers were broken. Tens if not hundreds of thousands of Rome's residents were crammed into single rooms, basements, caves, sewers. It was worse, the speaker said, than living two thousand years ago…

As I watched, I munched quietly on a dish that reminded me that it was time to go home, battered cod and chips, or at least a fish fillet with rosemary sautéed potatoes. Rome had been everything I had wanted and more. I was sated in more ways than one.

The speaker was only partially right. It was true that life for a few was far better in Roman times, but for the majority 'the plebs' as they were called then, life was almost exactly the same, and they would have experienced exactly the same problems with their Roman landlords. Both Cicero and Juvenal write extensively on the topic, bemoaning the poor quality of apartments while Crassus, the wealthiest landlord in Rome, was known to frequently set fire to his older buildings to claim on the insurance and build taller ones. It was in fact workers' riots that led to the democratic Roman Republic finally becoming the dictatorial Roman Empire.

The men cheer their speaker and hoist him high on their shoulders when he finally finishes. But just like their ancient brothers these workers are really only here for the free watered-down beer, and a ladle of grey ragu dolloped on top of a bowl of life-saving pasta. Politicians are seen as entertainers not leaders. Nobody thinks anything will really change. Fate is in the hands of the gods.

I asked earlier where the Romans went, but the simple truth is that they didn't go anywhere. There was never a people called 'The Romans', they were never a people, a race, a nationality. The Roman Empire was a system, a collection of integrated communities and unions with a shared currency, a shared defence policy and shared tax and legal frameworks. Everyone in the empire was an immigrant from somewhere, free, more or less, to work where they wanted and rotate between provinces as part of their jobs, public service and education. Even Rome's emperors came from all around the world: France, Spain, Algeria, Bulgaria, Turkey, Serbia and Britain, to name but a few. There was no concept of nationality in that Roman Union. There was no such thing as The Romans.

Nor did the Roman Empire disappear overnight, as the schoolbooks would have it. The legions did not leave Britain and turn the lights out on their way out of the door. Instead, a series of plagues and invasions ravaged the city of Rome itself and, slowly, her armed forces retreated back to defend the major centres of their culture and economies in the provinces began to stagnate. Rome fell, not once, but many times, over a period of hundreds of years and, when it did, most Romans simply stayed where they were. Governors all over the empire continued to do what they could with what they had. Slowly these local governors became kings, and the old Roman forts their castles.

The loose union of states that formed around Christian Rome in the early Middle Ages was still the old Roman Rome and so it was in Rome that Charlemagne chose to be crowned as the first Holy 'Roman' Emperor. It was loyalty to old Roman Rome that held the central European alliances together in the Middle Ages against the Mongols and the Turks and, despite Martin Luther and Henry VIII's best efforts, it is Roman Rome and Christian Rome, that still holds Europe together today. We are all still the children of that eternal city, Englishmen as much as anyone. Although we do not today have the same Latinised tongue as much of the continent, three times a governor of Britain was elected as Roman Emperor and that is more than can be said of either France or Germany.

I said that I'd not be political in this travelogue, so forgive me for a brief exception. The Treaty of Rome is a long overdue return to our shared heritage, a step towards how things were thousands of years ago and how they have always been. The policies and the procedures may well need tweaking, but it is our past and our future, because it is morally, culturally, militarily, and economically right and has already proven itself successful over hundreds, if not thousands of years. It is surely inevitable that Britain, too, will sign up soon. It is, after all, our birth right: we are as European as anywhere else.

View-Master™ Reel (Rome)

SPUTNIK

A Little Companion for Mankind, 4th October 19557

I t was a Friday, St. Francis of Assisi's day, and although I am not religious, I was once again eating a fish and chip dinner. It was traditional and more importantly it meant that the decision about what to eat that day was taken for me. Back then a piece of battered fish cost a shilling and a cone of chips three pence. I didn't have a television, but I had the wireless on in my room and I was listening to the evening news as I ate dinner. There was supposed to be a Sibelius concert later that evening which I was looking forward to, but it was suddenly cancelled.

At half-past-seven, the Soviet SS-6 launcher, based directly on their R-7 rocket platform, blasted a polished metal sphere, fifty-eight centimetres in diameter into orbit around the earth. The Russians called it 'Sputnik' which means 'Little Companion' or 'Co-Traveller', a beautiful name for a beautiful object. Its orbital inclination meant that it was visible to the naked eye, its flight path meant that it covered most of the inhabited world and, as it flew, it emitted a series of bleeps on a twenty-megacycle range, two up, two down, that even a radio ham like me could easily detect with basic equipment.

The whole world was stunned. You couldn't imagine how much so. Ever since I was a boy, cartoons and films had been full of the futuristic fantasy of mankind going to space and suddenly, that time was now.

Every night I listened out for our little companion as it peacefully crossed all national borders. We were surely entering a new age where nationality would become meaningless and war unfeasible.

BRUSSELS WORLD FAIR

Evaluation of the World for a More Humane Future, 1958

I got a chance to see Sputnik for myself the following year and I can't tell you how desperately excited I was. Sputnik 1, the original, had orbited the earth for two months before falling back and burning up in the upper atmosphere, of course, but its sisters had gone on tour around the world in order to demonstrate peaceful scientific progress and Soviet technical superiority. The Railway Workers Union had organised a three-day all-inclusive trip to the World Trade Fair in Brussels, partly to sing the praises of the socialist system and partly to highlight the lack of investment in Britain's railways. We were by now noticeably beginning to fall behind the rest of Europe. I was obviously not a member of the RWU, but did not mind in the slightest who it was behind the funding of the subsidised tickets; I just knew that I wanted one.

By the time they arrived, Sputnik 2 had carried 'Laika' into orbit and any criticism of the Soviet's capability instantly vanished. This was not a simple radio transmitter lobbed into space as a publicity stunt. This was a fully pressurised capsule with a life support system carrying a dog. Nobody was under any illusion that a man would soon follow. The American Government had already publicly approved a six hundred percent increase in funding to N.A.S.A., and who-knows-what, secretly, but it was the R7's ability to land a nuclear payload anywhere in the U.S.A. at any time that really frightened them.

Sputnik 3 followed in May 1958, a much larger capsule full of scientific equipment and a payload clearly big enough to fit a man. The rate of Soviet progress was shocking everyone and overturning false assumptions. If they could do this, what else might be possible? Governments everywhere started to get very nervous.

A filthy old steam engine, known as an 'Ozzie' by the railway union men, belched its way down the line to Dover, where none other than the TS Canterbury herself was waiting for me once again. She sat beside the dock with a no-nonsense, 'let's get on with it' look about her that I had to respect. She was, to me, Miss Seawright in boat form and I was glad to see her. Once again, the ship was packed, quite literally standing room only, but, unlike last time, the weather was tolerable, so I sat outside on the deck, collar turned up against the wind as the sea spray and a thin rain scoured my face. Thick, black smoke billowed from her yellow funnel and, with a ferocious blast on her foghorn, England disappeared.

The hotel in Ostend was immediately opposite the train station, with potential views over the harbour or of the St. Peter and Paul Church. It was a low-key place meant for blue-collar workers, free from any pretensions. A stew of some unidentifiable type was slopped out for dinner, where we ate on trays in the canteen. While my room mates went out looking for female company, I sauntered along the seafront in search of something more satisfying to eat. It seems we were both successful, so, having enjoyed my late-night snack, I decided it would be far less stomach-churning for me if I slept on a sofa in the hotel lobby rather than in our shared rooms. It was, after all, far comfier than the bed.

An original postcard from the Brussels fair.

167

Next day it was early to the fair. I was not to be disappointed. There were many brilliantly clever buildings like the Philips Pavilion, a Corbusier-designed concrete tent shaped like the flames of a campfire, the Czech pavilion like a glass boat, the British one like a series of folded paper hats and, of course, the silver 'Atomium' representing peace among nations, dominating all.

At the very centre of the five-hundred-acre site, the Soviet and American pavilions sat facing off against each other, like boxers or perhaps brothers, both still willing to talk and listen, but equally both ready for a fight. It was a fascinating comment on the escalating 'Cold War' and what was to become the start of the space race. Four showy buildings clad in chrome celebrated the American way of life, including music, colour television, cars and ice-cream (something that we know is more closely associated with Russia, but never mind). The Soviet pavilion, by contrast, was a self-supporting glass box, reminiscent of the original Crystal Palace, charismatically futuristic, delicate and yet brutalist at the same time. The defiance of gravity was to be a recurring theme inside, with flocks of sleek aircraft and rockets rising like birds in front of giant cardboard dioramas of the Moscow skyline.

Sputnik displayed in the USSR pavilion.

The hall was cleverly designed to show off the U.S.S.R.'s technical achievements, in such a way that it seemed to form an inevitable, logical story, each stage of which had been personally directed by the giant figure of Lenin, or so we were meant to believe. Sputnik itself floated magically, suspended in mid-air, silver body and thin antenna glinting in the light that flooded in. Another version lay in pieces on the floor for visitors to see how it worked and how the components had been packed into the R-7 launch vehicle. Pictures on the wall forecast how a family of the communities of the future would live in space stations or on Mars, perfect communist societies. It did not seem like propaganda, it seemed logical, scientific, inevitable. I wished my university chums were here to see it, too; one young lady in particular would have been in her element.

Suddenly, I felt as if a shadow had crept over me. I wandered back outside. I needed to taste fresh air and to feel the sun on my skin again. I felt sad and I didn't know why. I walked away from the U.S.S.R. pavilion and through a small garden with little, humpbacked bridges over little streams, past the notably racist Belgium pavilion with its message of African colonisation and found myself at a small wooden pagoda containing a single golden rose. It was beautiful, too, but didn't alleviate my sadness. The Finnish pavilion was made entirely of wood and smelled of pine forests inside. It was dark, pitch black, except for a single shaft of light falling on the face of Sibelius, a composer whose work was still banned in the U.S.S.R. I remembered how I had been looking forward to the Sibelius concert when news of Sputnik broke and it looked like he had been put on pause again here. I made a promise to buy a recording of the Finlandia and Karelia Suites when I got home. The British pavilion was a masterpiece of contrasts, with a futuristic plastic exterior and a traditional wooden interior. The austere Annigoni portrait of Queen Elizabeth floated in the darkness above the crown jewels, which I thought missed the entire point of the exhibition, but an abrupt turn and there was the Dounreay atomic reactor, the past and the future on either hand. Electricity, though common in public places, was still very much a power source for the future. Back then only twelve million people had access to electricity at home and for many of us, it was a single socket and lightbulb that frequently lost power and 'browned out'. The reactor at Dounreay was to produce 600 million kWh of power, out of virtually nothing. I wondered what a future would be like where electricity was bountiful and freely available to all. What a leveller of society that would be. There was humour, too, in the British pavilion and humour of a particularly English kind. I stepped into the library of a great country house, elegantly proportioned and lined with shelves containing all the great British classics. I looked up, feeling something and suddenly realised that it was open to the sky and that the books were made of stone as were the chairs. This was not a library at all, but in fact a garden.

The award-winning Philips Pavilion from Expo '68.

There was more, far more. Too much to fit into the limited time we had and literally all of it was fascinating for a multitude of reasons. The French pavilion, all five storeys of it, was balanced on a single square metre block of stone. There was a magnificent Catholic Church, a whole Congolese village, a toy fair and an old Flemish

Square newly built for the occasion. Overhead chairlifts floated quietly and at night there was colour and light everywhere, in the air, under the water, even the statues and columns on buildings glowed. Fountains slowly changed colour, too. It made me wonder what humanity could do if it worked together more often.

Now, as I write, nearly half a century later, my enthusiasm and optimism seems a little naive. Europe has mercifully seen decades of peace and even the notion of war has become an impossibility, a side effect of which is arguments between nations and cynicism and scepticism. But back then, we were all obsessed by the horror of the war and determined to create a peaceful brotherhood of nations, sharing and guided by liberating science and technology. The science fair embodied that: what it displayed was evidence that the future we envisaged was both real and happening right now. In both the East and the West, it ushered in an era of liberating reform and rising prosperity. Naive as we were, our excitement was justified.

The sadness that I had felt in the Soviet pavilion lingered with me, a shadow at the back of my mind. At night, free of distraction, I tried to confront it, to get some measure of where it had come from. I was again sleeping on a sofa in another hotel lobby, my room mates being in the midst of enjoying what Brussels nightlife had to offer. Companionship for one pound per hour.

I had seen the future and been excited by it, but I also knew full well that, although mankind had finally reached space, I personally never would. I was thirty-five and, despite being relatively fit, had numerous health issues. I would never don a spacesuit and walk on Mars and, most likely, I would never see a world where electricity was free to all. My friends from university were settling down and getting married. Some of my closest friends now had children, children that perhaps one day would get to travel to the stars and be part of a United Europe. I, however, was alone in the world and would have to watch from the side-lines, either powerless to help or unencumbered by a legacy, depending on how you liked to look at it. I had no idea that one day I would have children of my own and, if you had told me that in 1958, I would have laughed very bitterly in your face and staggered off to the bar.

We stopped at Bruges on the way back and it was a delight to see the floodlit old town, a gentle calming light on warm brickwork. I felt a little more comfortable with the past than with the future. I walked into the square where the belfry glowed golden and orange and listened to a carillon concert in the darkness and the cold night air. After the exuberance of the day, the quietness was very refreshing. I felt much more at rest.

The following morning, we arrived back in Ostend, in time for a lunch of fatty pork and a crossing almost as bad as that in '53. It was difficult to keep lunch down and many of us felt that it wasn't that much of a loss if it did come back up again! The members of the Railway Union were trying to cram in as much drinking as they could in their remaining hours of freedom. It did not help their stomachs. Despite the cold spray washing over the sides, I fought my way on deck to get away from my fellow passengers' boasts and continual retching. I realised that I was not like them, not in many ways, nor was I like my university friends. I was free, free to help shape the future in a way that someone with a family and children simply could never be.

The white cliffs of Dover appeared on the horizon, a grey smudge that slowly, inevitably grew closer. For three days I had floated free from the real world and caught a glimpse of the future. If I wanted to do something with my life then now was the time. As Gandhi is often falsely credited with saying, it was time to start being the change that I wanted to see in the world.

View-Master™ Reel (Brussels)

LUNIK

The Sea of Showers, 1959

On the night of 13th September, Luna 2 became the first man-made object to successfully reach the surface of the moon. It conducted a number of tests as it descended towards the surface, providing data shared with the scientific community that was later used in the moon landings. It carried a 400kg payload to the surface, proving that Soviet guidance and control systems were just as good as their American equivalents and that Soviet technological capability was not limited to their rocket platform. It came as a huge blow to the Americans, who were now faced with either giving up on the unofficial competition or an almost exponential increase in spending on the Space Programme. They chose the latter which presumably was just a proxy for foreign policy expansionism.

For a while the Americans thought that they were catching up with the Soviets and certainly that their control systems were better. An American satellite, Explorer, with advanced electronics, was launched from the Juno rocket followed by two more including Explorer 6, the world's first weather satellite that took pictures of the earth.

Juno, or Jupiter, was a variation of the U.S. military's Redstone intercontinental ballistic missile, which in turn was a development of the Nazi's V2 rocket system, developed by none other than the man in charge of the Nazi rocket programme, Dr. Wernher von Braun, who was now a top N.A.S.A scientist and upstanding American citizen.

AUSTRIA & BAVARIA

A Country That Never Existed, 1959

A friend of Miss Seawright was thinking of moving to the Barbican in London. Her husband, an admiral who seems to have managed to have avoided both World Wars, had recently died, leaving her with a very respectable pension and very little to do in Cornwall. The Barbican was a brand-new type of housing complex that I was very excited about, that had just opened in the shattered ruins of London's financial district, cleared, so thoughtfully, by Wernher von Braun. It had been constructed in line with the best socialist principles, with communal facilities, shops, a cinema, outdoor spaces to play chess and bowls, a lake and shared central heating and power. Like the Soviet buildings it copied, it was built in an architecturally brutalist style which was not everyone's cup of tea.

Lady Collins liked the idea of going to the 'talkies' in her dressing gown, but she was not a fan of the exterior of the towers themselves. She sighed and put away the brochures getting out her old photo album to change the subject. Glossy black and white photos of a smiling young couple on their bikes in the mountains looked up at me, because before she was the wife of the Royal Navy's Commander in Chief in the Mediterranean, before she was a refugee from the Nazis, Lady Collins was a pretty Bavarian girl that wanted to sing in English and become a movie star. The long, blonde locks were dyed now, but the deep blue eyes were still the same. She didn't understand why the war had happened. I'm not sure that any of us have explanations good enough to have made shattering her memories worth it.

I loaded up with cigarettes at Victoria, mostly packets of Embassy, a few Dunhill and an American Pall Mall at an exorbitant five shillings, before taking the usual foul train down to Dover, where I was secretly hoping to find the Canterbury. She wasn't in harbour, but only because she was already on the other side of the Channel valiantly churning her way back to Blighty. I wonder briefly what Dr Von Braun would make of the deplorable state of public transport in Britain, but I'm sure public transport is not a problem he has to deal with in America. Anyway, I said that I wouldn't be political in this travelogue.

We passed the Dunkirk beaches where the annual memorial services for the dead and thanksgiving for the deliverance of the living was being held. The couchettes were comfortable enough. I'm 6'4" tall but not that fussy, but I was woken up when the train stopped in the middle of the night to pick up passengers from a train that had broken down. Some of these poor people, mostly British, spent the rest of the night standing between our beds. I offered mine to a woman and her husband, so, instead of sleeping we spent the rest of the night sitting cross-legged on the mattress playing cards like naughty children. Card counting seemed to give me an unfair advantage so I deliberately lose a few rounds and smile. Never have I seen such a crowd pour off from a train as I did at Innsbruck the next morning. But from there it was just a short run to Seefeld in time for lunch and, hopefully, a brief snooze.

Seefeld, whence Lady Collins, née Krenkel originally hailed, had been both a pilgrim site and an important trading post on the route between Augsburg and Venice since the Middle Ages. The Holy Roman Emperor Maximillian I founded an Augustine monastery here, partially to take control of the production of shale oil found in the nearby hills. But by the time I visited it had lost its former importance and had the atmosphere of a big village. It was yet to acquire the rash of hotels, saunas, swimming pools and casinos that now litter the site.

Trees surrounded the village like a warm blanket wrapped around its shoulders, an excellent spot for a quiet walk. My passion for climbing mountains had somewhat waned over the years, although it had not disappeared entirely. I wanted to be close to them, at one with them, but not fighting them. I had no need to prove myself to anybody anymore. There were beautiful views of the village below me through beach, ash and fir trees. Steep rises alternated with level root-crossed stretches like a gigantic flight of stairs and occasionally there were small pools of turquoise blue water. The path steepened again and began to twist. Beech turned into conifers. Now there was no sound, except the occasional cracking of twigs underfoot, no view, no sense of direction. Only an occasional shaft of sunlight showed that the day was still young. A slightly larger pool, a small lake, glowed like a vivid green jewel in the forest. Animals scampered in the undergrowth. Skirting it, there came a final steep rise and the trees ceased abruptly, leaving a small green amphitheatre and there, across the valley, blindingly white, the whole range of the Zillertal Alps, peak upon peak. It was totally unexpected, the light, the vastness of the view. It struck me like a blow after the darkness of the trees. It was magnificent!

View down the valley from the Reither Spitze restaurant.

I had not really liked my experiences of chairlifts in Switzerland (I had still not forgotten that event with the milk churn). They were double-seated and swept up over the hillside at great speed, inevitably propelling one sideways. The Reither Spitze was, however, different. Single, forward-facing chairs carried one silently through the woods, the only sound the tick-tick, tick-tick, as the cable went over the pylon, and the gentle tinkling of cow bells

177

beneath my feet. Peaks appeared and disappeared above the trees and the scent of pines was all pervasive. Eventually the trees fell away, and a cable car provided the final assisted ascent to the summit and a large welcoming restaurant. Having not seen anyone on the way up, I was always amazed to see so many people at the top. Where did they come from? How did they get here?

The mountain was not very high, yet once again I looked over the rim of the volcanic bowl that contained Seefeld and out across the apparently endless ranges of mountains of central Europe. How ridiculous that some of it was labelled Italy, another bit Germany, Austria or Switzerland! It was clearly one and the same thing. It was the Tyrol. I sat on a ridge of ice and snow, with white and blue peaks on my left and on the right, the rich, green valley and glinting lake of Seefeld. The sun was blazing in my face, the air biting cold. I felt like a king, or at least an Admiral's wife.

The Achensee Steam Cog Railway, unchanged since my father visited it.

The Achensee is the largest lake in the Tyrol. In summer it can no doubt be very picturesque, but it was bitterly cold in mid-September. Neither the little red train, nor the big white steamers puffing about, did anything to enliven the grey, wind-lashed waters at the base of the hills. I sought shelter in a jolly hotel on the waterfront in Pertisau and waited for the rain to pass. As I sat sipping my hot chocolate, I reflected on the meaningless futility of national borders, how one side of a field or mountain can be one country, the other a completely different one, and yet the same people and plants grow on both sides. I thought about the road to Germany and the numerous wooden bridges I'd seen built over babbling streams, crossed by brothers and sisters going to and from work. These national borders hadn't existed until a hundred years ago. Now villagers and postmen had to show their papers to customs officials every time they crossed the street.

A rare photo of the crossing my father refers to from 1910, showing the Austrian side with Alois Hitler's customs hut.

Showing the crossing as it is now from the German side:

An officious and violent clerk called Alois Hitler had been one of these border officials at the small town of Braunau. His son, who he regularly thrashed with the leather belt of his customs uniform, grew up with a pathological need to wipe such borders out. That's not any type of excuse, of course, but the recent creation of artificial borders continues to cause huge problems the world over.

At Vent I took a chairlift with all my gear to Stablein and the Breslauer hut where I was to stay overnight and pick up my guide. The hut is a brick-built climber's hotel 2,840 metres above sea level. It is basic but functional, with rows of bunks in dormitories, hot showers and warm food. For me it was a chance to acclimatise, once again, to the thin air and the cold. I was by now very out of practice. I have, over the years, trained myself to go to sleep for a fixed period of time, almost anywhere. It is a trick people learn quickly in the army, but instead of getting a good night's rest before a long day, I found myself fretting and turning, panicking that I wouldn't be able to do it. Nearly everyone in the room around me was going to climb the same mountain, but they all seemed much younger than me. The Wildspitze was Austria's second highest mountain with twin peaks scraping the sky, but the route up was not particularly difficult, not compared to the Eiger, and I didn't really have any need to worry. Yet worried I most definitely was.

The Breslauer Hut guesthouse.

After a high energy breakfast of porridge with bits of bacon and honey, I set off with grim determination on my face and plenty of chocolate and Kendal Mint Cake packed into my pockets. The ascent was gentle enough, the path marked by red and white striped posts. Posts turned into small cairns with fluttering red ribbons as we zigzagged up further towards the Mitterkarferner Glacier. We hit the snow line and stopped in a gully to attach crampons and rope up. They put me middle of the chain, in the old-man spot, a spot that would get dragged off the mountain if either end slipped! Despite the freezing wind, I felt hot. My heart was racing in my chest and my hands were shaking in my mittens. The view back down the valley towards the hotel was spectacular, but I was not enjoying it.

We set off, at what seemed like an agonisingly slow pace across a huge sheet of featureless ice. The wind accelerated across it, lashing my face. Behind my snow glasses I literally closed my eyes and leaned into the wind, walking like a robot, placing my ice pick carefully and counting my steps. There was nothing to see anyway. There was no enjoyment in it all. At the head of the glacier the rope tugged sharply to the right. I opened my eyes once again to see that we were at the bottom of the south ridge. We sheltered behind a large boulder to eat and drink. More porridge, with chunks of chocolate broken off without taking off our gloves and a scalding hot liquid that was somewhere between beef consommé and black tea.

I felt no inclination to move. Less than fifty metres above me up a steep shale embankment knee-deep in snow, was the summit of the Wildspitze. I knew I was bloody-minded enough to make it to the top, but I could hardly be bothered. Getting down safely would take a lot more concentration and I was tired. Where had my enthusiasm for mountain climbing gone?

The summit of the Wildspitze, the highest mountain in the north Tyrol.

It was dark by the time we got back to the Breslauer hut. There was back-slapping in front of a roaring fire in the bar and toasts with glasses of burning Jagermeister. I joined in for a bit, bought a few rounds and offered my Embassy cigarettes around, before beating a hasty exit back to the dorm where, I'm afraid to say, I threw up, collapsed on my bunk and fell asleep immediately. My mountain climbing days were over.

Innsbruck

If the Tyrol is a single cohesive multi-state region, then Innsbruck is its self-proclaimed capital. The Imperial city has been guarding the Brenner Pass through the Alps since Roman times, when it was called 'Veldidena', a name reflected in some of the city's suburbs. At first metals and valuable minerals flowed back from Augsburg to Verona and from there to Rome, but culture also flowed the other way, and it was here that the first Renaissance palaces outside of Italy were built and here that they constructed the first opera house north of the Alps. Innsbruck is a pleasant city with grand architecture, sitting on a bend of the River Inn. The mountains loom high over the pastel-coloured classical facades, the Habsburg Imperial Eagle hovers over every roof. It was briefly the home of the Holy Roman Emperor Maximilian I. His successors, the Archdukes of Austria, built Ambras Castle here and funded a university in the city; compensation for Vienna taking over as the new administrative centre. It must be a delightful place to study, if you are rich, which most students aren't.

It was raining when I arrived, and the golden roofs shone and glittered with an additional sheen. After spending a period in the hills, it was nice to wander past the colourful shops on the Maria Theresa Strasse, to gaze at their tempting displays, full of luxurious fabrics and to explore the dark cobbled alleys. I was supposed to buy Lady Collins some sort of souvenir, but it was all very expensive.

After the war the Allied forces occupied Austria. Like Germany, the country was divided into controlled regions and, like Berlin, Vienna was also split up into zones. The Americans had once again, miraculously, ended up with the best bits, including Innsbruck. The occupation had lasted ten years and Austria had only recently become an independent country again, so the Americans were still here in numbers, enjoying the winter sports. The shops were clearly targeted at American budgets.

In the centre of the Altstadt is the 'Goldenes Dachl', the house with the Golden Roof. The house was built for the emperor Maximillian I, and, although the roof tiles are copper rather than gold, the effect is the same. A gilded, ornate balcony wraps itself around one side, allowing the Emperor and his wife to see what was going on in the market below. Presumably there were fewer crystals, candles and general tourist tat being sold there then. Opposite it is the royal chapel with its life-size bronze statues of great monarchs, real and imaginary, that came to pay homage to the Emperor, or perhaps more fittingly to the mountains.

Despite surly service, which seems to be an Austrian speciality, there were no shortage of 'Konditorei' and cafés, selling cream cake, apple strudel, bowls of steaming stew and hot chocolate. Less than a minute's walk from the 'Golden Roof' was Café Kroll, famous for its Apfelstrudel. Almost opposite that, inside the Hofburg Imperial Palace, was Café Sacher, home of the world's most famous chocolate cake, the 'Sachertorte'.

Innbruck's Marie-Theresien Strasse.

The café had retained the look of a nineteenth century salon, with red carpets and velvet wallpaper, glass chandeliers and moulded coving. Muted classical music drifted from hidden speakers, newspapers rustled and teaspoons clinked against china. Everything carried the magic insignia of the letter 'S'. I am told there are 34 individual steps involved in making the cake, which is made here using the original equipment and ingredients. I find it dense and slightly chewy, and it is not in any way helped by the addition of this aerated cream that the Americans seem to love with everything. I would have much preferred a slice with some of the vanilla ice cream that came with my strudel. Perhaps I shouldn't have eaten the Sachertorte straight after the Strudel. Never mind, if I come back another time, I can experiment eating them in different orders.

My hotel room had a small Juliet balcony, and despite the cold, I sat there later that night with the door open sipping a cup of hot chocolate. All the ingredients came separately and you had to mix them together yourself. It was slightly hypnotic and very relaxing watching the ball of chocolate slowly dissolve into the warm milk. It was the Spanish who brought chocolate to Europe from South America, of course, and Queen Anne, wife of Philip III who brought it to Austria. The Bourbon family went crazy for it, buying plantations in America and the entire supply chain, which is how they ended up with a chocolate biscuit named after them. I find them strangely extravagant and dull at the same time, not unlike the family itself. A Dutch chemist, Johannes van Houten, worked out how to separate chocolate powder and chocolate butter for easier storage and transportation and German and Swiss chocolatiers, such as Herr Lindt, who worked out how to make bars of a smooth creamy consistency out of it in the nineteenth century. It is strange to think how much history revolves around the mundane pleasures of tea, coffee, sugar and chocolate and how many millions have died for it.

Behind all the baroque royal buildings sits the dark curtain of the mountains and, above that, shining brilliantly in the night sky was the moon. Somewhere in that distant jewel, in the remote Mare Imbrium crater, sat little Lunik, Luna 2, whose first and last job had been to plant a flag. I, for one, would rather it had carried chocolate cake to our shared travelling companion, but with a scoop of nice vanilla ice-cream on the side, not that American squirt cream.

Bavaria

From Innsbruck we took the Fern Pass through the mountains, a road our Roman friends knew as the 'Via Claudia Augusta', passing on the way the site where Wernher von Braun and his team of V2 Rocket scientists surrendered to the U.S. Army. There were no great peaks or hair-raising turns, but the pass was lovely. Three lakes of different sizes and colours at different levels glinted through the trees. The road wound its way gently down through cool green shade, where waterfalls splashed from boulder to boulder and the mountain backdrop as the Romans themselves must have seen it all those years ago appeared and disappeared through the branches of the great firs.

The dark forms of the mountains tower over Innsbruck's Hotel Stubaierhof.

Under the mighty mass of the Zugspitze sat Garmisch-Partenkirchen, our base for the next few days. It is a very sophisticated resort and a very pleasant town, or should that be towns, as the difference between the more modern Garmisch and the fresco-filled, cobbled streets of Partenkirchen is still quite noticeable. Tourists are dealt with in a smooth, pleasant way that shows practice and professionalism rather than any real warmth, but there is no hint of resentment or the slightest scent of what is still only the very recent past. The town itself is sensibly laid out following the old Roman road from Verona to Augsburg, which acts as the high street. It was the host of the 1936 Winter Olympics and its sports facilities are still what draws people here, the American military included, who took over the old German army military hospital and expanded it as their base. The old merchant townhouses are slowly being turned into genteel, detached family houses with matching barbeques and station wagons in their back gardens. The presence of the Americans has created a cultural microcosm, warping local products to meet international needs. BBQ sauces, flavoured southern spices, ice-cold milkshakes and strawberry gateaux abound.

In the rolling green hills above Partenkirchen sits a large Art Nouveau house in immaculate grounds. It is the house of the composer, Richard Strauss, who created most of his most famous works here. Its construction was funded by the proceeds of his controversial opera, 'Salome', based on the controversial Oscar Wilde play. I wondered if the decision to pick something contentious was driven by the need for funding the build. The house is now a museum where visitors can voyeuristically poke around his office, bedroom and kitchen. At the back there is a glass conservatory with an aviary, which presumably acted as inspiration for many of his famous 'Lieder'. Beyond the conservatory there were a few catering tents and a small stage. Blankets were laid out on the lawn and candles had been lit along the paths. Strauss' work represents the end of the German Romantic movement and is often seen as being slightly trivial compared to giants such as Wagner and Liszt. That said, whereas they are often regarded as being very divisive, Strauss is an entertainer that provides plenty to please everyone. I spent a delightful afternoon listening to a group of relatively junior understudies perform 'Der Rosenkavalier', Marie Theres' glorious aria echoing off the surrounding mountains. The final trio of the comic opera I found incredibly moving. As the Marschallin steps aside, letting go of her younger love and younger self, confusion and remorse gradually transform into acceptance and grace. It was a fitting parallel for Germany's post-war behaviour as a whole.

Bavaria is a large agricultural region of rolling plains, water meadows and forests, that stretches from the Alps to the Danube. It provides more meat, dairy and wheat than the rest of Germany put together. It has been feeding Central Europe for thousands of years.

However, it contains few sources of mineral wealth and is strategically hard to defend. It has therefore been invaded constantly throughout history by everyone from the French to the Prussians, the Swedes and the Poles. Despite changes in allegiances, perhaps because of them, maybe because it has been treated as a remedial rural backwater and not a military threat, Bavaria has managed to stay completely independent with its own distinct cultural identity. It is a staunchly Catholic area, has its own language, quite impenetrable to Germans, its own style of cooking and clothing and, until nineteen-eighteen, its own king. So, when we talk about Germany, we have to remember that we are talking about a country that didn't exist until the twentieth century at all.

Neuschwanstein

For many tourists the star attraction in Bavaria, with some justification, too. The perfect fairy tale castle, so much so that every fairy, including Mr. Disney, has used it. The exterior, perched high on a spit of rock, is truly spectacular, especially when the valley fills with mist as it does most mornings, and I found the inside, although not to my taste, to be artistically just as good. How extraordinary to see, as I queued to get in, photographs of it being built. Cranes lifting stones and steel beams into place, bulldozers smoothing out great piles of earth, trains bringing wagons of material to the site and large nets of metal scaffolding growing out over the valley like vines. The castle itself is, you see, a modern building, much less than a hundred years old, but there is no way that you could tell that to look at it. The detail is extraordinary. I am not being deliberately perverse. One such place had to be built, and mad or not, King Ludwig II of Bavaria did so. Oh yes, it is vulgar, in bad taste, and undeniably, as architecture critics of the day described it, kitsch, but it is a tremendous work of the imagination and one that is consistently, and superbly carried out. From the entrance courtyard to the throne room, from the grotto to the music salon, it is consistent with itself and the Wagnerian vision it embodies. Despite everything, it is perfect.

Schloss Neuschwanstein. The 'new swan' castle – completed in 1892.

King Ludwig, widely believed to be a closet homosexual, was desperately in awe of Richard Wagner and everything that he did. Wagner, one of the greatest dramatists of all time, personally oversaw much of Neuschwanstein's decoration, lifting whole scenes, such as the throne room and the 'Singer's Hall' from his operas. As one progresses around the tour, the theme changes slowly from Tannhauser and Lohengrin to Parsifal.

The Throne Hall at Neuschwanstein Castle.

It is, unquestionably, a work of genius, one that interestingly borrows heavily from Arabic, Romanesque and Byzantine architecture. I wondered what Cairo's Mohammed Ali Pasha would have made of it. Perhaps it would be too much even for him.

Although I enjoy romps such as the 'Flight of the Valkyrie' or the 'Flying Dutchman' as much as the next man, I find much of Wagner's work difficult to enjoy. It is, in truth, too difficult to safely engage with. For me, like much of Wagner's music, Neuschwanstein is beautiful, but insular, painful and sad. It is the reflection of the tortured mind of a man not quite suited for the real world. My son, a 'Wagnerphile' as I have mentioned, and someone who I have literally seen stop breathing during Tannhauser, explains.

Far more than being just a dramatist and composer, Richard Wagner was a musical theorist, who experimented with the human body's reaction to sound and our innate love of symmetry and need for resolution. Wagner created rich tapestries of music that were deliberately intended to bully and cause pain, not only reflecting, but causing the intense emotions in the story. Rapid, almost chaotic, movement up and down a scale is frequently used to create confusion, escalating repetition of a falling stanza bludgeon us like waves, shifting tonal centres upset us, while extreme chromatinisation, uses tones and chords outside the scale of the rest of the passage of the music to inject fear. Many of these techniques come partly from Arabic music as my father discovered in Egypt. All of them are widely used in filmmaking today and their effects on humans can be watched on an oscilloscope. Nowhere is this better represented than in his tragic love story, "Tristan and Isolde", which is sometimes described as being the start of atonal modern music and by many classical musicians as being simply too traumatic to play.

A new road was being driven through the forest to bring people to the Passion Play at Oberammergau – and there you have the perfect duality: the attraction and destruction of that attraction in the same hand. Oberammergau was a staunchly Catholic village in the middle of nowhere. There was no education, no modernisation, no visitors for hundreds of years, so it had to entertain itself, by re-enacting scenes from the Bible, the only stories it had access to. Now this naive charm has turned itself into a multi-million-dollar entertainment business, with dedicated hotels, travel agencies and theatres. The place has become self-conscious and greedy. Even in the years when there is no play, the open-air theatre, with its auditorium covered in a great concrete dome, charges tourists for entry to see the costumes, props and old recorded footage. The village is undeniably pretty, as are many others in the valley, with frescos on the outside walls of the houses, but souvenirs are everywhere, bringing back memories of Lourdes and the Vatican. Why is it that religious souvenirs are so offensive? The selling of indulgences, the selling of forgiveness, has always been central to Christianity. I do find it a particularly dislikeable religion.

Close by Oberammergau is the delightful small town of Mittenwald, famous among musicians at least, for its violin making. Violins hung in most of the shops on the Obermarkt and many private houses, for all the world like smoking sides of bacon! The town is of course 'touristy', but it manages to be so by celebrating itself. It truly is the stereotype one wants to see.

With German Nationalism as dead as the Third Reich, the people of Bavaria have reverted to what they know best and what they understand. They have entrenched themselves in a desire for the peasant lifestyle, a love of the landscape around them, something that they call 'Heimat'. It is this that has spawned a resurgence in 'traditional costume' and traditional crafts. People who would have happily worn smart suits and dresses to work a decade ago, now prefer to wear 'trachten' to church – leather trousers, long socks, a bit of badger stuck to a felt hat, a gingham dress and apron. Their homes are simpler now, too, adorned with simple pine tables, wood-burning tile ovens and decorations made from straw. It is curious to see a people evolve backwards, but it is a wise move in an uncertain world and a political wilderness. They know they have taken a wrong turn and are retreating to solid ground to start again.

Cute though much of it is, I force myself to remember that Bavaria was the spiritual home of the Nazi party, the origin of the Brownshirt movement, the Munich Beer Hall Putsch, the Nuremburg rallies. Mittenwald itself is rumoured to be the last resting place of a huge cache of Nazi gold and diamonds, its exact location encrypted in a copy of Gottfried Federlein's 'Marsch–Impromptu' annotated by Hitler's private secretary Martin Bormann.

Hitler's copy of Marsch-Impromptu with Bormann's additions highlighted. The typed text 'Wo Matthias Die Saiten streichelt' (Where Matthias plucks the strings), is believed to refer to one of Mittenwald's most famous violinists, Matthias Klotz.

Yet there was little that I saw here to suggest that Bavaria's being the home of Nazism was anything other than geography. Hitler was an Austrian who grew up in the Austrian border town of Braunau am Inn, and Munich, which suffered terribly during the depression with over 40% unemployment and hideous food shortages, was simply the nearest city to him.

Although Hitler's policies were popular among farmers and his personal power base was in Bavaria, or rather the Tyrol as a whole, his political power came from the Nazi party's support from middle class and industrial Germany. In the 1932 election, only 13 seats in Bavaria went to the N.S.D.A.P., the significant majority remained in support of the Catholic B.V.P., and Bavaria's central parties, which today both form part of the C.S.U. (the staunchly catholic variant of the C.D.U.). Germany's burden is not for Bavaria to carry alone, but one we must all share.

There was a small service of remembrance being held at the little war memorial in the main square of Mittenwald. Wreaths were being laid at the foot of a statue of a soldier. It was strange and, to me, intensely moving, to see the figure in the, to us, reviled 'Jerry' 'coalscuttle' helmet, be treated with love and respect. I can honestly say that I never killed a German directly, although I was shot at by them numerous times, most notably in Bristol when a Heinkel He 111 bomber chased my signals truck along a road in Bristol, the bullets from his guns ripping up the tarmac as if it were a puddle of water, shattering the windscreen and slicing through the Bedford as

191

if it were butter. No, I never served on the front line, although my actions may still have counted for the deaths of many.

Guns are ugly, noisy, smelly things. They are crude, unreliable, not particularly effective for either party and are bloody heavy, too. The German infantry man on top of the monument certainly looked keen enough to put his down. I wanted to reach out and hand him a violin instead. Poor bugger.

Mittenwald's pretty town centre.

Eighty-five million people died, countless more were injured, countries and empires were ruined, all for the sake of one that never existed in reality. I don't mean to denigrate any of it, but the whole war and everything that led up to it, especially German Romantic Nationalism such as I saw at Neuschwanstein, seemed so bloody silly. Too silly for a young lad from Mittenwald to die for!

We have already seen that there is no such thing as Germany. There are certainly distinct regions like the Tyrol and Bavaria, the Rhineland or the Black Forest, and there are wider notions echoing the Holy Roman Empire, too, but Germany is not a concept that has existed in reality until now. Nor logically did the concept of Germans exist, until our creation of them after the Second World War. I was to see for myself that people who are clearly 'German' and who speak German, although 'German' is not a single common language that anyone speaks, live as far apart as France, Czechoslovakia, Serbia and Estonia. Germany as a nation was only created in 1871 by the unlikely alliance of Protestant Prussia with Catholic Bavaria. When it came into being as a legal entity, Germany immediately had to invent an identity for itself and a mythical past with shared heroes that everyone could rally around. Authors and artists were summoned to start 'realising' an imagined Germanic past including Goth, Vandal, Lombard, Saxon, Dutch, Russian, Swiss and Austrian characters. Coins were minted with their faces, a hall of heroes, literally called Walhalla, named after the Scandinavian Hall of the Fallen, was built beside the Danube as a German Nationalist theme park. National costume was nationalised into the standard dirndl and lederhosen image that we know today and stage set designers were asked to build fantasy castles across Germany. It is no wonder that Germany has had such trouble with state borders, because Germans, if such a thing existed, lived all over Europe and were given images from all over Europe to call their own. It took less than fifty years for this completely made-up nationalist mythology to cause two world wars, destroying the reality of the state that never really existed. Their real history is so wonderful, they shouldn't be making rubbish up.

VENICE

A Most Serene Republic, 1959

Venice is surely on everyone's list of places to see. It is a city whose image we all know well, a carnival of beautiful palaces built either side of a network of bridges and canals. We know it for its operas, its paper masks, its gondolas and ice-cream, but we hardly know it at all. For nearly a thousand years it was the brutal capital of a military state, whose navy ruled the Mediterranean. It is only two-hundred kilometres from Innsbruck over the Alps, but it takes nearly seven hours to get there by train. More tunnels through the Alps are planned to reduce this.

The train followed the Isarco river south from the Brenner Pass to Vipiteno, a hill fort with a fourteenth-century clock tower and a flourishing wine trade. It continued on through Bolzino to Trento, a fascinating place that sits high in the Italian Alps. It is, of course, a Roman town, and its name is derived from the Latin for 'Three Teeth' referring to the mountains that surround it. It has grown rich from the silver mines dug into the nearby hills and above the lintel of the old Town Hall a Latin inscription is still visible: 'Montes argentum mihi dant nomenque Tridentum'. ('The Mountains gave me silver and the name of Trento'). The town is German speaking and for most of its life it was part of Austria. Trento suffered badly in both wars and was officially confiscated from Austria and given to Italy after the Great War.

In the centre of the town is a splendid square with a very fine fountain outside the magnificent cathedral home of the Council of Trento. As I walked around the square differing compositions appeared, framing the low arcaded openings. The cathedral was plain, almost Gothic, epitomising the simplified and less wasteful approach of the counter reformation.

3Trento's cathedral showing a mix of Roman & Tyrolean styles.

The valley around Trento was incredibly lush, with every type of fruit and vegetable, hemmed in between its great cliffs. The valley gradually narrowed and became stony, the cliff drew even closer, and the valley turned into a gorge. Just when I was wondering if there would be a way out, the hills suddenly fell back, and the broad plain of the Po Valley stretched out to the horizon. Then the road ran arrow-straight out across the flat marshland of the 'Lagona Morte' to Jesolo.

Back then Jesolo was little more than a group of buildings, a few hotels and a church. The slender trees came all the way down to the beach, where every so now and again, a stone buried in the sand would announce the site of a future shop or a new hotel. From the site of the central piazza to the lighthouse, a distance of about two miles, there was nothing but beach on one side and marsh on the other. Along the edge of the lagoon, on a larger strip of raised ground, was the little village of Cavillino, once a rival of Venice, and having as its symbol the 'Little Horse' hence its name. This once maritime power had a shop that served the locals and a single bus stop. How times change. Beyond this the road ended at Punta Sabbione. Here was the lagoon, the sea, and the ferry to Venice itself.

It was a wild, bleak and lonely place, flat and silent. It is extraordinary to see it today, entirely built up with hotels and casinos. Only a year or so after I visited, the area between the lighthouse and the square became the largest caravan site on earth. I understand that it now receives six million visitors per year. I got there only just in time.

Jesolo's main hotel and beach in 1959.

I first saw Venice as it should be seen, from the sea. A small motorboat came chugging over the quiet water. It picked up its few passengers and returned. It seems odd to say a 'sheet of water' but the lagoon seemed curiously flat, the water still and silent, the few islands merging with the dark line of the mainland. There seemed to be few buildings apart from the bulk of the Arsenal itself. We rounded the dark mass and suddenly there it all was – quite magically. St. Giorgio on its island, the Salute, Doge's Palace, and all in complete contrast to the stillness of the lagoon, bursting with life and activity; motorboats rushing everywhere, water slapping and sparkling, men shouting and laughing. A sleek grey warship was moored there and higher up a white cruise liner, but the magnificent buildings in that incredible and unique setting were pure Canaletto. By the time we stepped ashore, I was already overwhelmed.

What is it about this place? I cannot describe its magic at all. It is in part sheer beauty, but somehow it also an encapsulation of our need to be near water, our urge to explore and our desire to trade. There is on the buildings an elegance that is imposed, touched as if by magic by the water, dancing and sparkling like diamonds in the sun, still and open, reflecting sunlight upwards under carved stone arches, giving a sense of life, of beauty to what might otherwise be just an alley. Walk through the poorer areas and stop in any nameless campo, and there will be windows of exquisite grace behind the washing, a fine well of deeply carved stone, a doorway of architectural merit behind the flaking paint and crumbling stucco, and topping the composition a campanile, leaning a little, but exactly the right height. And being traffic free, there is little sound here but some singing birds and the laughter of children.

The Grand Canal Venice in the mid-fifties.

It was not always so; Venice was never supposed to be like this. Towards the end of the fifth century, at a time that we would describe as the Fall of Rome, the Italian peninsula was suddenly overcome with famine and plague. With the Empire split into two separate centres of administration, and the majority of the legions out guarding remote provinces such as Britain, the Goths swept in the backdoor and sacked Rome itself. It was an action repeated many times over the next hundred years. The Governor of Britain rushed back with his legions to protect Rome, successfully, but at the cost

197

of losing control of Britain. As more and more Goths, Vandals and Lombards poured down from the Alps, seizing the silver mining town of Trento on the way, the people of northern Italy fled to the coast for protection and a series of communities were established amongst the lagoons on whatever dry land could be found.

Many times Venice's buildings collapsed into the silted mud and sand, but it was to be the sea that made Venice successful, not only protecting it, but providing food, trade with Byzantium who gave it the eastern Emperor's support, a source of great revenue, and ultimately a maritime empire of its own.

The great sights of Venice all hold a dark past. St. Mark's with its blaze of gold and jewels grabbed from piracy, pillaging and blackmail. The Doge's palace, created as a prison for holding Christian slaves before their export to northern Africa, and the Academy, which now holds so many great paintings that the mind became bewildered, was once the exchange where slaves were castrated and sold to the highest bidder. A denarius, roughly 5g of gold, for a white female in a healthy condition, 2g for a male in working condition or 4g for a eunuch that could read and write. Venice grew rich trading with the enemy, and then richer still by double crossing them.

The Arsenal lies at the centre of Venice, a naval harbour protected by towers, huge walls and sea gates. It was here that Venice built the fleet of fighting ships that were to dominate the Adriatic Sea. They used Byzantine money, slave labour, Roman naval designs and Greek fire to achieve dominance, expanding their city towards the sea as funds permitted, with bridges, canals, bulwarks, fortifications and warehouses. An empire of unstoppable mercenaries.

It was the crusades that really made Venice what we see today, however. By the twelfth century, Venice controlled the shipping lanes between Europe and the Levant, not only militarily, but through a complex arrangement of treaties with the Moors and Byzantium, both of whom paid for Venetian protection. Two hundred ships were involved in the transport of the crusader army for the first crusade alone, with extra fees charged for raids on the Islam coast and fortifications. So it was for three-hundred years, Venice taking coins from both sides to achieve a stalemate in the

Holy Lands and controlling the spice trade. By the sixteenth century, Venice was expanding her own reach inland, grabbing Cyprus, where Otello is set, and other colonies along the Dalmatian coast, all the while upgrading the grandeur of the capital, every glorious palace built on the waterfront representing a either a subjugated province or people.

Niccolo Machiavelli was an Italian diplomat and philosopher. His name has become synonymous with the deception, treachery and crime that Iago displays in the opera Otello. His most famous work, 'The Prince' is written about Venice's rulers and how the Republic rose to power. Despite the cold beauty of their gold and marble city, it is hard to empathise with the Machiavellian Doges that ruled the waves, and it is troublesome to compare them with the actions of, say, the British when building their empire. I find it hard to disagree with Machiavelli's observations on life and realpolitik.

I went in search of ordinary people and release in the little quiet corners of the city, overcome with a kind of mental drunkenness. Here an old man tinkered with an outboard engine in the graveyard of a church, there a man sold slices of roman style pizza from an oil drum on top of a marble tomb. How wondrous it was with the ease at which these people lived amongst such magnificence. I thought back to my experience in Holland where cities were being recreated: 'What you had before but better...' and wondered if anything we could learn from Venice could be applied there. But such a place, magnificence on such a scale, could never be built again, and it occurred to me that such attention to detail required control, total control and power on a phenomenal scale, something that the council and mayors of Rotterdam simply don't have access to.

One evening after dusk, I stopped on the Rialto Bridge and watched the last light fade. I found a piece of marble into which my shoulder fitted comfortably and there I rested. Below on the dark water a nameless tenor sang the well-known songs of Italy to a group of tourists in gondolas that could be rented at horrific prices. A tourist show, yes, but as the words of 'O Sole Mio' soared high and clear in the darkness I found myself strangely moved as if I, like Venice, had found my place of peace in the world.

It is sometimes forgotten that several foundations were established in the safety of the lagoon at the time that Venice was built. The lagoon was not quite as safe as it appeared, malaria causing many of them to fail. The lagoon is in fact littered with islands containing lonely church towers swathed in mist, graveyards drowned beneath nettles and brambles. Small farms and a wooden jetty are all that remain of most of them. A few are open for artists to explore and picnic amongst the nature trails, but one is nearly as grand as Venice itself. Torcello.

The old basilica on the abandoned island of Torcello.

The boat nosed into an island no different apparently from any other in the lagoon and moored against a makeshift wooden jetty. We scrambled ashore to find ourselves standing in an overgrown copse wreathed in nettles. Flies re-enacting the plagues of malaria, whined above the silty green water. The path leading from the boat dock was well made and seemed too elaborate for the place. There were patterns in the cobbles and every ten meters or so an iron bracket in a sconce waited for a lantern. Between the hedges there were traces of wall footings, and ahead a small group of farm buildings, with tiled roofs and complex chimneys. The weather-beaten crumbling brick facade was covered in boards offering ice-cream for sale and the time of the next boat, but around the back marble statues decorated the lawn and colourful artworks could be seen plastered across the pig shed walls. Immediately opposite the building was an elegant humpbacked bridge that led nowhere, elegant Arabian arches sculpted into its sides. A little further another long low building was being used as some sort of shed, machinery and stripped engines lying in the shadows of thick iron spiked doors. More frescos could be seen in the darkness inside, and above the roof a high campanile holding bronze bells. As we walked further, the shapes above the trees slowly resolved themselves into a huge cathedral, a small octagonal church, a city hall cum restaurant and a few houses grouped around a small green that had once been the town's piazza.

Torcello is a sparsely populated island at the northern end of the lagoon. First settled in 452 AD, it is referred to as the parent island from which Venice was later populated. It offered safety from the Goth invasions sweeping the mainland for a two-hundred-year period. It sheltered the Bishop of Altinum and received the sacred relics of Saint Heliodorus, who became Torcello's patron saint.

The Basilica of Santa Maria Assunta on Torcello.

The Basilica of Santa Maria Assunta was built in the seventh century when nearly twenty thousand people, lived and worked on this tiny island. It acted as a focal point not only for the residents of the island itself, but for the communities of fishermen and salt workers on the neighbouring islands too. It was constructed in a style common at the time but virtually unique to us today, for it represents a merging of established Byzantine practice, with a new western style that was to become the gothic movement. It physically represents a point when the Eastern Roman Empire, the world of Constantine, began to let go and Europe was beginning to emerge from the ashes. Torcello, an old Roman outpost, paid for its expansion and its new cathedral by sheltering celebrities of the day and supplying salt to Constantinople. It was designed and constructed by experts from the Empire in the East. Less than a hundred years after the Basilica was completed, Charlemagne, King of the Lombards and the Franks, visited the cathedral on the way back from being proclaimed the first Holy Roman Emperor in Rome. Torcello remained in his orbit. In the apse, the traditional Byzantine mosaic of the Virgin stands on her blazing field of gold looking down the length of the nave to the west wall and the mosaic of the 'Last Judgment'. Elongated, austere, this is no sweet maternal Mary from a wealthy background that could be found in any church in Constantinople. No, this is a new Mary, a tough disciplinarian, someone that could see off the Goths and the Mongol hordes and guide her children through the cold and the darkness. This is a new Gothic Mary, Mother of God, who demands spiritual obedience from her children in return for protection from a world no longer controlled by Emperors and the Senate and no longer policed by legions.

But by the fourteenth century the harbour at Torcello had begun to silt up and when the Black Death ravaged the Venetian Republic in the early fourteenth century, the island was the first to fall victim. It never recovered. By the fifteenth century, traders had stopped calling at the island and the Bishopric was moved to Murano. The monastery of St. Francis della Deserta is all that remains of Torcello's active religious community. Lying at the end of a tortuous channel to the side of the lagoon, remote and inaccessible, it suits the quiet monks that live there, content that their work is done. Its cloisters loud with the song of the swallows that overwinter there.

The telephone wires march on wooden legs across the water to the other islands, following Torcello's residents to Burano and Murano. In plan, Burano is similar to its parent island, but that's where the similarity ends. The boats pull in beside a stone jetty, lined with brightly coloured houses. The little piazza with church and town hall are full of people buying souvenirs. The church is of no consequence, the town hall a school of lace making, which is the island's main export. The overall effect was of a busy, cheerful, colourful mini-Venice.

Murano, however, was drab and proletarian; busy with its glass making around the roaring furnaces. There was no colour even in its cathedral with its superbly arcaded apse. I had lunch at a local trattoria. The inhabitants at their zinc covered tables were astounded. The proprietor's wife hurried out with a cloth for my table. Pasta, lamb stew, fruit and a jug of white wine – not too bad. In fact, one tenth of the price of the same meal in Venice just across the water.

The famous roofline of St. Marks is not connected to its interior ceiling.

Speaking of Venice itself, I do not feel that I have done St. Mark's justice. St. Mark's, of all the exotic churches, is one of the greatest. Venetian merchants going on long voyages undertook to bring back something with which to enrich the church. They nearly always did so, most famously the bronze horses captured from the siege of Constantinople in 1254 after the fourth crusade. The result is opulent, flamboyant, oriental, lavish and very strange. It was not my style at all, but its impact was so great that it can only be admired.

Canaletto's painting of the West Front clearly shows the steps up to the church. Two of them. Yet when I visited just two hundred years later, there were three steps down to it from the square. The floor inside is as uneven as a frozen sea – the great marble slabs tilted one way or another as the foundations slowly subside. The cathedral has sunk over half a metre into the lagoon in that time at a steady rate of almost half a centimetre per year; conclusive and shocking proof that the loss of this great city, like the loss of the great republic, is inevitable.

The church seems dim on entering, candle smoke covering much of the gold and glass. It takes time for the eye to see the sheer richness of the jewel covered stone that covers the walls. Mosaics, paintings and carvings cover every inch, with marble slabs and columns growing like vines in a forest. Everything leads up to the glory of the Palo d'Oro, the great screen behind the altar is entirely covered with gold. It glows in the darkness like a banked fire.

The interior of St. Mark's Cathedral, Venice.

Behind the narthex, a steep dark and dusty stair led to a flaking notice 'Museo della conservazione'. To the Museum of Cathedral Works. These places fascinate me, even more than the cathedrals themselves. I have visited many before in English cathedrals, faded manuscripts, charters with great seals, pieces of sculpture and ironwork, plans and drawings looked after by the same one little old man. This one in Venice was the same as its English counterparts.

After a happy hour pottering about I found a little door at the end of the museum. 'Prego. Di andare avanti.' The old man indicated that I could go through. This I did and found myself on a gallery high in the church. Here I was right up near the gigantic mosaic figurines illuminated by the sun streaming in through the west window. Below the body of the church still seemed dark and full of people, the murmur of their voices a steady undercurrent of sound. But up here with these gently glowing giants there was just silence.

St. Mark's as painted by my father. Oil on chipboard.

Another door, actually part of the west window itself, led to an outside balcony right beneath the hooves of the four Greek horses, that now rest here after travelling so far. Other ninth century relics here at St. Mark's were famously smuggled out of the Holy Land under a pile of pork. The domes that you see from the ground are empty wooden structures, they give a familiar skyline but one that is not actually connected to the brick domes on the inside.

The square was crowded below. The tables at Florian's were full despite charging over two pounds for tea and sandwiches (£80 at today's prices) and the orchestra was playing under the arches. To the left, past the Doge's palace boats and gondolas, full of wealthy tourists, bobbed about and danced. To be above it and to look down on that superb square 'the finest drawing room in Europe', to see the milling throng and the air full of whirring wings and to hear the music was to experience the carnival touch that has always been the speciality of Venice. It was the most splendid exhibit that only the 'Museum of Cathedral Works' could offer.

Machiavelli said that Mankind was always in a state of movement, that which was not up and coming, was going, departing into the night. So it was with Venice. As the empires of Byzantium and the caliphate contracted, so did Venice's economy. As the enlightenment spread through Europe, so Venice lost its competitive advantages. With the discovery of the Americas, trade with the East went into decline. Military decline followed economic decline and Venetian colonies became the focus of Turkish wars. It was Napoleon who finished it off, invading through the Brenner Pass in 1796, following the route of my train exactly one thousand, one hundred years after the first Doge was elected. Venice had done well for a funny little fishing village in a swampy lagoon.

Without ceremony the ferry pulled away from the quay, men in rubber boots and gloves guiding the great copper chains back into their rusty housing. Clouds of diesel smoke drifted across the face of the evening sun. Venice was always able to turn the smile on and off like a light switch. It was beautiful yes, elegant and cultured certainly, but it was not a place that you could trust. Not ever. Trees began to bubble up over the roofs of the houses, until the shadow of the Arsenal wiped them away. Suddenly Venice was gone and perhaps fittingly, all I was left with was the gently lapping water of that great lagoon.

Venice is still sinking, and at an increased rate. Not only is the city sinking but global warming is causing water levels to rise. Massive projects are underway to try to save the city, including the MOSE system that places huge gates between the lagoon and the sea. But the level of investment required to save the city is greater than that currently available. The city is expected to be 'lost' by 2100. Its most famous resident, Machiavelli would say that it was fate…

View-Master™ Reel (Venice)

PARIS

City of Light, 1960

A new decade and the 'Winds of Change' could be felt blowing, but were they ill winds or favourable ones? I did not know. Technology was blooming all around us, and the old colonies were beginning to drop away and find their own way in the world. Were we finally going to be able to let go of the war and move into the future? I thought so, and I was excited at the prospect of the world finally growing up, but I was also beginning to have some concerns about what that future might look like and who was leading us there. Paris was moving on too, but it resisted every single step, like one of its residents refusing to let go of their famous black stoles...

Rue Jacob was a quiet little street on the left side of the Seine that frequently flooded in winter. In 1783 the hotel where I was staying was then the British Embassy, and this was where Benjamin Franklin negotiated the American Independence Treaty from Britain. He refused, however, to sign it on British territory, so on September 3rd, 1783, he and John Adams signed the treaty at the York Hotel six doors away where he was staying. This is also where Hemingway used to stay on his trips to Paris, while Wagner stayed regularly at number fourteen. The 'October Group', Queneau, Vailland, and Sartre met at the Green Bar at number ten, and the feminist writer Simone de Beauvoir went to school next to my hotel. The area looks genteel, but it is really a hotbed of intrigue. Subversive almost.

For me, Paris was like an itch that I felt the need to scratch, yet every time I went there, I left it feeling slightly unsatisfied and had to come back again. Once again, I was just passing through, but I was trying to engage with it more emotionally this time, and less like a thoughtless tourist.

I started by exploring the sites on this side of the river. The Musée Rodin, Les Invalides, the Jardin de Luxembourg and the Pantheon. I took coffee at 'Les Deux Magots' beneath the large green awning, which socially, was no small accomplishment. It was the haunt of Hemingway, Joyce and Sartre, arguably the home of surrealism. Certainly, they defined their manifesto here. The Surrealists had their own club table, visionaries Man Ray, Ernst and Miro, could insult any newcomer they were feuding with. The interiors were untouched since the days of Art Deco, with chandeliers, banquettes, brass full-length mirrors, but the prices were bang up to date. It was hard to imagine Oscar Wilde who was a regular patron and lived and died only minutes away on the Rue des Beaux-Arts, splashing out on duck à l'orange, with his deliberately meagre allowance of three pounds a week.

Les Deux Magots.

It was four years since I had last visited, and by then Paris was changing. It was finally beginning to recover from the War. The facades of buildings were literally turning from black to white. Reconstruction was starting everywhere. None more so than at Notre Dame. Dilapidated and crumbling buildings were being torn down and replaced by offices, forcing up the price of land and shifting middle class residents to the suburbs. Paris once more was becoming the city of the cultural elite, haunt of film stars. For the first time in a long time the Eiffel Tower was having to share the skyline with cranes.

I found the Roman Arena – a dusty oval where small boys played football and revisited the Jardin des Plants which seemed just as pleasant as last time but not quite as magical. In the middle of the garden stands the magnificent Grand Mosque, a delightful haven of peace and tranquillity, that having spent a little time in Egypt I was keen to see. It is of course a relic of France's colonisation of large parts of the Muslim world, paid for in part by the French government's insistence that the Ottoman Empire pay to bury its own dead. Beside the exotic bell tower, that rivals, and in my view surpasses, the Eiffel Tower for beauty, a blank white wall with a small door invites one into a lovely garden with pools and fountains.

Paris' Grand Mosque.

The mosque itself was fashioned from cedar wood so delicately fretted that it looked like lace. The only mark of the passing of time was the regular call to prayer. A thread of sensuousness ran through everything. Far from being a bowed apology it was a proud advert for Islam.

I noticed all sorts of 'odd' things now that I was not rushing to see the great 'must sees'. I found myself stranded at Sacre Coeur

211

during Pentecostal Mass and was impressed by the professional theatricalism of it all. Later I found myself at the Zoo, which I visited almost as a joke, but found rather impressive. It is quite a thing to be looking down on a vista of trees and seeing a tiger looking back at me with nothing apparently between it and me at all. I sauntered through the Oriental Musée, the Musée de L'Art Moderne and also the entire length of apparently endless boulevards. I went of course to the Opera House to watch Coppelia and also strangely to the Folies Bergères. The ballet was lovely, although it was the glittering audience and the sense of occasion that made it feel different from Covent Garden. The showmanship was also what stood out at Les Folies too. With its superb sets and semi-dressed actresses and barmaids it has fascinated tourists for a hundred years, although its complete absence of 'smut' really classifies it as a family show. The French if they go at all, love to take their families.

At last, I sat beneath the trees at midnight in the Place du Tertre in Montmartre once again without francs, watching the flame of the candle on the table, motionless in the warm night air. The vibrant artistic community was more reminiscent of the era of the great artists. I was still unsure whether I liked Paris, but sitting amongst the canvases, with as few francs as Toulouse-Lautrec, or Van Gogh had when they sat in the same square, I felt at least that I'd done it properly this time. It was, perhaps, beginning to grow on me.

The next day at Orly airport, a Lufthansa Convair 440 was waiting patiently to take me onward with, worryingly, an armed guard at the foot of the steps.

A Lufthansa Convair 440.

BERLIN

City of Shadows, 1960

Berlin. My real destination. It was a quiet flight, quiet in every sense. There were only about twelve of us on the plane, academics, professionals and civil servants all sat bolt upright, with plenty of reading material. There was none of the excitement in the air that normally accompanies a trip, nor did I feel anything other than trepidation, even the engines seemed strangely muted. The silence was only broken when the stewardesses came round with drinks. My stomach felt a little unsettled, perhaps it was the rushed breakfast at the airport, but more likely it was the name of that city staring out at me in bold black print. I accepted a black tea 'with lemon', as a substitute and set about trying to memorise the map.

After a brief stopover in Hanover, we proceeded along tightly controlled air corridors to the city itself, landing mid-afternoon at Templehof, where only fifteen years before Dornier bombers had lined up in front of that hideous flag. I find all flags fairly offensive, but that one will always be exceptional! I had no idea what I would find here, who I would find here or how I would react to what I found. I wanted to be open-minded, I wanted to be generous and forgiving; Berlin has a long history and the Nazi flag had only flown over it for twelve years, but there was so much cultural baggage, in the name, in the landmarks, even in the font the street signs were written in. I still wasn't sure if I could trust myself.

Berlin is a city that is mired in grief. It wears its pain like a widow's weeds. It is overcome with a palpable atmosphere of sadness and decay, emanating from the ashes of war. Never have I seen a place inhabited by humans, quite so broken and dispirited. This was nothing like Bonn or even Cologne.

West Berlin is a tiny political enclave in the centre of the old city, which itself is stranded all alone inside the German Democratic Republic. It has nothing to boast about but boast it does. It is a tawdry place full of brash people that seemed to be passing through the place, businessmen, salesmen, politicians, rather than people living there permanently. It felt, to me, like arriving in a crowded bar, rather than anyone's home. The streets were crowded and full of hastily thrown up cement buildings covered in neon lights. Noise was everywhere.

I had expected to see an occupied city divided into sectors, with barbed wire along the streets, check points & soldiers in jeeps patrolling. In fact, this was not the case. Berliners were free to move about and the streets, at least in the West, were full of bright red bubble cars, scooters and the ubiquitous German 'Beetle'. There were few signs of the British and French presence, except for the occasional information board beside a dusty section of road informing me 'Vous Quittez Le Secteur Français', as if anyone cared. Nor were there many US soldiers on the streets, but everything seemed to have an American 'smell' about it.

I found myself sat under the red and white awning of a café on the Kurfuerstendamm having ordered, out of pure curiosity, the 'Hawaii Toast', a peculiar dish consisting of a slice of toast topped with tasteless plastic cheese, a whole ring of pineapple and cherry jam. It was not unpleasant in itself, but it was hard to swallow. What was it doing here and who was selling it to whom? I washed it down with a plastic cup of filter coffee that was somehow both burnt and overly diluted and asked the same question as I stared out at the rows of glass-fronted shops and the silver clad 'American Bank'. Heavy printed crockery, luxury furniture, shoes and cocktail dresses, all of it flown in from abroad. Who was buying it, who was it for? Certainly not the starving families struggling to survive in the ruins of bombed-out buildings. Large yellow buses thundered by advertising AEG fridges and sparkplugs. But again, to whom? Above the burnt-out dark skeleton of Kaiser Wilhelm Memorial Church, known cheerfully here as the 'broken tooth', a flashing Mercedes star proudly revolved. From making the Fuhrer's car to replacing religion in just 15 short years. It was a worrying vision of how the future might be if we weren't careful.

The 'Tiergarten' was really the only part of West Berlin that I liked. I don't normally like zoos, but I'd enjoyed the one in Paris, so I gave it a go. After the war it had been rebuilt to give the animals a more natural setting. I managed to find a stand that sold ice-cream, slightly disappointing if I'm honest, and it was here that I again sampled the culinary and cultural horror that is currywurst.

Images of two iconic buildings appear in everyone's mind when they think of the Battle for Berlin: Russian tanks pouring through the bullet hole riddled frame of the Brandenburg Gate and Russian soldiers raising the red flag above the burnt-out ruin of the Reichstag. 157,000 people died in just twelve days in the city, 250,000 more were injured. The two buildings stood next to each other at the heart of the city, surrounded on all sides by a ghost-filled empty open space.

The Brandenburg Gate after the war in the ruined centre of Berlin.

The Americans had started to renovate the Reichstag and the Brandenburg Gate had been patched up. I would have left them as they were, all alone in a park in neutral territory. There was nothing more that needed to be said about the destructiveness of war and the nationalism that caused it.

I entered the 'Democratic sector' through the front door, with only a cursory nod from the People's Police. They had no interest in checking my papers, nor the slightest inclination to take bribes. Their uniforms were smart, and their guns well maintained. They seemed cheerful enough and were nothing like the Blackshirts that we were so used to hating. To my surprise, Unter den Linden, previously the main shopping street in Berlin, was completely deserted. The wind rustled in the leaves of the trees that lined the once busy boulevard. There were no cars at all, and very few people. A few locals sat outside in a small café and in the distance a man with string bags attached to a bicycle walked slowly towards FriedrichStrasse; otherwise there was nothing. The contrast with the Western enclave could not be more striking. Unlike the gaudy colours of the West, the buildings that remained standing here were all faded pastel tones and stained with soot. Rubble was everywhere and, whereas in the American sector ruins were the exception in every street, here it was almost the opposite. The war could have ended fifteen weeks, not years ago, here. It was terribly, terribly sad. East Berlin has a strange smell to it too, instantly recognisable but hard to describe. There was the mixture of wet stone, cheap tobacco and brown coal that I recognised from other places, but that was just part of it; here there were overtones of sulphur, burnt metal, cleaning fluid and carbolic. No matter how many times I crossed the border, that peculiar smell followed me everywhere.

Beyond Unter den Linden lies Marx Engels Platz, dubbed as Berlin's equivalent of Red Square. It is a laughable affair with wooden benches stacked high on all sides in front of giant red posters of Marx himself. Crude anti-western slogans that nobody would have been taken in by, were daubed on the walls. Behind it the dark looming hulk of the Berliner Dom, an utterly burnt-out, pitch-black shell towered over everything. It was very sinister, death embodied. Everywhere I went I saw people working and living amongst the ruins. Rightly the government of the GDR was focusing on renovating facilities for the city's residents, schools, hospitals, housing, therefore leaving the major public buildings to lie in ruins. It was logical, but to an outsider it seemed shocking, almost vindictive. Much of old Berlin, places such as the Museumsinsel with its Royal Palace and multitude of museums full of fine art, would once have been highly restricted spaces only accessible to the elite. Now the wrecks of these same prestigious buildings lay awaiting demolition among the weeds, and anyone was free to wander over them, chasing rabbits and the other wildlife that has begun to reclaim these places for themselves. I sat in the long grass, contemplating the difficult choices that East Berlin had to make every day, at every level. It had a set of very clear priorities and was just trying to survive as best it could. It was odd to see a city struggling so.

I took a boat along the Spree to see Berlin from the water, the reason why the city was here and for hundreds of years its main source of income. The water was heavily polluted and full of the debris of war but for the two men whose boat it was, their hunger-panged frames confirmed instantly that this was still their main source of food. They were courteous enough but glared at my black suit with sullen, accusatory eyes. Who was I, what did I want? What could they say? They were both still of fighting age and fit enough to fire a gun. Actual Nazis unquestionably, but equally defeated, traumatised men who had, and still were, suffering great pain and loss. They dropped me back by the Tiergarten where the Berlin Philharmonic under Herbert von Karajan were performing in one of the university buildings. The Western enclave had its own special currency worth five 'OstMarks' and money could be exchanged anywhere easily, so despite their backgrounds I paid them both well in Western Deutsche Marks. They were extremely grateful, and I have to say that I too felt like I had passed some test. A weight had been lifted off my mind and I was now free to enjoy an evening of Brahms. To this very day, whenever I hear the 'Academic' or 'Tragic' overtures, I think of those two poor souls and their little leaking boat. Instantly the dark outlines of Berlin's ruins come into my mind, and somehow still that strange smell.

The picture I have painted so far is rather one-sided. There were many nicer memories of Berlin which is not all doom and gloom, especially as you go further out. It is both intentionally, and with the assistance of the Allied forces, a place with many parks and open spaces, and there was a lot that appealed to me in the quiet capital of the GDR. Everywhere there were little cartoon propaganda boards and newspapers, particularly 'Neues Deutschland', which were displayed for free on every street corner. Outdoor activities were encouraged and facilities for children and academics were superb.

Treptow Park.

As with cities everywhere, the majority of the population were deserting the old city centre and moving into new custom-built high rises in the suburbs. From Friedrichstrasse I caught the metro out to Alexander Platz to see the construction of the new showcase known as 'Stalinallee', where thousands of people and machines were labouring to create rows of tower blocks and cranes choked the sky. The station is dark and gloomy with virtually no light coming from either the blackened glass roof or the feeble tungsten lights, but in a few minutes, one could rattle out into the countryside and be surrounded by gorgeous lakes and trees. I caught the Metro to the Wannsee, where the boats that cruised back and forth across the lake were considered part of the Metro service and are therefore covered by the cost of a single fixed-price Metro ticket. As a result, they were hugely popular pastimes. A large open-air lido had been constructed along one side of the lake where the locals liked to swim, and the surrounding woods were full of wildlife. It was lovely, but there were too many people there for me.

On the eastern side one could wander freely from the dull ruins of the city to the country. Quiet streets of grey buildings gradually revealed shady mud lanes.

Part of the Altstadt in Köpenick (East Berlin) as remembered.

The large formal parks began to join up and slowly trees returned. It's amazing how resilient nature is. There are a number of delightful little towns that Berlin has swallowed up on this side. One of these is Köpenick, a mediaeval town with its own lake, nestled at the foot of the hills, surrounded by forest. It is reached quickly on the S3 Metro line, the 'Schnell-bahn', but felt like a different world entirely. Fourteenth and fifteenth century brick buildings line the cobbled roads and there were more horse driven carts than motor vehicles. In fact, I only remember seeing a handful of cars during all my time in East Berlin. Berliners, understandably, like to eat outside so I sat with them, beside the Müggelsee in an open sided barn and tucked into a fantastic plate of smoked eel and fried potatoes. A small jazz quartet was playing quietly in one corner and a few benches away a couple were reciting poetry. The notes mingled with the smoke on the air. It was heavenly, or as heavenly as an anti-religious state can be. Everyone was drinking a pale and slightly hoppy beer, which came in a glass far larger than I was accustomed to. In my slightly intoxicated state, I could see how Berlin had been, before the nationalist politics of the eighteenth, nineteenth and twentieth centuries, and how it could perhaps in future be again as a quiet international academic community. But every time I closed my eyes, and I tried not to do so too often, the roar of the traffic in West Berlin, the blaring of horns, the cacophony of neon lights and even the nasal screeching of Hitler's speeches came back to me. I knew it was not to be, not in my lifetime anyway.

I ate relatively well in East Berlin which might surprise you, both in public canteens and in quiet restaurants, with a book as my only companion. There is an emphasis on functionality rather than luxury there, it is true, but I'm not sure that's a bad thing. The chairs are cheap pinewood and uncomfortable to sit on, the decor is minimalist and gloomy, but as long as you have the right expectations, food was plentiful and nourishing. I told you that I like university towns and I could have happily lived in East Germany. There was a simplicity, perhaps a naivety about the place that I admired. Sauerkraut and potato fritters were everywhere, as was a strange kind of fried pasta, and I particularly remember a dish of chewy meatballs and capers, which I have never been fond of. The choice was always limited, but this was a city still deep in the throes of a war. I was always grateful for what was on offer and shocked by how cheap everything actually was. Money here was virtually meaningless. Light however always seemed to be in scarce supply, during the day whatever daylight filtered its way through soot-stained windows had to suffice; at night the light was from foul smelling tallow candles, or the occasional electric lamp that flickered just as much and threw out no more light.

There was one more event to attend and although a new concert hall was being built in West Berlin, the 'Pregnant Oyster' as it was known was not yet ready, so it was in the Eastern sector that most concerts were held. I had seen the shattered ruins of the old Schauspielhaus on Gendarmenmarkt, the old lime market in the centre of Berlin, and fifteen years later, not even the slightest attempt had been made to clear the site let alone renovate. By all means pull the whole thing down, but what chance did the city have of healing leaving it like this?

Incredibly the 'Staatsoper', halfway down Unter-den-Linden, was fully functional. As always in East Berlin it was dark, and in the shadows of the building, a long line of men, dressed like myself in slightly shabby black suits, waited silently, illuminated only by the moon. It felt like a school trip. There were excited whispers. The great Konwitschny, a disciple of Furtwrangler himself, had come from Dresden to conduct Beethoven's Seventh for us. The rumours were rife that old 'Konwhiskey' as the wags were calling him, was drunk again. If so, the performance was none the worse for it. In some ways life in Eastern Berlin is not unlike going back to university. For me those were happy times, certainly simpler times, but I can see that this might not be so comfortable for others.

The neglected 'Gendarmenmarkt' fifteen years after the War.

We emerged two hours later, satisfied and happy, into almost total darkness. The streets were unlit, the buildings pitch black shadows looming over us, but there was no sense of fear. The city was safe, crime absolutely unknown. Trees rustled gently in the breeze and the occasional bird could be heard cooing softly. I looked up to see where the moon had gone only to see behind the dark silhouette of the silent buildings the bright neon lights of the Kurfuerstendamm and above them all the Coca-Cola red news ticker marking the time of a very different symphony about to enter its final movement.

The U-Bahn scurried westwards one last time. Three times the announcer nervously called out: 'This is the last station in the Democratic Republic. I repeat, this is the last station before the border!' Nobody moved. There was a slight panic in the young woman's voice. Men hid behind their newspapers. You could have heard a pin drop. 'Very well…' the announcer seemed to say, 'Don't say that you weren't warned…' The train moved shakily forward, and everything went black.

There are good people and there are bad people, but these are always the minority. Mostly there are just average ordinary people and people are people all over the world, including in Berlin. Berliners are typically tough, bloody-minded, and practical. They have to be to survive. I wondered if it had ever been any different, and if the Berlin of the Nazis had ever existed, even during those twelve long years of their rule. It seemed more likely that the people of Berlin had simply knuckled down and got on with life, then as of now. But if perchance Hitler's Berlin had ever existed in reality, which I doubt, then it certainly wasn't to be found in either of those tragic little towns co-existing in the middle of the woods on the River Spree. I wished both of them well, especially the Eastern one, which my heart instinctively goes out to, and which treated me so very well, but I feel that Berlin's story is only half done.

Not everyone felt the same way as my father about life in the GDR. Since the creation of new modern passports in the nineteenth century, travel between countries in Europe was by no means "free" and required significant paperwork. Leaving Germany had been made virtually impossible by the Nazis and the war had of course made it harder for people, especially Germans, to leave their towns let alone their countries. East and West Germany were officially different states and although there were allowances for family connections, travel between the two was severely curtailed, as it was between the different occupied sectors. Berlin (and also Vienna) provided a loophole in the legislation. Although it was not easy for a West German to travel to East Germany, they could travel to West Berlin and cross with no physical barrier into East Berlin and from there walk freely over into East Germany. Given that a West German Mark was at least five times the value of an East German Mark this happened daily. Likewise, citizens of East Germany could travel to East Berlin and simply catch the underground to West Berlin and from there onto West Germany, or America. By 1961, 3.5 million East German citizens, 20% of the entire population of the GDR, had got on board aeroplanes at Tempelhof airport, without paperwork or money, and flown to the West. Forty percent of the entire workforce of East Germany vanished in three years. The effect was worst felt in the professional sector with a disproportionate loss of doctors, teachers and scientists.

It has been calculated that in the three years since 1958 the loss to the East German economy was 22.5 billion dollars. Yuri Andropov, the CPSU Director of Relations with Communist and Workers' Parties of Socialist Countries, was asked to chair an investigation into potential solutions. The East German government was desperate for something to be done, feeling that the country was becoming a non-viable wasteland. The East German leader Walter Ulbricht appealed directly to Khrushchev for approval to build the wall, a solution that both Andropov and Khrushchev had earlier rejected. On Sunday the 13th August 1961, the border between East and West Berlin was closed.

The photo shows curious onlookers on the Eastern side.

Twenty-eight years later, on the 9th October 1989, the wall finally came down. It now seems likely it was actually an unintended accident that became irreversible. By then Erich Honecker, the man who had hoarded and hidden the materials needed to build the wall so cunningly and overseen its efficient construction, had lost control of his party and his country. The GDR was effectively dead before the wall actually fell. The world's televisions showed pictures of thousands of East Berliners flooding into the West and collecting their 100 free Deutschmarks. But what the cameras didn't show was that when the partying was done, most East Berliners returned to their homes and work in East Berlin, as normal, the next day. That was true freedom, and Berliners were practical as always.

On 3rd October 1990 the German Democratic Republic (East Germany) was formally reunited with the German Federal Republic (West Germany) with a reunified Berlin as its capital. Over thirty years later and the wall is now ancient history, but the GDR is still not completely dead, at least not in people's minds. I suspect that my father would want to point out that there remains to this day a generation of Europeans that grew up in East Germany and were shaped by its philosophy and mannerisms. It was almost as if they were orphaned when the GDR collapsed. It was all that millions had known when they were effectively abandoned, first by their own leaders who fled with money into hiding, then by the Soviet Union that had bigger problems of its own and then, arguably most brutally of all, by their own new (but still West German) government. Even today the unemployment rate in the East is twice that of the West, GDP per capita half, while annual income has increased to two-thirds. It was not in the end a reunification, but an entirely one-sided takeover.

View-Master™ Reels Berlin

I have chosen to include here View Masters of Berlin as it was in 1962, with the wall up, rather than of it in 1960 when he actually visited. We are familiar with the images of the wall from newsreels and history books, but they are still bizarre and shocking to look at. In photos of the wall, it should be noted that the contrast between the two sides is artificial and semi-deliberate. The land next to the wall on the eastern side was an official militarised zone, the buildings were not supposed to be occupied, although due to a lack of housing many squatters lived there. The dark and quiet ruins did not reflect the living conditions of the average East Berliner, and as Andropov pointed out, they present an obvious opportunity for critical comparison.

West Berlin (1962)

East Berlin (1962)

A NEW DAWN

Off We Go! 12th April 1952

The world has changed!

Mankind has entered a new era, as we knew it would, an era of travel beyond the world all of humanity calls home. The concept of countries, borders and warring nations has surely been rendered obsolete by this achievement. From now on we are all simply citizens of Earth!

The French magazine Je sais tout's depiction of Vostok 1.

On 12th April, a new star rose in the east, Vostok 1, carrying aboard Major Yuri Alekseyevich Gagarin and the dawn of a new era. Less than four years have passed since Sputnik blazed this trail. I am stunned. I feel proud and humbled and excited for the future all in equal measure. I rush out and buy every newspaper and magazine I can find, 'Scientific American', 'The New Scientist', 'Nature', even a 'National Geographic'. I borrow French and German papers from the library and pour over them with a dictionary.

What a journey it must have been, the ultimate form of travel, to the stars! How I wish I could have been there with him. I will try never to complain about crowded British trains again.

ITALY REVISITED

A Renaissance, May 1961

Berlin has left a scar on my soul. I had expected to feel many emotions when visiting the city, anger, resentment, maybe even glee, but this deep sense of sadness and loss was unexpected. I still feel as if I have been immersed in an ice-cold lake. Traumatised. I need a change, somewhere warm, somewhere colourful, somewhere I can trust...

Italy had always treated me well and having been relatively well paid for a difficult job, I headed straight there. I had no elaborate plan, no itinerary meticulously worked through with Thomas Cook; it was spontaneous, and I was making it up as I went along. Tuscany turned out to be all the better for it.

I impulsively bought a ticket for the night train to Florence. It was a very long stint, officially fifteen and a half hours but in practice far more, as the engine gave way to other trains at virtually every set of points along the route. Slowly images of a world of blackened concrete, smoke-stained glass and dimly lit stations disappeared as the sun eventually rose. Breakfast came in little shaped trays and cartons of hot coffee were handed out at Milan. For me they could not have come soon enough. I had struggled to sleep and had spent much of the night reading articles about Gagarin's flight in the 'British Scientific Journal' and 'Scientific American'. It was easy to imagine myself in that narrow metal bunk staring down at Earth, the sound of the giant Vostok-K engines humming in the background.

Slowly my reverberating capsule re-entered Earth's atmosphere. At last, the fiery red glow receded over the glass to reveal the sun shining over the tops of the gas holders and Brunelleschi's dome. I had arrived in Florence.

So, it seemed, had the Queen & Prince Philip, who were on a tour of Italy. I saw more of them in Florence than I ever did in England. 'Elisabetta! Filippo!' The cries were everywhere. 'Viva la regina!' I wondered what inspired such enthusiasm for people they didn't know. Was it just fantasy and escapism, from those struggling in the dirt? Why did the presence of foreign royalty inspire fanatical devotion rather than resentment or anger? I confess that I have never seen the attraction of the Royal Family. I'm a committed republican, but one that doesn't have the money or the energy frankly, to prioritise replacing them, and what would we replace them with anyway? General Secretary Macmillan? No, they seem to keep the masses amused, so for now they can stay.

Repair work theoretically underway in Florence's main streets.

I have to confess that I did not like Florence, which might surprise you, but it could never have lived up to the expectations placed upon it by centuries of history and culture. The 'Athens of the Middle Ages' was in reality, noisy, dirty and run down, although not as hot as I had expected it to be. Italy's post-war 'economic miracle' was just taking off as the benefits of EU membership hit. But the work was all in the north, the factories in Turin and Milan, and people were leaving semi-rural places like Florence in droves. In 1961, the city had only just begun to start shaking off the effects of the war. Not only had it been bombed by the allies, but the Germans had also occupied the city for a year and had deliberately destroyed much of the historic centre including its bridges over the Arno, in order to delay the inevitable Allied advance.

Collapsed buildings in backstreet Florence used as an impromptu car park.

Despite being known as the home of the Renaissance, of Michelangelo, Leonardo da Vinci and Botticelli, Florence has a long and decidedly bloody history, not least because for nearly five-hundred years it was the financial centre of Europe. It was the home of the mercantile elite, the Vatican's bankers and the 'Ordinances of Justice'. The most famous of these being the Medici family, who were raised to the status of kings. But as with Paris, much of the old mediaeval city, the city of the Medici, was pulled down during modernisation in the nineteenth century which is a shame. In fact, the city has been in significant decline for two hundred years. What's left is a muddle of historic relics stranded in a modern sprawl that the current city cannot afford to repair or really maintain. There were of course many incalculable treasures to be seen in the museums of Florence, so many that the mind became sated. But museums alone do not constitute a place. The Uffizi Museum, which holds the illicit art collections of the Medici family, could take almost a year to visit, so although I can remember most of the paintings I saw, only a few stood out as moving. I liked Bronzino's little jewels of portraits, Lorenzetti's 'Visitation', and Botticelli's 'Birth of Venus' surprised me by being far more lovely than its reproductions indicate. At the top of a bare staircase, without any explanation hangs Fra Angelico's 'Annunciation'. It is theoretically a simple painting, relatively uncluttered save for the two main figures. It is designed to be approached slowly from below, lines of perspective and vanishing points drawing the eye in slowly, but hypnotically. Both Mary and the angel have been stripped of glitzy decoration and unnecessary adornment, and instead the viewer's eye is guided to their faces, full of obvious sexual tension. While they silently communicate their hopes and fears, the eye is once again drawn past them, towards the symbolic locked garden. It is stunning and was presumably highly scandalous in its day. Amongst the sculptures I remember the Gaddi Torso. The young man's muscled body straining violently against whatever was restraining it. David by contrast was lifeless and told no story of pain.

Italian troops welcome Hitler to the Uffizi Museum in 1938.

What moved me the most perhaps, amongst all these gems, were two simple Rembrandt self-portraits, one as a young man, one an old. How fitting, as I look back on this travelogue now. The poses

233

were identical, the canvases the same size. The whole of that man's life, his hopes and passions, perhaps ours and Europe's too, were etched into the young face, his past, his failures and disappointments enshrined in the old. It was inexpressibly sad.

The Uffizi proudly tells me that it was one of the world's first museums, open to the public since the sixteenth century. It sounds very honourable, but I wonder what it means in reality beyond the already rich charging the public to view their stolen private property. In a city where 50% of homes have no running water or toilet facilities, who is paying to see the Medici's art?

The famous cathedral does not so much dominate the skyline as lurk around the corner of the city's streets, its big black eyes peering into every dark and narrow lane. The exterior is clad in white and green marble, which seems to attract the dirt, and makes it look damp and mouldy. I felt it also gave it an unnecessary air of austerity and artifice. The interior by contrast is surprisingly plain apart from the chaotic mosaic floors, which are the main attraction. It's like walking on a tutti frutti gelato and slightly disconcerting.

The dark eye of Florence's cathedral peers down its narrow streets.

Florence was dirty, tired and sordid, but it had a card to play, its glorious past, and unlike Britain, that continues to trade on an imagined history that never really existed, Florence's past glory was only too real. From every dark nook and cranny, history suddenly poured out onto the streets. Banners appeared, men in full armour were seen with glistening swords, and gradually in that casual Italian way, a procession formed. The banners lead the way followed by many drummers, then mounted knights and men at arms. Their armour was not imitation but the real thing, the edges of their swords sharp. Waxed beards flared and eyebrows knotted. Renaissance faces, with that high arrogant nose that Cosmio Medici would have recognised instantly, glared out from under raised visors. A great stream of violence, men marching to the solemn beat of the drum. A living re-enactment of an irresistible force streaming over the Ponte Vecchio towards the Boboli Gardens. No voice was raised, but the message was clear. This was as much a land of 'bread and circuses' as in Caesar's day, and the rich have always been able to afford the best bodyguards.

I left Florence and jumped on a bus headed out into the rolling hills of the Tuscan countryside. Fiesole, a little town high on a hill, was at most half an hour outside the city and was everything that one could have expected from Tuscany. There was the superb view right down the Arno and the fresh air after Florence was like wine. There were the splendid Roman remains including a fine theatre where I could have sat for hours. The little Franciscan monastery, perched on the edge of the hill, so different from, and yet so similar to, the one in the Venetian Lagoon. I watched the sun set over the valley and was completely at peace, so much so that I had forgotten to find somewhere to spend the night. An 'agriturismo' came to my rescue, providing a comfortable room above a barn, where I slept wonderfully amongst the stacked wood and hay, until I awoke early to find I was sharing my modest lodgings with an entourage of giant Longhorn beetles! I'm told that they are harmless, but as they say here: 'Ogni scarrafone è bello a mamma sua' – 'Even a cockroach is beautiful to its mother…'

Another bus, south to Poggibonsi, a town completely destroyed in World War II and now being slowly rebuilt. It was completely featureless, and I remember it only by its name. But just outside, a printing works sat high on the hills, where Machiavelli's books first saw the light of day. The bus stopped for the 'English Tourists' – did the driver mean me? I hope not – to photograph a bullock cart creaking towards us.

Rival families towers compete against each other above San Gimignano.

More Italians piled out than English, they apparently had not seen one before either and used the opportunity for a quick picnic under the trees. I completely forgot about the bus and ambled off down the hill towards the absurd but splendid towers of San Gimignano which had caught my eye, wobbling slightly in the haze. There were so many of them that surely a collective madness must have once seized the little town.

God it was hot, too hot for a completely unplanned walk of an unknown distance down a dusty track in a dark suit during the middle of the day. I even had to stop at one point, loosen my tie and take my jacket off. Scandalous!

The central piazza was like a furnace, every stone reflecting the heat of the midday sun back at me. Although the town was perched high on a hill, there was no wind or breeze in the narrow streets. In spite of this 'St. Gym' as it was known locally was a lovely place, seemingly untouched by tourism, living its own life, busy and intense. The fossilised window in the Town Hall, from which Dante once addressed the city goers, looked out on exactly the same view as it did then. The round steps leading up to the church were still the debating forum for the town's elders. The floor of the Piazza turned out to be the roof of an enormous cistern built by the Romans, which was still the town's source of drinking water. Everywhere I went views opened up; an alley, a flight of steps under an arch; a tiny, deserted piazza surrounded by those great towers, impossibly high, perforating that green carpet that is so quintessentially Tuscany. It is these images of that rolling green landscape that form my most vivid memories of Italy.

Thinking of debates, out here, as in the big cities, the big fight is between the conservative church and the popularist left. Between the Socialist Party and the Communists. The left has over seventy percent of the popular vote, but here the working man stays fiercely loyal to the Catholic Church, which continues to provide Italy's paper presidents and prevent any 'red alliance' controlling the government. Everyone formally backs the PCI, (the Italian Communist Party) but the only thing red in the Executive or Senate is the wine.

The 'Partito Comunista Italiano' was the largest party in Italy after the war, its membership peaking at over 12 million in 1976. Despite taking control of most city councils and demonstrating 'uncorrupt', and 'efficient' government in Central and Northern Italy, it never actually gained an executive government majority.

A packet of cigarettes was hastily exchanged for a plate of delicious olives, some slices of cured meat and a jug of fresh orange juice. I tucked in gratefully. On production of a second packet the narrow rubber tyres of a rusty old Lancia Ardea could be heard crunching slowly across the gravel. My transport onwards, for when I had decided wherever it was that I was going.

Right in the centre of Tuscany, in the middle of a vast hilly landscape, between the Arbia River and the Chianti hills, lies the city of Siena, a less famous, and all the better for it, version of Florence. I liked it instantly. It has fantastic sites of course, such as the cathedral, the Palazzo Pubblico, the Piazza del Campo, but everywhere you go it delighted me with its honesty and simplicity.

There are steep cobbled lanes under high stone arches, bubbling mediaeval fountains where women still washed their clothes, and dusty brick courtyards where cats sat blinking in the sun. Everywhere the air was filled with the scent of cypress trees.

Tuscany's rolling hills as remembered by my father.

A great black and white cathedral dominates the skyline like some great ship. I joked about its 'Liquorice Allsorts' appearance, but I think the joke may have been on me, as in retrospect the effect is rather good. On first entering the Piazza del Duomo, the ornate west end facade with its unblinking eye and harsh horizontal stripes struck me as almost monstrous. Inside it was even more severe as the colour scheme of white with black stripes was reversed, so that the black became dominant, crushing my frivolity.

For me it came nearer to the English feel of a 'cathedral' than any other religious building that I have seen in Italy. It has a Gothic dramatism about it that is particularly effective, belittling the world and drawing the eye upwards towards the light. A male choir chanted in the darkness heightening the effect. The idea of God may be a simple childish myth, a mental comforter, but the showmanship put in place here, even if it was just machinery to keep the masses in place, was just as effective on believer and non-believer alike. 'Soli Deo gloria' – Glory to God indeed! I hope he, or she, if they exist, judges me for my actions rather than my beliefs.

The dramatic interior of Sienna's cathedral putting Florence's to shame.

Tucked away on one side of the nave in the little Sacristy were a collection of brilliant little frescos by Ghirlandaio and Pinturicchio. It is curious, and a little unfair, how the works of Michelangelo are the highlight of the country's finest museums and yet the art of the men that taught him are simply gathering dust in the side chapels of rural churches. How much nicer would it be if our museums told more of a story displaying them side by side for us to see the evolution of ideas, as they occurred man to man.

Once again, I found myself making my way upwards towards the roof, as I had done at St. Marks and elsewhere, trying to get a glimpse of how the building, and the Renaissance as a whole, worked behind the scenes. Memories of scaling the mountains in Switzerland came back to me as I scrambled up the crumbling vertiginous staircases and rusting metal ladders without a safety line. I sat down on an unparapetted top of one of the great unfinished buttresses to take in the view, a sheer three-hundred-foot drop to the ground on either side of me. From my vertiginous seat, the white stone of the cathedral cascaded chaotically down towards the roof tops, which in turn flooded out into the streets, before themselves tumbling down the hill towards that huge green plain spread out all around me as far as the eye could see.

From Sienna a train back to Rome, and a brash new hotel in a brash new suburb, hopefully free of beetles, long horned or

239

otherwise. It was a long journey to the Piazza Venetia, where the bus dropped us in front of the Victor Emmanuel monument, a conspicuously vulgar wedding cake stuck on the side of the Capitoline Hill.

The Cathedral at Sienna as remembered.

After seeing so many wondrous works of art on my trip, it was a little shocking to be confronted with this monstrosity with its fake history and its blatant, and equally fake, nationalism. It was in this square that Mussolini's fascist forces paraded and where traitors were hanged. They had long since taken down the symbols of that era, but it still stank of nationalism and false pride. I found it impossible to reconcile the mood of the square with the rich cultural world of the Florentines or Tuscany's gentle rolling countryside.

The stay was short this time as I was intending to catch a train to the south. I was there just long enough to renew a few old friendships and to find a couple of new things. The fountains of the Urns, the Tortoises, the Ara Pacis, the Augustes, and the Piazza Navona where I ate dinner. I took a dozen English tourists staying in the same hotel to see Moses in the Spanish Square and got a free cup of tea for my troubles, which made me feel very smug. I marvelled at the gauche travesty of St. Maria in Trastevere and visited the curve of apartments that are built on the foundation of

240

Pompey's theatre, where Julius Caesar was really killed and where it is said that even the devil cannot stand. I saw a procession to St. Peter's with the floodlit bodies of two dead cardinals lying in state like Lenin and Stalin in the mausoleum, and had one last drink in the Piazza Republica before my train left, thinking that however naughty the fountain is, it really is rather splendid.

The train went south through Terracina on the old Via Appia, where there had been a tough little battle during the war, and on to Naples, which frankly you can keep. I know that there are fine things there in the various museums, but it was, and some would say still is, a poor and violent city, with clogged sewers, broken pavements and dark narrow backstreets full of danger. Back then the socialists were in charge, and new tower blocks were beginning to go up in the suburbs, but very little was being done to provide work or police the backstreets. The city was more or less left to the mafia who are the only people offering any order amongst the chaos. It made me angry and I was glad to move on.

Pompeii

Pompeii – such an evocative name. It lies just outside of Naples and was overwhelmed not by lava but by dust. Its inhabitants were suffocated to death in a stifling atmosphere and stifling it certainly still was. The city lay in ruins, of course it did; I had expected that. Not only had a volcano erupted over it and buried it under twenty feet of mud for centuries, but the Americans had actually bombed its fragile remains during the war and the Italians had, for reasons best known to themselves, run tanks and armoured cars through it. So, I was surprised quite how much of it there was left at all. In fact, more of it was being uncovered every day. Not just dusty grey stones or bits of old blackened metal either, but incredibly fragile items too, made of cloth or leather and brightly coloured items that still held their own against the strong Italian sun. The museum is full of them, a collection of simple domestic articles, combs, pins, toys, and incredibly even notes and letters that really bring the famous body casts to life.

Even the best museums can often seem dull and academic, and what makes the one at Pompeii unique is its collection of body casts, made from the spaces left in the ash by the bodies of its previous residents. It is strangely moving and slightly voyeuresque, to see what are clearly very real people, frozen in their intimate moment of death. It is almost too personal. Despite the cool air conditioning I was glad to get back outside, for despite being dead for two thousand years, Pompeii has a surprising energy to it; an inexplicable vibrancy.

Death cast of a man and his wife found at Pompeii.

The site is large, for it was a Roman city after all, not a town. The standard tour covers just a small part of it. But back then, visitors of a curious nature, such as myself, were free to turn off the main routes and duck down backstreets as they saw fit, and there really was a lot to see. The Amphitheatre was awe inspiring of course, and the artwork in the House of the Forum, or the House of Mars and Venus has to be seen to be believed, but these are not what remain most vivid in my mind. I left the rest of the group behind and began wandering off down the narrow lanes, deserted except for the occasional cats or goat, except that it didn't feel that way. Less than twenty yards from the gate the modern world had all but dissolved, replaced by something every bit as vivid, pragmatic and very down to earth. My shoes squirmed in the ruts cut in the flagstones by heavy cartwheels, shops and blocks of flats loomed overhead. I passed one of the town's thirty-one bakeries on a corner, dough still baking in the oven and sat down to quench my thirst at a Thermopolia, or snack bar opposite. There was a clear counter out the front and a back room where food and drink still stood on the tables. There were traces of duck, goat and pig dishes covered in a spicy sauce, crispy side dishes, wine, beer and caffeinated pick-me-ups in disposable cups. The walls were covered in the remains of political slogans and advertisements, including one for a lost cat, one promoting a local plumber and, astonishingly, one advertising travel abroad! The ancient world of Rome was, all of a sudden, shockingly real and fighting to be heard.

I think what makes the Romans appeal to me so much is how modern and accessible they really were, grabbing a coffee on the way to work, collapsing in the stairwell of their multi-storey apartment blocks after too many beers on the way back, taking out advertisements in the local rag and adopting the services of call girls in seedy hotels. They are undeniably us as we are now, and yet they are also brutally ancient. Ancient Pompeii has more life in it than any of the Italian towns I'd visited on this tour, even Rome, and would positively wipe the floor with Florence, but everywhere you go in this exciting city there is also the unmistakable stench of blood and animalistic violence. Towering over it all, stands the dark profile of the still gently smoking volcano.

Vesuvius looming over the Temple of Jupiter in Pompeii.

I must be the only person who is unable to see the attraction of Sorrento. Byron, Keats, Goethe, Wagner, Dickens and Nietzsche all loved it. Maxim Gorky lived here during the twenties and my daughter decided to get married here, yet I struggle to understand what draws people to this nineteenth century resort perched on a gloomy shelf of rock; its only access to the sea two steep slopes perpetually hidden in shade. The nineteenth-century architecture is satisfactory, but uninspiring, consisting mostly of the now tired holiday homes of the vanished Italian gentry and slightly run-down hotels. Whilst the alleys and smaller streets were pleasant enough to walk through, they are choked with tourists and hawkers selling cheap tat from stalls. There is that fairly impressive view of course, but it is no better than many other places and nowhere near the class of Positano, Amalfi or so many other resorts along the coast. I took a ferry out to Capri, a mandatory day excursion for many, which has much to recommend it, not least the cave of the Blue Grotto and the ruins of Tiberius's 'Villa Jovis' where the old Emperor died and the mind of Caligula was first twisted. I was amused and intrigued by the very thin electric vehicles that drive through the narrow lanes but depressed by the number of shops for tourists. It is not a real place for real people anymore, but perhaps it never was. Taormina is a similar resort. High on a rocky cliff, it is in every way superior to Sorrento, but for me Sorrento has something that Taormina does not, the image of a very beautiful young woman in a long flowing white dress, highlighted against the backdrop of the emerald sea and the bright blue sky. My daughter. That alone makes it the crown jewel in the Amalfi coast for me.

The Amalfi coast is a fifty-kilometre stretch of the Sorrentine Peninsula where steep cliffs drop down to small beaches and pastel-coloured fishing villages cling to the rugged shoreline. The sea really glitters like liquid emerald, foaming viridian near the shore. The occasional dark island and white fishing boat only add to the brilliance. Yet again I found myself reaching for a paint brush, but there was no time to stop. The road swept steeply along the coast in a mixture of vertiginous cliffs and scrub covered slopes with next to nothing to keep vehicles on the road. Crumbling tarmac, gouges in the earth and broken trees a constant reminder of those who had been less careful. It passes above the roofs of hotels that cling to rocky ledges and villages that tumble down to the sea like a box of upturned bricks.

The Amalfi Coast.

We stopped at Positano, which really has become the 'in' place and is therefore completely artificial, but none the worse for it as an exception. Tiny colourful houses, most of which have been converted into shops, zigzag their way down to a small beach. It is surrounded on all sides by cafés and pensione, like the stage in a busy theatre. I ate a bowl of very overpriced scialatielli, while I enjoyed the show. The calamari was chewy and the pasta cold, but the dish came with some of the best black olives that I have ever tasted. I pushed the remains of the expensive seafood to one side as the waiters did their rounds and reflected on the joys of simple tinned and pickled foods from my childhood. I was determined to find a decent backstreet canteen for the working man where locals ate, somewhere. Amalfi itself, another pretty Italian town, was blinking sleepily in the sun in a fold in the hills. How odd to think that this little place was once a military power in its own right, the Amalfi Navy taking the fight to the Byzantines, the Normans, the Venetians, the Arabs and then the Turks. The well-placed forts around the town were the only indication of the town's mighty past. In mediaeval times it was famous as a centre of law, engineering and mathematics, the gilded Cathedral of Sant Andrea the only reminder of this. The life of the town ebbs and flows around the foot of its colourful staircase. I confess that I would not have minded studying here, engineering anyway if not the other two.

Beyond Amalfi the hills begin to drop, the villages become more workaday. The fishing boats pull up on small gravel beaches, pottery is displayed on blankets by the roadside and piles of tiles lie baking in the sun. Finally, the road swings round a headland and runs down to the plain and the modern city of Salerno where I had actually booked a hotel.

On the night of 9th September 1943, the combined Allied forces under the command of General Mark Clark, landed 165,000 men on the shore at Salerno under the cover of a sustained aerial and naval bombardment. The plan was for Montgomery's Eighth Army to delay the Germans further south, while the US Fifth Army captured Naples cutting Italy in two and the Wehrmacht off from their supply route. Salerno was chosen because it had landing beaches favourable to invaders and had nearby airfields and major roads that could be used by Allied forces after a successful invasion. But the German Commander-in-Chief realised that this was the plan and pulled back most of his elite Panzer divisions, so it was in fact the British who got trapped in southern Italy. Just hours before the invasion began, the Italians surrendered, withdrawing from the War, an event the Germans had also anticipated. So, instead of finding a quiet town defended by half-hearted Italian troops with outdated weapons, the Fifth US Army ran into the full force of the well prepared and battle-hardened German Wehrmacht.

The history books do not describe the disaster that followed. General Clark considered evacuating his forces only to realise that pulling out would cost as many lives as staying and fighting. Over 100,000 Allied soldiers died. 600 members of the British and American Corps mutinied. Salerno itself was flattened.

Not far inland from the modern city of Salerno a crop of tall Doric columns topped with sculpted capitals rose up out of a sea of roses. They were not the stark white of marble, but the glowing golden brown of limestone so familiar in my hometown of Bath. The roses were mostly deep red and every so now and again I caught the sight of them at strange and unexpected angles through the columns as if the earth had been slashed open and was bleeding. Paestum had not always been this quiet. Before the era of Pompeii, before the sea retreated to where it now sits, this was a bustling Greek city called 'Poseidonia'. The site is huge, one hundred and twenty hectares and now stands more or less empty apart from the three temples dedicated to Hera and Athena. Other features, such as the Forum, the Sacred Way and the Amphitheatre were built by the Romans who captured the city in the Pyrrhic war, four hundred years later and gave the town its current name. How odd that two thousand years ago they would have looked upon this historic site as I had looked at Florence or Amalfi.

Away from the main tourist sites the grass had grown high and the sound of its gentle whispering permeated everything. There was a great sense of peace and tranquillity here, not only from the satisfying form of the temples and the wide openness of the site, but also from one knowing one's place in the enormity of time, a connection to the past and the transience of everything, even perhaps of that sparkling emerald sea.

Ostia is an almost complete Roman city, more so even than Pompeii as it has been neither bombed nor plundered for stone, being mostly made of brick. Here three or four storey Roman buildings still towered over the deserted streets, and rows of shops and warehouses stood quietly waiting for their owners to return. It was difficult to comprehend. If it weren't for the excellent mosaics, I might have said it was little older than the buildings from the late nineteenth century that lined the road from the capital. Ostia was the Port of Rome until its basin silted up in the tenth century and, as with the Venetian Lagoon, the marshland became infected with malaria. Unlike at Pompeii with its grand houses and temples, here trade was the dominant force, the mosaics reflecting the theme. The fishmonger had all manner of fish surrounded by leaping dolphins, the butcher all sorts of animals and a ship's chandler with sails and ropes. Hoists and cranes hung over the street ready to swing into action and there was a surprisingly advanced public toilet still fully functional after all these years.

Everything spoke of a busy thriving town, its size a testament to the enormous amount of food and goods that was needed to support Rome. At its height, nearly two million people lived in the capital, a number not achieved anywhere else until the nineteenth century. It is undeniably one of the reasons why they seem so modern to us, and yet by 400 A.D. that number had shrunk to less than two hundred thousand. That ultimately was why Ostia died, not with a sudden bang like Pompeii, but with a long slow economic fizzle.

The themed mosaic floors in Ostia's marketplace.

The beach at Ostia was amazing, a hidden gem. Just thirty minutes' drive from the centre of Rome, its golden sands slope gently down to the sea. As always, I found myself itching for a plate of fish and chips and I was sure that the working man's Roman port would not let me down. A swarthy looking man bobbed up and down inside an old brick hut as the smell of paraffin filled the air. He handed me out the Italian equivalent, 'Tellina a Passoscuro', a heap of steaming spaghetti mixed in garlic and olive oil, dumped out into a bowl made of newspaper and topped with a dollop of buttery clams and parsley. Simple, cheap but delicious, and probably the best meal I had in the whole trip.

Instead of returning via Rome, I concocted a slightly petulant plan to fly back from the military airport at Pisa which had recently been opened to commercial traffic. This apparently caused a great deal of consternation among the local brass but meant that I got to see one of Venice's counterparts and Amalfi's thalassocratic big brother, albeit briefly. A marvellous group of white marble buildings float above the city, each sculpted with superb workmanship. The cathedral with its bell tower, the Campo Sancto, Hall of the Knights.

With all of the emphasis on the famous leaning tower, we often forget that Pisa, situated at the mouth of the Arno River, was during the Middle Ages a great nautical power like Venice and the capital of its own republic. It is this former military and commercial strength that attracted people like Galileo to the town and left it with the architectural legacy that we see today. Its beauty, as in Florence where I started, was created largely through violence.

The existence of so many independent republics in the same space, Pisa, Florence, Venice etc., may sound a little peculiar, even silly to us, but it is a reminder that there are many forms of government and identity other than that of countries and nations, including those such as city states, that have historically flourished for centuries when operated within a wider Union or Alliance.

I returned to Bath warmed and re-invigorated by my Italian expedition, happy in the knowledge that Europe's past held the key to its future. Living conditions were improving rapidly in Italy and the future seemed bright for us all.

View-Master™ Reel (Italy)

EUROPE

A Curtain of Iron, 13th August 1961

This day is painfully seared into my soul, although it is not a date on which anything specific happened. I said that I would try not to be political, but this must surely be an exception. A darkness descended this day upon Europe. Our continent, our shared home, was cleaved in two, shattering communities and arbitrarily creating lines on maps that do not exist in reality. I felt it cut through my heart like a surgeon's blade. Those far wiser than I argued that it was the only way to stop war in Europe. But whose war? Who wanted another one so soon? Who among us even has the strength to get to the starting line for one?

It was rumoured to be a temporary solution, but it was no solution at all, temporary or otherwise. It turned rebels into martyrs, made tolerance a test and dragged negotiation into disrepute. It was the policy of bankrupt brinkmanship on both sides. What mindless sabre rattling brought us to such a point and so soon after the last war? What hope is there of a sane future for Europe's children if we burn what is left of today? Where were the fanatics and the loudmouths when the plans were being drawn up to create a stable German government to hand over to, where were they when the plans to redefine the access routes to the capital were put aside? Reconstruction funding has been diverted to the military.

Rarely has a country more needed help and reconstruction, a people more needed role models and good stewardship and yet, instead of withdrawing troops from the occupied zones in line with peace treaties and international law, the occupying forces send tanks instead of teachers and park them belligerently under the linden trees. How is this behaviour different from that of the fascist forces that tore our world apart? When do those who sit and think quietly in the background get to have their say in running the world instead of these empty vessels? We are making the same mistakes over and over again.

In the very same year that mankind first ventured into space carrying our hopes for a new peaceful future, we have soiled our planet like this. How many lives will it have to take to move beyond this senseless notion of nationalism if eighty-five million deaths were not enough? The lights are being turned out in the once shining cultural jewels of Prague, Warsaw, Budapest, and Belgrade, as whole countries are being downgraded to buffer zones and death strips in a pointless board game of the worst colonial nature.

CHÂTEAUX OF THE LOIRE

Escape to the Country, 1962

The Americans have made it into space. This has to be a good thing for the world, perhaps Britain will follow one day but it seems unlikely anytime soon. I am amazed how much money is being poured into what is clearly a propaganda race. How long before the moon starts to look like Berlin: bright lights, Coca-Cola and advertising billboards in one base, quiet queues and libraries in another? I can't help wondering what could have been achieved on Earth with the same amount of funding. Let us hope that it brings some benefits.

The division of Europe had left me angry and sad. On my return from my travels the previous year I instantly started making plans to visit cities in Central and Eastern Europe, to follow the Danube or visit Poland or Czechoslovakia. But my funds were running low, and I was unable to make my mind up where to go, then work got in the way. I was feeling generally grumpy, which is unlike me, and in truth I think that I had lost some of my motivation for travelling. I am not quite sure why. Summer drifted around again, and the grand dames of Bath were drifting off to their summer retreats in Torbay, Cornwall or wherever they went. Miss Seawright wondered where I was off to and when I said that I had nothing planned she wondered if I was ill. Perhaps I was. The division of Berlin and the race into space had done something to me. Neither event was expected on my life's plan.

A newspaper was dropped onto the counter in front of me. An advert for a coach tour had been ringed in red pen on one of the back pages. 'Châteaux of the Loire' it said in large capitals.

'Don't think about it. Do it!', Miss Seawright commanded me.

Miss Seawright was always trying to set me up in some awkward social situation and get me married off to the niece of someone she knew and wanted to get leverage over. I was therefore cynical about most of her suggestions. I shrugged like a sullen schoolboy, but ultimately did as I was told.

In an act of minor defiance, I had slightly changed the itinerary to give myself a few days in Paris by myself before getting on the coach. We are all supposed to love Paris, a city synonymous with so much European culture and history, and yet for me, as you know, the jury was still out. I was still in two minds about the place.

The Paris I found this time was a very different one from any that I'd seen before. Algeria had finally gained its independence, but its troubles were far from over. Colonel Argoud had just been arrested for attempting to assassinate De Gaulle and the disgraced Black-Foot refugees were roaming the streets. As a result, armed police were everywhere, presenting yet another side of the city for consideration. I had been allocated a room in a quiet but prestigious hotel on the Rue Cambon, which had unfortunately been completely sealed off with barbed wire as the French Treasury occupied the other side of the street. Hotel guests could only enter from the Rue St. Honoré end, on foot where all luggage was searched in front of a heavy machine gun position. The city felt restless, edgy, defensive and alert. Revolution was bubbling out in the new suburbs as France's colonial legacy refused to be suppressed. I mooched about, and saw some of my favourite paintings, but I had no interest in Ms Chanel's offerings and could neither stand idly by nor get involved with what was happening, so I was glad when the coach finally left.

A quick run past Château Rambouillet and Poitiers, where we stopped for coffee and a quick look around. Coffee in France, unlike Italy, is not a quick experience, and patrons are expected to take their time whiling away their mornings in a comfortable chair with a newspaper. Even the method of brewing requires time as the famous 'French Press' sits by your cup obstinately refusing to be pressed down. But time was something I didn't have, and I would rather have settled for an Italian 'shot'. I got a compulsory look at the famous statue, but I felt no sympathy for the 'The Maid of Poitiers'. Then it was off across the river and through the woods towards Tours. As the coach made its way through the wooded countryside, its occupants chatting annoyingly amongst themselves, my thoughts turned to those migrants and refugees arriving on the shores of France from Algeria and other places, who were seeing their motherland for the first time. But neither the Algerian nationalists nor the old French colonialists were welcome here. For decades France had tried to postpone the inevitable, the violence rising as the Algerian Front de Libération Nationale's request for negotiations slowly turned into a demand for revolution. There had been a massacre on the streets of Paris and finally De Gaulle had seen the light and swapped sides, much to the horror of right-wing paramilitaries and Colonel Argoud. The parallels with France's own struggle for independence against the English during the Hundred Years War could not be clearer. Naturally I thought of the role of Joan of Arc, the 'Maid of Poitiers', in that conflict, and by extension the role that so many brave Muslim women had played in the recent Algerian War. They had participated actively as spies, combatants, bombers (famously) as well as nurses, cooks and informers. The war was over but French Algeria did not die quietly. Its problems were just beginning, and nobody came out of it looking good. I knew Britain was struggling with the same problem, but so far we had been slower in reaching for our guns, certainly since the fiasco in Egypt anyway.

On to Tours and the hotel, which was to be the centre of my itinerary for the next few days. I had already posted ahead a little light reading material which was waiting for me. Tours is a pleasant enough university town that prides itself on the 'purest form of French in France', but at the hotel I only heard them speak English. The old square was very pretty, surrounded by 15th-century half-timbered houses, all listed as historic monuments. I enjoyed a lunch of bean filled brioche and dried pears while rapidly turning the pages of 'Ronsard & Moliere'.

The following day we went to Blois. Unlike the castle at Chambord this was in the middle of town. I remember the mediaeval courtyard and the big spiral Renaissance staircase, the Chambre de Roi with its coloured roof beams and King Henry's initials in the floor tiles, a huge and finely carved fireplace and of course, Catherine D'Medici's famous poison cabinets.

Catherine D'Medici was both an Italian princess and a strong regent who held the country together during the reign of no fewer than four weak French kings. She was widely hated during her lifetime but – although a large number of people were seen to die around her – her infamous cabinets are far more likely to have held state papers than poison.

On to Langeais, the home of 'Fulk the Black'. This I really liked. It looked like a proper castle, its huge barbican with working drawbridge thrusting out into the streets of the village, its ramparts pierced for the dropping of missiles or boiling oil. This was a proper military building from the Middle Ages, not a royal hunting lodge from some renaissance duke. Deep down, some part of me was still up for some kind of fight. Quite who I wanted to fight I had no idea, but I felt like I was a man looking for his cause. Surprisingly Fulk's castle was elegantly furnished inside and with entirely authentic pieces. This was not the standard for historic buildings at the time and was certainly not what I had imagined for my bearded pirate king. The hall where Anne of Brittany had married the King of France and given him her country was notably memorable, as were the living quarters and the gardens with their view over the River Loire. As if a country and its people could ever have been treated as personal possessions and wedding presents. How ridiculous.

The right bank of the river was a mass of cafés, restaurants and places where you could sample the wine and soak up the sun. It was an offer I was happy to accept. The French papers were full of the news of the ongoing Algerian troubles and worries about Cuba. Khrushchev had ordered the deployment of mid-range nuclear missiles to the islands just off the American coast in response to the American sponsorship of mass defections in Berlin. The R-7 rocket platform, which only the year before had launched Gagarin into space, could cover the distance from Havana to New York in just five minutes. But what could anyone's motivation possibly be? To my mind the answer was West Berlin. The Soviets had pulled out of Vienna as a compromise, but they had expected full control of all of Berlin in return. Now they had lost even that as an option. The Americans were determined to get their way in all things. Despite their supposed love of capitalism, experience had taught me that for them it was an almost religious matter of principle not bribery, as

Britain learned the hard way in Suez. The Soviets trod a less aggressive path, but for them no form of ideological retreat was possible either. Was another war inevitable? If it was, the Loire was not a bad place to be.

Troglodyte houses built into the cliffs of the Loire Valley.

The Château de Chenonceau is probably one of the most famous castles of the Loire valley. It was built on the foundations of an old mill that extended out across the river, giving it a unique, magical appearance. It reminded me a little of Pulteney Bridge in Bath.

The Château de Chenonceau as it likes to be seen.

On the day that I visited, it did not look quite how it liked to be photographed. It was cold, misty and damp. Bare branches and low hanging clouds would indeed play havoc with the cameras, but for me the castle was all the more magical for it. Nor was the river placid. The sound of its mighty roar drowned out all other noise and one could only marvel at how powerful a mill it must have been back then and wonder at how it had been built with the technology of the time. Heaped up by the construction of the pillars, the flooded river nearly touched the peak of the arches as it hurled itself through, steaming in the cold air.

Intriguingly the château has a long history of being on both sides, politically as well as physically (of the river); most recently during the war when it acted as an escape route from Nazi-occupied France, a gallant role which caused it to be both occupied by the Wehrmacht and then bombed by the Allies. Today it is owned privately by the heir to a chocolate empire and on such a cold wet day, I for one was not saying no to a 'chocolat chaud'.

The Château d'Azay-le-Rideau was next on the list. It was built on an island in the Indre River and is surrounded by willow trees. With its rounded turrets buried in greenery it was to me the prettiest of all of them, and to this day it forms the image I see in my mind whenever I hear Tchaikovsky's 'Sleeping Beauty'. When I took my son to see the ballet at Covent Garden, visions of myself wading through its weed-clad lake immediately came back to me. I must have looked ridiculous standing in the middle of the weeds dressed in a smart black suit, tie and waders, but I couldn't resist going in. Still, I'm glad that nobody has a photograph of it, although everyone on the coach did have cameras.

We stopped at Chinon and Fontevrault to see the Abbey, and the ruins of Henry's great castle stretched out on the hill in the afternoon sun like a giant lion.

These were once English lands, and this, the great road north to England. The great Abbey was plain and austere, and empty except for the tombs. Four of them. Henry II and his amazing wife Eleanor of Aquitaine, one for Richard I, King of England, the 'Lionheart', a man who neither spoke English nor ruled that land and who died a coward's death whilst on the run, and finally one for the French Queen Isabelle, wife of the man that ruled England instead of

Richard, King John. These were people who, like the Château de Chenonceau, straddled both sides of the Hundred Years War as it suited them: French queens ruling England, English kings ruling France. Yet none of them would recognise even the names of those two countries that we so vehemently fought for. It is all nonsense.

(Eleanor of Aquitaine was a really fascinating woman and if you don't know much about her then I do really recommend Alison Weir's excellent biography.)

Speaking of nonsense… We were due to stop at Saumur on the way back to Paris where my plane was waiting, but the château was shut. There was an outbreak of general panic on the part of the courier and the whole coach hurried to the Hôtel de Ville. A gendarme was rapidly dispatched from the Town Hall to find the custodian of the castle who was by then not at home but at the Château. The coach returned to the castle to find it open, and its host, who had been enjoying a leisurely lunch, was surprised by all the panic. By this time, I had lost any interest in the castle itself, whose rooms seemed to be filled with a succession of horse skeletons, horses' hooves and even stuffed horses. This at least explained the lack of other visitors and the custodian's tardiness. We staggered out to be met by the gendarme who apologised for the contretemps and informed us that the Mayor wished to offer us a glass of wine by way of an apology; back, of course, at the Hôtel de Ville. Tongues hanging out we returned to the Town Hall, only to discover that a De Gaulle referendum was taking place.

The hall was completely packed, and the Mayor had gone missing. Eventually the French equivalent of a town clerk did the honours and we drank a pale, slightly sweet wine and tried to converse in French. I find it hard enough to make small talk in English let alone another language but was pleasantly surprised to hear how much it limited my companions. Eventually the Mayor returned and proposed a toast to the 'Entente Cordiale'. The result of the referendum was apparently 'Oui', which everyone was delighted about, although I for one wasn't sure why.

'Santé!'

View-Master™ Reel (Loire Valley)

BRITTANY &
THE CHANNEL ISLANDS

The Seagull, 1963

It seemed that we were narrowly able to avoid nuclear war. The Soviets agreed to remove their nuclear missiles from Cuba, the Americans to remove theirs from Turkey. The US had agreed not to invade Cuba for a bit, and I assume that the Russians likewise agreed to postpone their plans for an invasion of West Berlin. Khrushchev and Kennedy appeared to be engaged in a personal childish rivalry of brinkmanship. Whatever happened behind the scenes to keep the peace it surely had little to do with either of them. It made me wonder how long either of these petulant politicians would be allowed to stay behind the wheel. Who would police the superpowers? Perhaps those appointed to protect their states…

John F. Kennedy was assassinated in November that year, many conspiracists suggesting by the CIA. Khrushchev was invited to step down from power by the KGB less than a year afterwards and was made an offer that he couldn't refuse. Castro felt that Cuba had been abandoned by the Soviets, but such was the price of peace. With all hope of the Soviets recapturing West Berlin now lost and Khrushchev effectively out of the way, Andropov began to experiment with alternative solutions to East Germany's problems implementing a series of economic reforms known as the "New Economic System".

My fortieth birthday had come around. Time to do something special, but what? I wondered what other people did for their fortieth and realised that I was not other people. I did not have family; I did not have work mates. I didn't mind that, I am insular and introverted, a 'loner', but it does make planning a big bash difficult. I wasn't sure that I should be celebrating at all in fact. I celebrated my thirtieth by splashing out on a mountain climbing tour, but of late I had lost the desire to travel a little and I no longer wanted to challenge the mountains. So, what, if anything, was I to do?

Miss Seawright as usual had the answer, an answer anyway. She reached into her bag and pulled out a little red notebook. I knew from past experience that this contained a veritable catalogue of suitable marriage candidates, and my heart sank. She knew someone, a friend of a friend, of course she did, knowing people was Miss Seawright's forte, and this 'friend', was a Royal Navy Commander who had just retired and who owned a boat. Sailing sounded like a good hobby for an international man that liked travel, besides, a bit of sea air and physical exercise would, Miss Seawright said, be 'good for me' and blow away some of those 'dusty cobwebs that filled my mind'. She scribbled the number onto a piece of paper and stapled it to a train ticket to Plymouth.

'He can't sail it by himself, can he?' she said by way of explanation. 'The last boat he was in charge of was the HMS Devonshire, and he made a hash of that too if I recall!'

I had no idea what I was going to find in Sutton Harbour, or who I was going to find either. Miss Seawright tended to gravitate towards a certain type however and usually that was not a type that I found good company. The boat, which I named 'The Seagull' turned out to be a twenty-four-foot Eventide yacht, technically a sloop I think, which was deceptively large on the inside. It had had a few outings from the boatyard over the last couple of years but was to all intent and purposes brand new and superbly kitted out. I learned that it had cost eighteen hundred pounds (About £45,000 today my son points out, reminding me to be suitably grateful). As for Richard, he was not what I had expected either. He was tall and thin with hooded eyes and a square jaw. It was true that he was nearly seventy, but it looked like he could still handle himself in a fight and would be happy to start one at any time. Far from being an administrative paper-pusher behind a desk, he gave the impression that he was disappointed that the war was over. He had spent much of it escorting the Russian convoys through the North

Atlantic to Murmansk. Neither cold and wet weather nor giant rolling waves had any effect on him. He looked me over harshly.

It would have made no difference if I had sailed before. Everything I did was wrong and had to be relearned. Coiling a rope, tying a knot, stowing items in a cupboard. Everything had to be done in a special 'Richard way'. He stood at the helm in his cable knit sweater, smoking his briar pipe, the brow of his cap pulled down over his eyes, constantly barking orders as I scrambled over the wet pitching deck, constantly tightening the lines to prevent the mainsail 'luffing'. I wondered if my Dutch friends would have fared any better. If he wasn't grumbling at me, he was grumbling at the boat. Apparently it was under ballasted and needed a bigger keel. Quite how he knew it was unstable in the constantly twitching currents of the English Channel I don't know.

As land disappeared, I felt a primeval fear creeping up on me. The same sense of panic that I had felt all those years before on the glacier in Switzerland. The sea is huge, and The Seagull seemed minuscule. It swirled all around and refused to be controlled. Away from land darkness enveloped us. I was alone, alone with only my dark thoughts and the gods...

An Eventide 24 in its original 1960s colour scheme.

On June 16th, 1963, Valentina Tereshkova became the first woman in space, launched in the tiny capsule of Vostock 6. She orbited the earth 48 times over three days, making it the longest and toughest journey into space yet. An ordinary girl from a cotton mill from the Yaroslavl Oblast according to the Soviets. But they have picked their 'ordinary girl' very carefully. She looks like a tough old boot and reminds me of a younger Miss Seawright. I will not complain about my situation.

> It is I, Chaika – The Seagull! Everything is fine. I see the horizon; it's a sky blue with a dark strip. How beautiful the earth is... everything is going well.

The Americans said that she was just 'Gagarin in a skirt', but Colonel Tereshkova was far more than that. Her flight was more complicated than any before hers, performing several experiments in space and logging more time in a single flight than the entire American space programme put together. She spent most of the three days in space vomiting, and her experience formed the basis of how future astronauts on both sides of the Atlantic dealt with nausea and ate in space. On return to Earth, she campaigned for women's rights around the world, particularly in India, where she championed the cause of enslaved women. She went back to university and earned a degree in aeronautical engineering, rising to become Russia's first female Major General. She became a politician after retiring from the air force aged 65. She has volunteered, and been approved, to be the captain of the first one-way human expedition to Mars, where it is her ambition to be buried. The world needs more 'ordinary girls' like that.

Colonel (now Major General) time in a single flight Tereshkova shortly after her flight.

Thoughts of Comrade Tereshkova floated through my mind in the dark cabin as I attempted to settle my own uneasy stomach with the scrapings of a tin of crab meat and a cold packet of chips I'd bought back in Plymouth. I drank a strong mug of black tea I'd eventually made over a Primus stove in the little galley, imagining how much harder such a task would be aboard Soyuz. Richard grunted, semi-satisfied. If I wouldn't make a captain, perhaps I would one day make cabin boy. He smoked constantly and pointed me in the direction of the VHF radio set up on a shelf in the cabin. It was straightforward enough to use and only about half the size of the ones I'd used in the War. It was reassuring to hear the electrical chatter of marine traffic in the otherwise enveloping silence. France was just a few hours away at six knots, less if the currents were kind, but it wasn't the part of France we were aiming for. As darkness fell, we pressed on under the stars. There was no concept of stopping until we were in lieu of land and able to safely anchor. Lights blinked in the darkness but got no nearer. We seemed to be sailing parallel to the shore rather than getting any closer to it. The first light of dawn was breaking before Richard or Admiral Onslow to give him his proper title was satisfied, turning the bows into the current.

The River Rance at Dinard.

The next day we sailed quietly into the marina at Dinard. Out of season, it was a very pleasant place. The seaside aspect of the town did not impose too much on the quietly wooded rolling hillsides that surrounded it, partly because the season had not fully started yet, but also because there were several small beaches rather than one great big one, as had been the routine in Italy. Behind the beaches were Victorian style properties laid with long privet hedges. The smell of fuchsias was everywhere and even the salty sea could not swamp it. In general, I am not keen on seaside 'resorts', but I would happily consider returning to Dinard, even sailing in with Richard, perhaps to take up painting.

The Admiral had things to do, people to see, a chandlery to visit and doubtless a few bars to frequent. How odd that we still use that word to describe a Marine supply store. It is a medieval word used to describe the storeroom in a large house where the candles and wax were kept. It was usually attached to the kitchen and often the same place used for the petty cash to pay servants and tradesmen. I love such curiosities of time and language.

I left him to it and went in search of my own adventure for the day and I didn't have to go far. The other side of the marina a blackboard was advertising day river cruises. The boat was quite large, a twin screwed launch that seemed to have no rudder but merely two levers on the bridge that varied the speed, or pitch of the propellors, a little like a tank. I was glad that someone else was in charge for a change. The launch started upstream, passed the woods above the town. Soon the great hydro-electric barrage was reached, and we slid silently through a narrow section. Although still sea water, the character of the estuary was that of a large lake. We kept to the middle of the river, passing holiday hamlets and isolated farms before going under a great road bridge with nothing but the beauty of mathematics to support its great weight.

Soon however, the banks began to close in and the lake became a river; open country gave way to thickly wooded slopes. Trees crowded to the water's edge and arched out, like the supports of the road bridge, nearly meeting overhead. The noise of the engines died away, and we nosed forward silently. The sun filtered gently through the trees and every so often a shaft would strike blindingly upon the water. A green light, heavy with midges, seemed to hang over the river like a fog, and the water was so crystal clear that the bows seemed to be hovering above the weed-coated bottom. The white eyes of fish looked up at us before disappearing in a silver flash. Silently, no one saying a word, we eased forward listening to the songs of the birds and the gentle bubbling of the water on the hull.

After a series of locks, each with its own Napoleonic era lock cottage, the fields opened up and high on a hill Dinan appeared. It is a splendid old town. The hill rises steeply from the river quay, passes under the gate arch of St. Jocelyn and arrives at the square with its surrounding complex of little streets. A small castle, fine ramparts with an excellent view down the river and a large, but modest church. The town was lively and vigorous, full of cheerful countryside characters in brightly coloured scarves and neckerchiefs, shouting over one another from across the cobbled lanes. They were friendly and the complete opposite of the black stoles and cold shoulders that Paris is famous for.

The journey back was of course the reverse of the morning's, but so different. The sun had come around behind us, and there was a cheerful feeling of being 'off to the sea'. The river gradually widened as the conversation flowed. Through the Barrage de Rance, back down the St. Malo side, past the tower of St. Saviour as we swung left to come into Dinard, the boat rolled gently in the waves of the open sea. It was a truly satisfactory and enjoyable day.

I ate fish and chips, or the French equivalent thereof, in the harbour and slept on the boat that night. It was odd to be alone in such an intimate space that was not mine. I fruitlessly turned the dials of the radio. searching the airwaves for the faint callsign of Vostock 6, somewhere far up above me in the sparkling firmament. It was marvellous to think that all my brothers and sisters across our great continent were looking up at the same scene, regardless of which side of the iron curtain they lived. I eventually found some Tchaikovsky and settled down with a cup of warm cocoa. The gentle rocking of the boat and the warmth of the drink, or more likely the paraffin fumes in the unvented cabin, soon sent me to sleep.

I had just enough time the next day to sneak in a visit to Vitré, one of the castles that once lined the border between Brittany and France, and billed, perhaps optimistically as the 'Carcassone of the North'. I had ordered a taxi from the harbour master's office which was duly awaiting me, after an only partially successful attempt at cooking myself porridge for breakfast in that tiny galley kitchen.

There is a part of me that admires the plucky Bretons for sticking it to the French for so long, the British part of me anyway. The old French-Brittany border, Chambord, Fougères, Vitré, is full of fortresses built to subdue the Bretons who simply wouldn't stay in line. Of course, most of these castles, like Fougères, were built by what we would consider to be English kings, such as Henry II to defend his land against Vikings, although the exotic buildings that now occupy the sites were built much later by pretentious dukes as showcases. You only have to go back a few hundred years and nationality gets very confusing, especially amongst kings. Were the Georgians German or English? Were the Plantagenets English or French? Is there a difference? No of course not, they are one and the same thing.

Brittany became part of the Roman Empire in 51 B.C. but surprisingly did not become part of France until 1790.

Château Vitré looked like a film set, with its conical slate tiled roofs posed on the edge of a buff, and just like a film set it was hollow and empty.

Castle Vitré on Brittany's Vilaine river.

The castle had been a Huguenot stronghold for centuries before being abandoned in the seventeenth century and used in the Napoleonic era as a prison. The Huguenots were a group of French

269

protestants who followed the Calvanist teaching coming out of Belgium and North Germany. Under the otherwise enlightened Louis XIV, the number of Protestants in France declined from nearly a million at the start of his reign to less than a thousand by the end. Their exile and the Wars of Religion did much to shape modern Europe. Britain in particular benefited from the expulsion of the Huguenots from France as large numbers of skilled workers with advanced knowledge of cooking, music, medicine and lacemaking flocked to our shores. One of those immigrants was a young lady called Solange Luyon, better known to us as Sally Lunn, who brought the recipe of a delightful sticky bun to Bath where she opened a cake shop on the site of an old Roman bakery. Today it is one of Bath's main attractions and a mandatory stop for anyone visiting the city. But I digress.

A Sally Lunn and a Bath Bun.

A "Sally Lunn" bun is a large bun or teacake, a type of batter bread, made with a yeast dough including cream and eggs, similar to the sweet brioche breads of France. Served toasted and sliced, (you only get one half don't panic – top for sweet filling, bottom for savoury), it was first recorded in 1680. The "Bath Bun" shown behind it in the photo on the next page, was invented nearly a hundred years later. A surprising outcome for a city that is basically a health spa. The Bath Bun is "pocketable" so was a more common purchase for my father. The Sally Lunn, as you see, is a more serious sit-down event demanding at least a penknife and napkin.

Behind the sad skeleton of the Château de Vitré lay an entire walled mediaeval town. Fortunately, it was nothing like the famous tourist trap to the south. A sinuous network of narrow streets full of dark timber-framed buildings slope off down the hill, their names 'Leatherworker Street', 'Pottery Lane' being clear reminders of their past. Traffic was allowed in, which along with the accompanying traffic signs, was the only anachronism. From a defensive perspective the lanes were intended to confuse, their corbelled upper storeys cutting out the light from the sky and channelling rainwater into central ditches. I wandered about all afternoon hardly seeing a soul, sampling a rather nondescript crepe, and a very acceptable 'Kouign Amann' pastry. At last, I awoke my sleeping driver and we headed back to Dinard.

With no sign of Richard, I followed my taxi driver, who spoke not a word of English, into a dimly lit tavern on the seafront. Strips of damp wallpaper the colour of a dark burgundy wine peeled slowly from the mouldy walls and the air was so thick with tobacco smoke that it was hard to see the trio performing on the little stage let alone read the menu on the chalkboard. A chipped cup and saucer was placed in front of me and a pint glass full of cider. An old tin bucket, that seemed to be steaming gently, was then dumped on the table between us by a grumpy woman with a cigarette hanging out of her mouth. To my surprise the cup contained not tea but a buttery creamy sauce and balanced around the rim of the saucer were three neatly charred scallops. I beamed with delight. My driver grunted as if he didn't care and plunged his oily hands into the bucket. He wagged the blade of a curved knife at me menacingly and in thick accented French said that scallops were for 'branleur'. I was unfamiliar with the term, but its meaning was still pretty clear. He was right, the mussels, scooped out of the bucket with my cup and cracked open with my penknife were infinitely better. It ended up being a very jolly evening.

The same however could not be said of my onward voyage to Mont St. Michael. Having been terrified crossing the Channel, or 'The Sleeve' as the French call it, the journey to St. Michael managed to be both boring and unpleasant. It rained most of the way, although the Admiral, who was clearly hung over, was adamant that it didn't count as rain, and the relatively shallow waters kept us pitching and tossing the whole way. The little town of Dol–de–Bretagne was indeed Dolorous with the tolling of a funeral bell echoing dolefully out across the water from the giant grey cathedral. We anchored up and went ashore. The run to Mont St. Michel was featureless until we got near enough to see it through the trees. It was a grey day, which did not help matters, and the bitterly cold wind swept along the flat sands stinging my face.

A stream of black vehicles seeped like oil from the foot of the hill and spilled out along the causeway, a queue of traffic for a religious site supposedly inaccessible from land. I have been to a few tourist sites as this notebook will show, and generally the place rises above the people. There is normally grace in what was, even if it isn't now, but whatever was once here was now lost, engulfed in a sea of tourism. There were so many souvenir shops, so many people poured into such a small space, that even my Russian friends, more flexible when it comes to personal space, would start to get itchy.

There were so many official and non-official touts here that they became aggressive as well as loud. Memories of the sick travesty that is Lourdes came back to me. As for the Abbey? Forget it. Such a controlled streamlined tour of the building that it was only the steepness of the steps that prevented the guides forcing us round at a jogging pace. It is a wonder that Debussy's piano prelude is not set at a higher tempo.

The views from the church terrace are of course superb, if you like a flat sea, but the Abbey's ever widening foundations dominate the mass of roofs that tumble down the hill to meet it. I have stood in fifty-mile-an-hour winds on the top of mountains and, while the weather at Mont-Saint-Michel was not comparable to that, I still had no desire to linger and was glad of the relative warmth of the narrow streets as I picked my way round seaweed clad coves looking for crabs until the tide came in, and Richard was ready to sail.

We waited for the current to change and made our way north to St. Malo, where we had a boozy lunch before I decided to walk it off with a walk around the town's ramparts. Blown down and rebuilt, the effect was still impressive. The 'Creak and Groan' museum in the old castle was an amusing if inaccurate depiction of history, but popular with children. The rooms were not only furnished, but waxwork figures had been placed in various postures to give it life!

Voltaire was reading in the library, head in hand. I felt I should apologise for intruding. The dungeons and torture chambers were lovingly lingered over by the guide. Whilst their mechanical devices were no doubt imaginative, they were I am sure highly impractical and unscalable. I am sure we have more efficient and scientific ways of getting results these days, but they would make a less interesting museum. As it was, it was all very jolly.

Mont St. Michel as remembered.

Not so the fort overlooking the yacht harbour. No attempt had been made to clear up the detritus of the war, as if the French, adamant that it had not been their fault, had left the task to the Germans and Americans. Shell holes, shattered pill boxes, tank traps and torn metal all still littered the grass. It was a terrible graveyard and not a place that I wanted to linger. Nature at least, was doing its best to wipe the scars from the earth. Weeds clawed at rusted iron and burrowed into concrete, and even the strongest defensive points were surrounded in shrubs. Perhaps if mankind continues to make the same mistakes, the planet will at least be able to clean up for itself, after we are all gone.

From St. Malo we tacked our way back to the Channel Islands which sat blinking in the sun like jewels on a felt setting. Jersey apparently was not where it was supposed to be. Richard blamed the French fishermen, so instead of sailing into St. Helier we bobbed along St.Ouen's Bay, rolling with the surf until we put in at Le Braye for sandwiches.

Guernsey was, according to Richard anyway, a much more sensible place, and was precisely where he had left it. It is peculiar to see the fierce rivalry between these two very similar islands, both part of the Kingdom of Normandy before becoming British possessions in 1066. It seems likely that the animosity stems from the English Civil War when the islands fought on opposite sides, but the list of crimes they hold against each other is endless, so the truth of the matter has long since been lost. Perhaps we should give Kennedy and Khrushchev their own little islands and let them slog it out in the sand.

St. Peter Port is not a foreign town, but it deserves to be, tumbling down its steep hill to its busy little port, where we tied up. The castle and the narrow streets, all full of booze and baccy shops, and the sequence of markets, one above the other like a colourful flight of steps. I liked it very much. It was lovely to feel completely alone amidst the wind and the heather of the South Cliff Path, high above the great waves smashing on the rocks far below. Deeply indented little coves revealed shaded beaches, that I wished I could explore alone with The Seagull.

The Herm Coastal Path as remembered.

I also liked the island of Herm just off the Guernsey coast, which was small enough to be easily walked around, its shell beach where intact shells, large and small, lay in their thousands. It held a whole range of scenery in miniature, a plain, a moor, a small mountain and a lonely manor house. I could imagine myself living here, all alone, with my books and maybe a few goats. And a pig, I like pigs; I had one as a pet when I was a child. Pigs are very clever. I was reluctant to return to the boat. Perhaps sailing wasn't for me after all.

My father hardly mentions it at all, but Miss Seawright jointly funded the purchase of the boat in his name, officially making him part owner of The Seagull. Perhaps she had other motives, a desire to get leverage over the Admiral, but most likely it was just a very thoughtful and generous gift for my father.

As the joint owner of The Seagull, he was officially entitled to take her wherever he liked, whenever he liked. But it seemed as if this never really happened. My father used to tell lots of stories about the boat, typically self-deprecating adventures that ended with some form of disaster and a mug of warm cocoa. In truth he wasn't sufficiently confident to take her out to sea by himself, so he could only really go somewhere if the other owner of the boat wanted to go to the same place at the same time. As a very private man, my father would have found sharing the cramped confines of a small boat quite arduous. They could have happily sailed around the Mediterranean and North Sea discovering our shared heritage together, but 'Two Men's Europe' this is not. Richard and my father continued to sail together for the next four years, but it was never to be a holiday for him. It was a hobby, a physical challenge, a distraction at best, albeit one to which he doubtless rose.

Plymouth was inconvenient for him to get to for a weekend, but the waters of the Bristol Channel were challenging, fast with dangerous currents, a high tide, and to be honest the scenery was boring. If The Seagull was at Weston, as she occasionally was, then France was too far away for a quick getaway.

Richard Onslow sold his share of the boat when he moved back to Shropshire, and my father was happy to cash in too. Admiral Richard Onslow died in 1975.

GREECE

Cradle of Civilisation, 1964

For generations a good education meant a knowledge of the 'Classics', read, if possible, in the original Latin or Greek. In Britain knowledge of such archaic languages continued to be prioritised over speaking the languages of our neighbours, or the learning of science, until the middle of the twentieth century. Perhaps you think me a little bitter, for although I can reel off stock phrases as well as any public-school boy, I have never made any effort to learn the language of true scholars. I don't see the point. As you have seen, I am also a fan of 'Team Rome', and the Greeks, whilst fascinating, have never quite had the violent earthly pragmatism I admire so much in my Roman chums. All of which meant that it was not until 1964 that Greece made it to the top of my travel plans.

This time it was a Comet 4B whisking me up into the darkness from Heathrow. They had sorted out the whole thing with the windows blowing the roof off by then! It was almost empty, so I stretched out across the seats and dozed off. We flew so high that there was virtually no turbulence, so I slept almost all the way through. We touched down at 4 a.m. but the air was already warm and still. It is funny to think that we can now fly from one end of Europe to the other in just two hours, and I think we have lost some of the magic of travel as a result of such convenience, but we should temper that regret with the thought that anything that makes mass transport, education and holiday-making more accessible, is to be encouraged. I stepped eagerly out onto the tarmac and above the smell of oil and the hot metal of the engines came the scent of pines and orange blossom. I love that moment when you first disembark from either a plane or ship and stand there soaking in the heady atmosphere of being somewhere new. It matters not to me whether it's cold and smells of diesel fumes, cheap tobacco and coal smoke, or warm and smells of forests and the sea, these first moments of acclimatisation are like a drug to me. Addictive. Impossibly, everywhere smells different.

Walking across the runway to the terminal building I was already too hot in my heavy suit. A man from the office came out to greet me, wearing an open necked short sleeved shirt. He was as bright and cheerful as if it were the middle of the day. The thought of taking my tie, or even my jacket off, was, of course, absurd. I would acclimatise soon enough, a process of mind over matter, helped by calm yogic breathing. I had been much hotter than this in Egypt, but never had I experienced such a rapid transition from the cool of the air-conditioned aeroplane to warmth like this. We were herded onto the bus like Intourist victims and loaded up with tickets, maps, and brochures before being driven off to our hotel. Half the bus were already singing, drunk on little more than the night air.

Athens is a curious city unlike any other that I had been to. There was a clear division between the ancient Greek and the modern. There was no gradual growth, no layer upon layer as in Rome, or London, or so many major cities. Instead there were stark lines, that made it hard to believe that there was continuity between the two. As a city it was cheerful enough, and certainly vibrant; the people alone saw to that. In the small lanes behind the big straight main roads, little shops fought for survival, as they do almost everywhere, a constant uproar of furious bargaining which seems amicable enough. Foreigners like myself are treated with an amused courtesy and rightly more than a hint of suspicion. Englishmen in particular have already taken their pound of flesh from Greece.

If the Acropolis still towers over the city, the city towers over the lovely little Byzantine churches. They are typically only about 40 feet long and no more than seven feet high. In many I struggled to stand straight at all. In one case a department store was cantilevered out over it. Another stood half buried under a more modern cathedral, completely stealing the larger building's thunder. The sheer number and the quality of these little buildings is fascinating, a reminder that the 'classical' idea of Greece that Englishmen pride themselves on as part of a decent education is, in fact, entirely erroneous. The concept of 'Greece', ancient or otherwise has never really existed at all. It was a series of ancient independent city states, a chain of ports in the Byzantine empire.

I was surprised to see that I had little reaction to the Acropolis itself, the supposed highlight of the tour. It was exactly like all the pictures that I had ever seen of it and the reality added nothing new. It felt too well-known, too photographed, and strangely empty. Its sheer size was impressive, and the approach zig-zagging upwards over the uneven stones battered the senses. But it was the brilliant purple and yellow flowers blooming between the rocks that I remember, not the building towering above it. Despite its mathematical elegance it seemed a little crude. Perhaps like the Ancient Greece beloved by Victorian English academics, the Parthenon is best seen from a distance, a pleasing philosophical construct, rather than a brutal architectural reality.

There was a similar lack of reaction at the Thesium in the Agora. The temple was in good order, the best preserved of all the Greek temples, yet in its low corner, overshadowed by the Acropolis, it made little impression at all. It was pleasant enough to wander about the place and the rebuilt Stoa gave a fine impression of what the original building must have been like. All the same, the experience left me cold. So what? I wanted to say. Perhaps I was hungry…

One site however did give me great pleasure: the Forum with its 'Tower of the Winds'. In the centre of the old marketplace the warm sun caresses the sides of a small octagonal construction with the bas-reliefs of the winds set into the top frieze of its eight faces. The structure combined a mixture of sundials, water clocks and wind vanes and seems to have acted as some type of meteorological station. Long after its mechanisms fell into disrepair it seems to have continued to act as a secret meeting place for one secret society after another, leaving the insides covered in cryptic messages and Turkish graffiti.

Comic images came into my mind. I imagined clandestine groups, dressed in capes and disguises, meeting up here under the cover of darkness. Several of these groups, rival factions perhaps, unwittingly meeting up at the same time, by the different faces. I imagined them all assuming the others gathered there were part of their group and chaos ensuing. I wished the weather station well. Long may such illicit subterfuge continue.

The 'Tower of the Winds', Athens.

So, were there really no high points to Athens? Yes, three and wildly different they were. The first was the archaeological museum. This was a vast collection, superbly presented for the time, but it probably seems completely ordinary now. The aesthetic blow in the first hall where the gold of Mycenae was displayed was tremendous. Then the thrill of the little statue of the boy joking and scampering off down the centuries, but above all, sending a great shiver down the spine, the overwhelming statue of Zeus about to hurl his bolt. And it was not only me that was impressed. I noticed that all conversation went quiet as people entered the gallery. Truly this figure was godlike, and everyone's instant response was awe.

The second highlight came during the 'Son et Lumiere' display. I sat on the opposite hill to the Acropolis, it is surprisingly cold there at night, and watched spellbound as the invading army surrounded the Acropolis, and hundreds of little red lights, indicating campfires, came on. Slowly the ancient monuments went dark. 'But the lantern of freedom was still alight...' reflected the commentary cheesily. There was a piercing trumpet call in the darkness and suddenly the Parthenon was blazing in an extreme white light, a beacon shining for all of Europe and all men. It was complete nonsense, propaganda for the masses, but I loved it!

The third highlight was purely subjective and very, very short. It was simply a taxi ride at night. I have always been a fan of public transport, and taxis in particular. They are by far the best way of seeing a place by getting out on the streets, and mixing in with the locals, sometimes quite literally in cities where taxi sharing is common. The driver had his radio going full blast with a strange haunting music full of quarter tones, that I remembered from Egypt. I still had not developed a liking for the music of Um Kolthoum, but I hadn't really tried very hard. The driver drove at great speed around Omonia Square, where they were considering moving the statue of Zeus to, and off through central Athens. The skyline was a blur of neon signs. The taxi swerved through the crowds that were still milling about the roads oblivious to the traffic. The combination of the big fat car, the music, the colour and the foreignness of the language made for a heady mixture. It was over far too quickly, despite the drunken pedestrians.

Following my previous little outing I decided to hire a taxi once again to set out towards the monastery at Daphni. In Athens, taxi drivers are rated as speaking English if they can master the words 'Acropolis' & 'OK Joe' which are nearly always spoken together regardless of the intended destination. To get one to go to Daphni therefore proved to be an interesting challenge. A combination of charades, maps, and my confused attempts at writing in Greek capitals, got us to the town, but instead of taking me to the monastery he dropped me at the prison. Neither did he drop me at the gate but much to my horror drove right into the courtyard. Did he think I was some kind of dodgy backstreet lawyer in my old black suit? I heard a strangely familiar clicking sound and turned to see the dark barrels of several Russian 'papasha' sub-machine guns pointed at me. I'd been in tight spots before, but I'd usually been better prepared for them. Who even knew I was here, let alone would miss me?

'Don't do anything, that can't be undone!' My own catchphrase echoed around in my head. I tried a few choice words in a smattering of different languages, but Greek was not amongst them. Eyebrows were raised a few times, but the guns weren't lowered. Neither

French nor English had any joy, and I thought that I'd better not risk German given that the Nazis had executed hundreds of Greeks just up the road in reprisal for a series of partisan raids. I held out my passport authoritatively, the embossed coat of arms clearly visible. Soldiers were all the same all over the world and soldiers liked people to have papers. In desperation I tried Italian. The guns were lowered, clearly enough water had passed under that bridge. I was tersely escorted to the church by a pair of heavy boots. It was a timely reminder that Greece was not all 'sun and sandals'.

Haidari prison was originally created as a barracks for the Greek military but following the German invasion of Greece in 1941 it was converted into a concentration camp, becoming the most notorious camp in the Mediterranean. Over two thousand political prisoners and prisoners of war were executed there by the Gestapo in just two years of operation. After the war, ownership returned to the Greek army who continued to operate it as a military prison until 1980. Hundreds of communists were executed here during the Greek Civil War and thousands of prisoners passed through its gates during the rule of the right-wing military Junta which ruled from 1967 until 1974.

Daphni monastery stood serenely in a grove of laurel trees, plain, austere, giving no hint of the blaze of colour inside. The sixth-century mosaics covered every inch of wall, with Christ Partocratic in the dome sternly judging all men. The mosaics were lovely in quite a different way from those in St. Marks, more austere, more primitive perhaps, making together an atmosphere that was a refreshment to the spirit as well as a joy to the eye.

The coach left Athens by the north, stopping for coffee at Thebes, now a small country town with a few sad remnants of the once mighty walls. We turned abruptly into the hills. Looking back, I was impressed by the tight compact nature of the town and villages in the plain below – no straggling, no ribbon development. They reminded me of coins thrown onto a green baize tabletop.

The monastery of Hosios Loukas sat in the middle of the wild mountains, an oasis from the harsh country and the bitter remains of the civil war. Silent children held up little bunches of flowers as we walked down to the monastery, making us feel guilty, but of what

I am not sure. The mosaics in the church were I believe even finer than those at Daphni.

Sitting on the rocky terrace afterwards I wondered how anyone survived the winter here, and how money that flowed into the church was redistributed amongst the community. What mechanisms existed for tourism to influence local policies? Could foreign tourism be connected to social services?

We moved quickly on, over the shoulder of Parnassus, the clouds dark and drawing close. The long white street of Aradora, then over the pass in fading light and down to Delphi. Such an evocative name. Were the name and the stories the source of the magic, or was the magic always there?

People say the museum is unsightly, but I did not think so. There seem to be tourists who'd like nothing better than for the people that actually live there to be hidden away completely. I did not think that actual village impinged much on the essence of Delphi at all, in fact the ancient shrine would have been less poignant without it. Everything needs a context. Even the new 'Hotel Delphi' was relatively inconspicuous, and its neon arches a cheerful contrast to the ancient temple.

Anyway, the contents of the museum now had a decent hall to display them. From the splendid series of archaic stone figures (you can sense the sculptor struggling with the stone) to the incomparable bronze 'Charioteer'. He stands motionless, no wind disturbs his robe. Smug? Contented? No, but totally focused. The fact that he is clothed may, ironically, mean that he was a servant with flesh not suitable to be on display. This would in turn explain his expression, a servant determined to do well for his master, or perhaps one that could expect punishment if success was not delivered. What scars lay under his cloak?

It was raining in the morning and the 'Shining Ones', as the cliffs above Delphi were known by the ancient Greeks, were shining indeed. We drove high above Delphi and then through the woods. I realised that this ancient Greece was not so much about temples and statues, but about rocky hills, scrubland, goats and food shortages. There was silence once again save for the occasional drip of water. Pine needles, a glimpse of shining stone. The rain stopped and with a dramatic suddenness a brilliant blue sky. Then as if on cue, marching en masse up the valley whole columns of goats began to envelop us, like a group of earnest philosophers attending a debate. Shadows swirled all around, vanishing and reappearing constantly. It was more educational than any museum could be.

Down again to the Theatre with the dramatic backdrop of the site. To the Temple, the Sacred Way. Down once more to the Sacred Spring, a featureless cistern carved into the rock, and then finally out onto the road to Thalos.

Brilliant sunshine streamed down from the hills next morning. At 5am I was out on the balcony gasping at the beauty before me. The long rays of the sun shone down from Parnassus, over Delphi and out into the plain far below. The entire area was covered with olive trees (over seven million of them apparently) making a spiky green carpet that stretched to the sea. The sky was a delicate washed blue, the rocks glowed pink and gold. I breathed in deeply, and wondered where I could get a tea or coffee at this hour and what was for breakfast. I shared a strong brew with one of the security guards in exchange for a cigarette. They are a universal currency. It was boiled over a fire in a little copper cup called a 'briki' and served with a dirty lump of sugar in a shot glass. I gripped the sugar between my teeth like a Russian peasant and sucked the strong liquid past it, smiling with a childish pleasure that I'd never get from smoking.

After breakfast we followed the road down to the sea, which was as flat as a millpond. Even the wake of rowing boats was visible long after they had gone by. The ferry was a spruced up old landing craft from the war and chugged slowly across the Straits of Corinth in a long diagonal. I leaned over the side, my tie blowing in the wind, and hoped that my glasses wouldn't fall off. It was slightly more than two hours before we made our way past the two Venetian forts that guard the entrance of the Port of Patras and landed, like the US Army on the shore.

I saw little of Patras, but what I saw I liked, especially the excellent lunch. Some of the goats we'd seen earlier perhaps and red mullet fresh off the grill, served in wraps with charred vegetables and a yoghurt sauce. I ate until I almost fell asleep in the sun. I'd been up since 5am if you remember, that's my excuse anyway. The oddest thing about the place was the harbour. It was without breakwaters, lock gates or any of the things we expect in England, just a long concrete wall that ships tied up at. Here quite large ships - ferries bound for Italy and Turkey, were lying quietly moored by the stern next to the bus stop, as if they were day boats for hire. From street to ship there was no transition at all. After lunch a short drive along the coast to our hotel. More woods, but by now they looked more established and less like scrubland. The trees here were deciduous, oaks and beeches, the woods more like in England.

Incredibly my father stayed in the Hotel SPAP Olympia, which was a railway hotel opened in 1908. Its luxurious rooms hosted not only hundreds of ordinary guests, but also kings, heads of state and personalities all keen to see the treasures of Olympus. The hotel was famous for its flowers and for its range of cocktails, neither of which he would have appreciated. It had undergone a significant expansion in 1957 adding a pool and extensive spa facilities, neither of which he would have taken joy in. He stayed in this luxury hotel for two nights, but it obviously did not compare well in his view, to the seafront cafe in Patras as there is no mention of the food!

Hotel SPSP Olympia.

The setting of Olympia is sublime, but it is of course, quite unlike the original town which was a cheerful industrial dynamo, that erupted every four years into noisy chaos. Now the great columns of the temple have fallen and lie like a pile of coins.

Olympia, like piles of coins.

Lesser temples have been recreated and now stand buried scenically in the trees, crumbling archways blending almost organically into the branches. There is no harsh brilliance here, like at the Acropolis, no magic as at Delphi, not even a sense of competition. What there is, however, is a gentle sense of peace and of timelessness.

The journey across the Peloponnese was fascinating, as the road, newly opened, rose and fell through the mountains, emerging with the breath-taking view over the Plain of Argos to the sea.

There were pretty white villages dotted about everywhere, sites with famous names, ruins unmarked and potentially undiscovered, a column here, a theatre, half grassed over there. After the barren desolation of the hills, the plain seemed to be teeming with life. We drove round the gulf to the curious little town of Nafplio, with its castle, the winged lion still proud above the door, sliding down the hill. Under Venetian domination, this bustling port was known in the Middle Ages as the 'Naples of Byzantium'. For thirty years, it stood as capital of its own naval kingdom, a successor to the dying empires of the Byzantines and the Venetians before being engulfed by Turkish forces at the start of the eighteenth century. It is yet another reminder of how different the world looked even in recent times, with whole communities of nations we now no longer know clustered around trade routes and a shared sea.

I stayed at the Amphitryon Hotel in Nafplio, a modernist building inside an old fort, right on the beach with superbly well-appointed facilities. The name means to play both sides off against each other, as the town has undoubtedly done throughout history and as, to a certain extent, have I. I am ashamed to say that I loved the place! Standing there on the old stones, looking down through the cypress trees at an almost purple sea. Nafplio seemed to have everything that I felt I wanted in a place; warm sands, old stone, hot sun, dark trees and that gorgeous blue water with a passing white sail. I found myself quoting Lermontov. If only there was someone to share this wonderous place with…

White sail out in the bay billowing in the wind.
Why sail so far away?
Why leave so much behind?

Winds must play on the seas and masts must creak in the wind.
Fortune is not what he seeks,
Nor what he's left behind.

Just along the road lay Tiryns. You've never heard of it I'm sure, and nor had I. But Mycenae and Tiryns were the two greatest cities of the Mycenaean civilisation. Between 1600 and 1200 B.C., its kingdom was the most powerful in the Mediterranean. Homer, in his 'Iliad', which I was hastily rereading on the coach, and the 'Odyssey', spoke of it as being 'rich in ancient gold'. The site was huge, and the heat radiated back unpleasantly from its ancient walls. It is a myriad of courtyards and dead ends designed to encourage trade and confuse invaders. The whole place is a labyrinth. No gold has ever been found there; presumably Homer, or more likely the Venetians, got to it first, but the frescos that remain are surely even more valuable. The modern world is doing its best to impose upon the ancient city, but it seems likely that after nearly four thousand years, it will endure.

The avenue was straight, and tree lined. At each end they crowded around hiding the view. Then suddenly they fell back and the great bowl of the Theatre at Epidaurus was before us, beautifully restored, its curves splendidly satisfying, the grey stone sweeping round like an embrace. People were moving about inside, climbing the steep steps, curiously remote. Yet every word they spoke was audible even from this distance. A masterpiece of physics. I wished that I had someone cleverer than I there to explain how it worked to me. Built in the fourth century B.C., there are 34 rows of seats divided into 34 blocks and it can hold 15,000 spectators, every one of whom can hear the action on stage perfectly without microphones. Our guide demonstrated this by lighting a match. It was like a small explosion. Instantly I wanted to run around testing it for myself. How would different types of frequency be affected by the stone? Would attenuation be a problem for higher pitched instruments? How indeed would the dreaded Um Kolthoum sound, wailing in such a venue with her orchestra? I could have stayed and played here all afternoon.

It was not to be, yet another famous Greek site beckoned. How were there so many of them? It seemed as if every hilltop and shepherd's hut had had some story made up about it. I was getting a little overwhelmed, and possibly bored. Mycenae the other half of the equation. Very well. At first almost invisible against the hills and then dominating the landscape to the exclusion of everything. The steep uneven path leads upwards to the Lion Gate. Squat, heavy and indifferent. It neither threatens guests nor welcomes them. Just inside on the right, the grave circles where those magnificent treasures were dug up by Schillmann, but I had no reaction to them. Not listening to our learned guide, I climbed the citadel to get a general view of the place. A feeling of unease came over me only gradually but grew steadily stronger. Standing in a little room in the bright sunlight, flowers growing through the stones, that lovely view across the plain before me, I nevertheless shivered. Other people were moving around, I was not alone or at risk, but something was deeply unpleasant here. Plenty of men have been murdered by their wives for sleeping with another woman, and there was no reason for me to care particularly about Agamemnon, a king. All the same I felt uncomfortable standing in what had once been his royal bathroom. Why? Was there any residual evil in that room or was it just a subconscious reaction to a popular myth? If there was any evil, surely it was not on the part of his murderer, his poor wife Clytemnestra, for she was the one who was wronged. It is clearly

287

the harlot Helen of Troy that was at fault in the tale, and she had no connection to this spot. I couldn't help wondering as I returned to my party, what if the crime had been the other way round, what if a friend had slept with Clytemnestra? Would Agamemnon have murdered her if she had been unfaithful to him? Or killed his best friend for sleeping with her? I think so.

Corinth was by contrast a relaxed and friendly place; its four Corinthian columns looked very picturesque against the view of the straits. Even the touts were cheerful and did not stop smiling when I said 'Ochi - No!'. The Acropolis here was very high and too daunting for me to try climbing in the midday sun, dressed as I was, as always, in suit and tie. So instead, I sauntered over the ruins, wishing that I had a travelling companion with me, murderous or not. The modern world and the motorway back to Athens lay just over the hill. It would have made a good spot for a painting contrasting the ancient white marble columns with the new black streaks of tarmac. But my paintings were always much better in my mind than in reality. I blame the canvas somehow…

The Plain of Argos as remembered from my father's travels.

I heard on the radio that a communist deputy had been killed somewhere in the north of the country and suddenly there were tanks on every corner and soldiers with machine guns patrolling the square. The joy that I had felt just a couple of days before evaporated, and once more I realised that I was standing in a country that was at war with itself, as divided as Berlin. The right-wing military Junta had not yet come to power, but they soon would, backed by American money, determined to crush a popular coalition of Socialists and Communists that were trying to improve the quality of life for the masses. It was time for me to leave. I caught a boat at Pireus Harbour out to the islands. It was fast, powered by an old aircraft engine crammed beneath the decks, causing the green waters to sparkle and sending a refreshing spray of cool water through the air. Silver slivers could be seen darting about in the water all around me. In what seemed like no time we entered the harbour at Hydra and tied up. I know it is a terribly fashionable place, a sort of Greek St. Ives, but as we tied up at the quay, I got a sense of how it must have been all those years ago, when the whole Mediterranean world was just a set of little isolated communities connected by a shared sea reached in such a fashion. Nets were being mended along the front, and sand and crushed stone loaded onto the backs of donkeys, for transportation through the narrow lanes. I was not there very long, an hour or two maybe, then off once again to Aegina with its colourful harbour

We stopped at an uninhabited island where we were told we would have lunch. It was little more than a mossy sandbank and I could see neither a building serving lunch or otherwise, nor anyone to serve it. Were we to pick our own lunch from the eggs left by the seabirds or fish it from the sea ourselves? I would have been happy doing either and had my shoes and socks off and trousers rolled up in preparation. From a boat moored further up, sailors appeared, removed their sweaters and put on white coats, and ran up and down the golden sand with chairs, tables, cutlery and trays of food. From this one small vessel, soup, fish, lamb, vegetables and a lovely cool white wine appeared. To it the detritus returned. The only downside to this lovely experience was that it left me feeling a little guilty about being waited on so, and the thought of those chaps sitting there waiting for us made me feel a little sick. I told myself that they would have been relaxing on the sand themselves not waiting in line, and indeed some already were. As I strolled along the island shore, I heard them singing, performing handstands, and jumping with real joy, like children, fully clad into the sea that had been the centre of their universe for thousands of years. I left them my unopened packets of Embassy and made my way back to the waiting boat.

I headed back to the mainland and watched as the sun burned orange and gold over the Bay of Salamis. Dusk would soon be upon us and then the bus ride back to the airport. I had come here, snobbishly, because of the culture and the history. But it was clear to me that it was the sun and the sea that I had enjoyed the most. At the last minute, I spotted in the distance a glint of white high up on the hill. In a world where the cliffs glowed ochre and the sea shone like bronze, it stood out like a lighthouse. There was no doubting what it was or why it had been built that way. I realised that as usual I had been looking at things the wrong way. The Parthenon was not designed for those that lived at its foot, not built to be looked at close up by the citizens of Athens, or for tourists to consider quickly while their taxi drivers smoked around the corner, but as a gift to all of those who lived and worked in these waters, and out on the surrounding islands. It unified them, as much as the stories it told of their heroes and of course their shared magnificent sea.

View-Master™ Reel (Greece)

VIENNA

City of Dreams, 1963

No European travel journal could be complete without a trip to Vienna. The city embodies what Europe was, is and will be, more than any other – except of course Rome, which I had already visited several times. Europe's heritage is born of three things, the Roman Empire, Christianity and trade along the Danube. The Holy Roman Empire, modern Europe's predecessor, combines all three and its capital was Vienna. We could add many more things to the list of what defines Europe, the struggles against Islam, the Turks and the Mongols, the feudal system, classical music, literature and art, etc.; but all of these things are intimately connected to this city that lies truly at the heart of Europe.

I had originally planned to visit the capitals of Austria and Hungary together. To fly to Vienna and get the train or perhaps a boat to Budapest, stopping at towns and castles along the way, but the Iron Curtain that has split our continent in two was officially impenetrable and my request for a permit to visit Budapest was surprisingly turned down. I was shocked. I had assumed that the anointment of the new bushy eyed General Secretary would usher in a new period of relaxed relations, but perhaps I was wrong. What did I know? The Soviets had invaded Hungary in response to the Revolution in 1956, a nasty business if ever there was one, but I understood that things were stable nine years later. Still there was no point in arguing.

My plane from Heathrow was another Comet. I'd been rather hoping that it would be one of the new sporty three-engined Tridents that BEA had introduced, but it wasn't to be.

A BEA Comet 4 in the 1965 livery.

It took just two hours to cover the distance to Vienna, which was hardly enough time for me to enjoy a complimentary lunch, cake and a glass of a rich red.

Vienna is a large and cosmopolitan city of over two million souls from diverse backgrounds. It stretches over terraces from the Viennese Woods where Richard Strauss set his tales to the tunes of Jewish zither music, down to his famous 'Blue Danube' which, by the time the airport bus pulled in, was glowing a burnished gold in the evening sun. You know that I'm going to tell you that Vienna started life as a Roman fort. The Danube formed the frontier of the Roman Empire in the northeast and forts were built along the river's length, not to expand, but to keep the barbarians out. It was far quicker and easier to supply these by boat, and Vienna, or Vindobona as it was known then, was the largest, and oldest military base on the Danube.

The Duchy of Austria was created by the kings of Bavaria as a military border zone. It was administered from the German city of Regensburg, whose bishops set it up as a land of markets and churches in order to generate revenue from and tame the dark forces in the East. Vienna has always played the role of a frontier town, a marketplace, a bridge between darkness and light. There is a certain malevolence to it as well as its obvious forced beauty. Until the eighteenth century it was ringed by huge walls nearly as large as Contantinople's, which shaped its growth. It fell to the heathen

Hungarians in the 1400s before being recaptured for Christianity by the Hapsburgs who went on to make it their home, and who made it their mission to defend the Holy Roman Empire against the pagans. Cash poured in and churches bloomed everywhere as a result. It took two hundred years to defeat the forces of Islam in a series of struggles played out over Hungary, Romania, Bulgaria and Yugoslavia, all of which became part of the Hapsburg's Austrian Empire, with the blessing of the popes of the day. The city that we see today was rebuilt in the late eighteenth and nineteenth centuries as a planned Imperial capital. The ancient city walls were torn down to make way for the 'RingStrasse', a large circular boulevard lined with grand buildings with the Hofburg Palace as the jewel in the crown. Tree-lined avenues, quiet squares and formal gardens sprung up. Baroque palaces bloomed and found themselves sandwiched between middle class apartment blocks. Cafés and shops appeared everywhere, as trade along the Danube blossomed.

It could not be more different from Berlin. At first it reminded me of Paris with Haussmann's lines of ornate apartment buildings and distinct districts, but as I neared the centre it began to look and feel more like London, with its busy streets full of traffic, and historic smoke-stained offices towering over ground floor shops. There is a real bustle about the place that reminds you that this is a proud imperial centre of commerce. Just like London there are dark and narrow lanes just off the main thoroughfares where water drips from broken pipes onto the cobbles and bomb-damaged buildings lean uncertainly on their crutches. There are a lot of slightly awkward parallels between London and Vienna, far more than there should be, I'm sure.

Vienna has got away very lightly with the War, and huge amounts of money were being spent repairing it, especially by the Americans who bombed it the most. Austria claims to have been the Nazi's first victim, the ones who were invaded first. I am cynical I'm afraid. The idea of an Anschluss with Germany dates all the way back to 1871. It's not a Nazi or even a German original concept. I have seen for myself in my travels through the Tyrol that the border is a nonsense, and I am old enough to remember when on the night of 13th March 1938 ninety-seven percent of Austrians voted in favour of unification with Germany. Even now, after everything that has happened, in a recent census forty-six percent of Austrian citizens declared themselves to be 'German' as their nationality rather than Austrian, as of course did Hitler, an Austrian, born and raised in Austria. But whereas Germans go about their business diligently, overcome by crushing shame and guilt, here I still see men, little men, postmen, policemen, bus conductors, clerks, etc., all strutting about in quasi-military uniform officiously ordering citizens to keep off the grass and pompously waving flags. I wonder how much has really changed here? This must have been how it was back then. There's no guilt here and lots of arrogance. You'd get the impression that they'd won the war and that the Holy Roman Empire was still in place.

Central Vienna, 1965.

Just ten years ago occupying forces withdrew from Vienna, which was set up as the capital of a new 'independent' republic. Austria has declared itself in its constitution to be officially neutral. Actual neutrality cost Switzerland and Holland dearly in the last war, if you remember. I wonder what sort of official neutrality Austria is talking about for the future. The historic buildings that line the RingStrasse are covered in bright advertising and the fancy glass headquarters of many international organisations and American businesses are popping up everywhere. There are seemingly more diplomats and businessmen here than residents, reminding me of West Berlin. That kind of 'neutral'.

I had compensated a little for the extortionate cost of the flight, fifty-three pounds (nearly £1,000 today) by saving a little bit on my hotel. It was a modest affair in a quiet side street in the district of Leopoldstadt. A dull beige rendered exterior with metal framed windows hid a colourful open plan interior with wood veneer panelling and bright orange armchairs in the lobby. A paternoster lift, which you had to jump into, ticked slowly around in the corridor. I worried about what would happen if I stayed in the thing to the top and jumped out hastily at my floor. From my room I could see the giant Ferris wheel in the Prater Park and, beyond it, the Danube.

I had planned too much for the next day and I rushed my breakfast to get to the museums early, which proved to be a mistake. I could grab a pastry anywhere surely... Red and white trams clanged their way through the traffic choked streets whilst men in western suits and women in polka dot print dresses filled the pavements. They marched almost in unison and crossed the road together like cattle under the watchful eye of the clocks that lined the street. I noticed that they waited until the lights were green even when there was no traffic. They are, as the Germans would say, 'Regelmessig', a word that means law abiding or compliant but is much stronger. They seem unable to break the rules, as though in fear of them.

I started at the 'Kunsthistorisches Museum', an ornate building out on the RingStrasse. Its exterior is covered in ornate columns and statues of great historical figures as if trying to bestow a grand heritage on the building's creator. A large bronze dome echoes the look of byzantine cathedrals giving it a legitimacy it doesn't have either. It is the kind of building that you might see in Trafalgar Square, and like its identical twin, the Natural History Museum, that sits on the other side of the street, it is a fake. It was built in 1891 and closed less than twenty years later at the outbreak of the Great War. Temporarily open again between the wars it shut shortly after the Anschluss with Germany as its priceless collection of fine art made its way into the hands of Nazi officials like Herman Goering.

Inside it is a riot of gold leaf, stuccoed ceilings, chandeliers and marble. It rivals even St. Mark's in Venice for gaudiness. But the art, my goodness, where to begin? A series of rooms cover the art of the ancient Egyptians, which I hardly looked at, and specialist rooms holding work from the Middle and Far East, but the bulk of the collection is the Imperial family's private collection of Medieval, Renaissance & Baroque European art, which sweeps away into the distance up the grand staircase as if masterpieces by Rubens and Rembrandt were simply family photographs and holiday snaps.

I walked silently in awe around the galleries and the rotunda, ignoring the stern looking guides who tapped their truncheons anxiously in the shadows. Perhaps they thought that this suspicious looking foreigner in a black suit was meeting someone illicitly here or making a 'dead letter drop'. I am told that Vienna's parks and museums are famous for such clandestine activity. Perhaps, like the surly waiters in the cafés, they were resentfully hiding in case I dared ask for something or had 'difficult' questions. There was far too much to see, and I lost all sense of time. I particularly liked Titian's Suleiman with his magnificent hat, and Archimboldo's Summer man, whose face was so healthy and expressive yet on closer inspection was entirely made from fruit. I do love Bruegel's miniatures of peasant life as well and some of Dürer's sketches made me laugh out loud, much to the attendant's displeasure. In the basement was an exhibition of carriages and historic military uniforms. It seemed to be far more popular with the locals than the galleries upstairs. Not being a fan of militaria, or for that matter the military in general, I decided to give it a miss and headed out for my next museum a short tram ride away.

There are palaces everywhere in Vienna, and the Albertina is another one of them. I'm amazed that there were enough royal princes and aristocrats to go around them all! Everything seemed to be designed to show off wealth. You can see why the workers revolution very nearly happened here when the Great War broke up the Austro-Hungarian Empire and crashed the Austrian economy.

Vienna was a hotbed of socialism, so much so that it was called 'Das rote Wien'. It was in Vienna's cafés that German philosophical socialism met Russian, and British, revolutionaries. In 1915 Hitler, Trotsky, Tito, Freud, and Stalin all lived in the same neighbourhood and drank at the Central Café. By the mid-twenties unemployment in Vienna exceeded 40%, with working class Germans from agricultural and manual backgrounds worst affected. When the Central Bank of Austria collapsed in 1934 riots broke out in the workers' districts and the army was sent in with orders to shoot anyone on the street and to shell the workers' communal housing. Thousands died in the rioting, tens of thousands more from starvation. Anger turned against the ruling elite and middle-class professionals, especially any that weren't pure German. Less than four years later Hitler swept to power and the common antisemitism became government policy.

The Albertina is a palace built near the Hofburg on the foundations of a tower in the old city wall. It was created for the Holy Roman Empire's Ambassador to Venice on his retirement and houses his personal collection of plundered Italian masterpieces. In 1919, Austria's new socialist government confiscated the building and its contents and evicted the Archduke without compensation. The following year the building was opened to the public as a museum. With more than sixty thousand exhibits ranging from da Vinci's superb 'Last Supper' to impressionist works by Monet and Toulouse-Lautrec, I was spoilt for choice. I am not normally a fan of religious paintings, although I appreciate the skills and techniques, but if you ignore the setting and the figure of Jesus himself, there is something delightfully down to earth and human about the expression on each disciple's face as they react to the news of Jesus' betrayal. James looks utterly stunned, at a loss for how to react, whilst the wizened old face of Peter boils with anger. I cannot help but feel that these are real characters from the streets of Florence reacting to an actual Machiavellian scandal of the day.

I was suddenly starving and found myself ambling through the quiet backstreets and leafy squares looking for somewhere to eat something, anything. Monuments to artists and composers were everywhere, and opposite one to Schubert I found a place that looked a little like an old stable with arched wooden doors opening up onto a small, cobbled yard. It was dark and very plain inside with wood panelled walls and a long wooden bar. It smelt of wet stone, cheap tobacco and steam. Men in dirty linen shirts with baggy trousers held up by braces were hunched over scrubbed wooden tables. The menu was chalked up on the wall in elaborate gothic script that I struggled to read.

A small bowl of lard, beef dripping, was dumped unceremoniously in front of me on the table with a basket of dried bread rolls. It didn't look or taste particularly inviting. The bread, called here 'Kaiersemmel' or 'Emperor Roll' disintegrated like plaster when I bit into it. It's meant for dipping, but the lard was as rock hard as the stone tiles on the floor. I confidently ordered the goulash, which is a Hungarian dish rather than an Austrian one. What arrived was a beefy stew with onions and very little paprika. It was closer to a Lancashire hotpot than what I understand a goulash to be, but it was perfect for soaking that bulletproof bread. I ordered the 'Kaiserschmarren' for dessert, purely because I could read the word. I was told that it is so named as it was the Emperor Franz Joseph's favourite dessert, but what turned up hardly seemed fit for an emperor. It was a pile of deep-fried shredded pancakes covered in plum jam, cream and toasted nuts. It looked like a total mess, but it tasted fantastic. It was one of those dishes that got better as it mixed together in the bowl. I can think of a few improvements, maybe cherry jam and sour cream, and fancied having a go at making it myself when I got home. I don't cook but I was sure that I could improve on the goulash too.

The Austrians called these old-fashioned bistros 'beisl' from the Jewish word for 'house'. It is one of countless little reminders of how deeply integrated the Jewish community was to the life and economy of mediaeval Europe. Christianity at the time expressly forbade the lending of money, or the gaining of it through activities that the Soviets call 'speculation'. Islam also places strict limitations on the ethics of financial matters. The image of the Jewish moneylender is a stereotype, but has a kernel of truth. For the best part of four-hundred years the majority of people occupying these middle-class financial roles were Jewish. The Hanseatic League borrowed money to build ships and develop towns, the Polish commonwealth used them to collect taxes, and the Medicis used them to grease the wheels of the supply chain extending Italian bank loans to northern communities beyond the Alps. Keen to raise money for his new city, Jews were granted autonomy by the Austrian Emperor in 1890.

By 1938 there were twenty-two synagogues in Vienna alone and Jews made up ten percent of the city's population. Eighty percent of the city's textile manufacturing was owned by Jewish families and sixty percent of its pharmaceutical businesses. It was from just such a family that Vienna's famous son Sigmund Freud was born.

Within weeks of the Anschluss, Vienna's estimated 200,000 Jews were rounded up into an artificially created ghetto in Leopoldstadt. A young SS Lieutenant named Adolf Eichmann (like Hitler an Austrian not a German) was placed in charge of coming up with a system or model for solving 'the Jewish problem'; a 'final solution'. By 1945 less than a third of Vienna's Jewish community was still alive.

The Hofburg. The most historically important of Vienna's palaces, the house of the Habsburgs-and the official residence of every Austrian ruler since 1275. Since 1955 a series of public museums containing the history of the city, the Holy Roman Empire and the Hapsburgs themselves. The complex includes eighteen different buildings and countless rooms and galleries. I had not left myself enough time to do it justice, but found myself simply walking past the Imperial Apartments, the Treasury with its Imperial regalia and the Silver Collection. Kings and emperors will always be kings and emperors and they will always want gold. It sparkles but has no meaning to the ordinary man on the street and who cares how they dressed for what ridiculously superficial activity.

Vienna's 'Hofburg'. The home of the Holy Roman Emperor.

I found the display of Holy Roman Empire relics curious but faintly ridiculous too. What terrible atrocities have been carried out in the name of religion. Austria, perhaps more than any other country, has lost countless generations fighting, not only for Christianity, against Islam, but for a specific version of Catholic Christianity. Maximillian, the son and heir of Emperor Ferdinand the First, was banished from the Hofburg for leaning even the slightest bit towards Protestantism and so his father built him the Stallburg palace in the grounds of the Hofburg's riding school and stables. I enjoyed the Royal Armoury, with its collection of impractical armour and non-functional handguns. In reality Austria has always been far behind its opponents technically. The Italians and the Turks, both of whom had better firepower than the Austrians, left their mark on the Hofburg, as did the Bavarians who made better armour and Napoleon even built his own palace on the site of the Hofburg's library once he had defeated the Holy Roman Empire. But just a few years later he was in turn defeated and Europe came together in the 'Redoutensaal' to sign the Treaty of Vienna, that created modern Europe. I stared up at the chandeliers hanging from the decorated baroque ceiling and watched their light reflect in the ballroom's countless giant mirrors. How odd, that I, a complete nobody, should be standing in the very room where so many emperors had stood and so much history had happened. What if we could go back in time and meet those people? What would we think of each other? Perhaps I'd rather not know.

I wandered back along the old Roman road that leads from the Opera House on the Ringstrasse, the site of the main gate in the city walls, to St. Stephen's cathedral built on the remains of the Roman temple that once lay at the city's centre. It is a wide pedestrianised precinct full of up market expensive shops selling the latest in clothing and furniture designs. But unlike West Berlin, where it was all just for show, here there are a constant stream of people going in and out with shopping bags crammed full of purchases. Everyone here seemed to have money. I wonder how many of those purchases are going eastwards.

St. Stephen's cathedral is a grand gothic affair, that has been extended many times in its lifetime giving it a slightly chaotic shape. Soot and air pollution have darkened the stonework giving it an austere appearance and the spire looks almost as menacing as Cologne's; but unlike Cologne Cathedral, here there is that slightly trite form of advertising that trivialises the experience. The unusually steep roof is fitted with coloured patterned tiles into which someone has chosen to layout the Habsburg coat of arms, and at the tip of the spire, the highest point on the Holy Roman Empire's cathedral, above everything, is not the crucifix as you'd expect, but the Imperial Eagle. Empires it turns out, are brands and need marketing images and slogans.

Saint Stephen's Cathedral (Vienna) with its patterned tiled roof.

Beethoven once stood on this exact spot and watched birds fleeing from the tower. Only when he realised that he could not hear the tolling of the great bell from the steps of the Great West Door did he understand how truly deaf he had become. His Eighth Symphony was premiered in the Hofburg's Redouten-saal on 27th February 1814, but by then he had become so deaf that the orchestra had to ignore his ungainly gestures and follow the lead of the first violin instead. I do think of Vienna whenever I play the eighth, which isn't that often. It is a fairly cheerful piece of work, that echoes themes from Haydn & Mozart. Technically it is very clever but there is no great emotion behind it. It does not really say anything, which is how I was beginning to feel about Vienna too.

Fortified by a large breakfast of scrambled egg with bacon, called 'Speck' here, coffee and pastries, I headed out to the suburb of Hietzing which was my focus for the day. The 'Stadtbahn' rattled out along the remains of the River Wien which at this time of year is little more than a gravel path in a concrete ditch but turns into a gushing torrent of muddy water several times of year. Hietzing was a delightful village outside the city walls at the foot of the Vienna hills. For centuries it had been the centre of wine production with vines climbing all over its sunlit terraces, and you could still see the crumbling remains of giant barrels and wine presses outside some of the ancient inns and farmhouses that survive. However, the area was destroyed by the Turkish invasions of the sixteenth and seventeenth century, and the razing of the land around the city during the siege of Vienna. Sulieman the Magnificent, who I had last seen at the Historic Art Museum the previous day, was determined to capture Vienna, and for almost three hundred years the Hapsburgs and the Ottomans fought over eastern Europe. Spain came to the Austrians' aid the first time, fighting alongside Bavarian and Italian mercenaries. A hundred years later it was much weaker and France, keen to weaken the Holy Roman Empire, chose to leave it to its fate. Protestant Germany sent troops out of solidarity, but it was the now forgotten Commonwealth of Poland that rode to the Hapsburg's rescue. Literally. By September 1683 Vienna had run out of food and Turkish engineers had breached the city walls. It was over. The Hapsburgs had failed to defend Christianity and now Islam would inevitably spread west along the Danube. That was when 18,000 mounted knights appeared out of the woods and the great Polish General Jan Sobieski led what is still the largest cavalry charge in history. It is said that on saving the city the Polish General paraphrased the famous quotation from the Roman General that had first founded the place. 'Veni, vidi, vici'. 'We came, we saw, and by God's grace we conquered!' Fabulous stuff.

The Treaty of Warsaw signed in 1683 was fundamental in shaping modern Europe. It created a strategic military alliance between the Christian rulers of Poland, Czechoslovakia, Hungary, Romania and Austria, forming a Danube-based power block in central Europe, that started to turn its back on France, Germany and Spain. It gave the

Hapsburgs a new set of allies, a refreshed economy, new trade routes and a new way of working that was to guide it until 1914 when Archduke Franz Ferdinand was assassinated, and the three-hundred-year-old treaty caused Austria's collapse. A side-effect of the Treaty and wars against the Ottomans was an increased distrust and enmity between France and Germany. After the Second World War the Americans were keen to get Austria to again 'face West'. But Central Europe, with the Danube at its heart, is very clearly its own region, one known to marketeers and economists as 'DACH'. It is a stand-alone self-supporting region, but unquestionably as European as Paris or Rome.

Schönbrunn Palace was the home of the Hapsburg Imperial family and is now Vienna's most popular tourist attraction. Built on land gifted to the Empress Maria Theresa it is a rococo extravagance set in nearly two hundred acres of formal grounds. It was here that the Hapsburg Emperors were born and died, and here, in the Chinese Room, that Charles I signed the Austrian Empire out of existence in 1918. It is as grandiose as you'd expect, but somewhat lacking in imagination or excitement.

1960s postcard of Schönbrunn.

I enjoyed the palace gardens far more than the palace itself. There are large lawns with formal views up to the 'Gloriette' on the top of the hill, but also lots of smaller areas divided up with courtyards dappled with light, small pavilions and fountains everywhere. The air was full of the smell of roses which grew in great banks like coloured cushions on a verdant green sofa and the sound of Schubert's 'Trout Quintet' which was being played by a small orchestra who were perched on garden chairs on the grass. Schubert was a resident of Hietzing and Johann Straus II lived around the corner from here. Around every corner was an artist sat at his easel capturing the scene. Earnest looking parents in dirndls and lederhosen lead small groups of young children round the official path, while staff in Imperial Era uniforms hovered in the background. Judging by the clothing it was as if the first half of the century had simply been deleted from history. I wondered if such denial of real history, a delight in the made up, would cause problems later, like it had already begun to in England.

I followed the scent of roasting almonds to the site of a small fair, where market stalls had been laid out in front of a few games for small children. There were stands selling wine and beer and numerous variations of sausage and sauerkraut as you'd expect, but also quite a few selling pot plants and wicker products. I filled my pockets with a hot paper bag of cinnamon roasted almonds which I picked at as I followed the 'Rundweg' off up the hill along avenues of beech trees.

The Palmhouse is exactly what you'd expect, hot and humid, a site of scientific interest for botanists, of which I'm not one, rather than pleasure. But the building itself is extraordinary, both for its sheer size and because of the curvature of the glass. From here I wandered on to the Tiergarten which is also in the Palace grounds. I have never been a big fan of zoos but having visited them on trips to Rotterdam, Paris and Berlin, they were becoming a feature of my trips abroad. Vienna's zoo is quiet, small but it has a good variety of animals many of which were sheltering in their pavilions. I did rather feel that they all looked a little sad, the polar bear and the orangutang in particular. Only the penguins were out enjoying the sun. They did rather remind me of the Austrians themselves in their little uniforms crossing the road in mass formation.

I exited the gardens at the Hietzing Gate and ambled back through the genteel streets of the suburb which are filled with the

Art Nouveau buildings of city architect Otto Wagner. They are typically tiled, like the Stadtbahn stations, with ornate railings and flowers blooming across their facades almost like stained glass in a church. They are not to my taste, but I do appreciate any effort and design being put into a building regardless of the style. Across the main street from the palace grounds is Hietzing Cemetery where Otto Wagner himself is buried. It is a lovely quiet space. Dappled light filters through the trees and squirrels bounce from branch to branch overhead. I have mixed feelings about cemeteries. I find them interesting and normally quite pleasant, but the idea of paying a great sum of money to leave an unimaginative monument to oneself I find presumptuous and slightly offensive. By all means plant a tree or something that actually contributes to the community, but in this day and age I believe we should all be cremated, and our remains sprinkled in with the fertiliser without ceremony. I was surprised to see that Herr Wagner's own grave was not decorated in his own florid Art Nouveau style. He has designed something much more ridiculous: a fake Roman temple complete with red marble columns, his name carved in gold glinting in the sunlight. It seems pathetic rather than glorious. Almost next door is the very modest tombstone of the famous Viennese artist Gustav Klimt which bears just his name in a modern font. I almost approved. I am not a fan of his, to me, almost erotic art, which uses techniques gained putting up wallpaper in the salons of Vienna's elite, but perhaps I will give him another chance.

Just outside the cemetery is the Viennese institution Café Dommayer, where Johann Strauss and his orchestra used to perform regularly. Tea and cake were provided to the 'band' free of charge in exchange for an afternoon of musical accompaniment. It explains so much, classical musicians are famously mercenary individuals. I went to peruse the glass cases of pastries and tortes. There were stacks of shortbread biscuits sandwiched together with jam and cream that I had to at least try – you were supposed to dip the already highly-caloried treat in chocolate – multi-layered nut and butter cream cakes that looked rather messy and lots of varieties of apple strudel with filo pastry. Amusingly, or perhaps not, there is a cake called a 'Punschkrapfen' that is a term used to describe someone that pretends to be left wing but is actually a right-wing bigot.

It looks like what we might call a 'French Fancy', with red icing and a chocolate interior. The red icing is simple enough to understand, and I'm told the chocolate represents the brown shirts of the SA. How peculiar. It makes me wonder how many other of Vienna's cakes have such hidden meanings, and it quite put me off ordering anything with chocolate, which is nearly everything. In the end I settled on a slice of 'Malakofftorte' which is like a Charlotte cake, sponge fingers covered in rum and cream with flaked almonds on top. Perfect with a strong coffee. I also purchased a cinnamon and apricot swirl for later, just in case I got peckish. By the time I arrived at the Gothic City Hall it had already gone.

Prater Park is one of the oldest amusement parks in the world. Opened to the public in 1766, it stands beside the Danube in what was once a water meadow and Royal Hunting grounds. For hundreds of years there have been beer halls, cafés and fairground rides here, and since 1897 the 'Riesenrad', the highest Ferris wheel in the world (which curiously was built by the British Royal Navy as a present to celebrate the Golden Jubilee of Franz Josef I. Why I do not know, I will have to ask Miss Seawright to find out.) Free to enter, it has been the site of illicit meetings since the day it opened, and there were no shortage of men in grey raincoats loitering in the shadows, or newspapers neatly folded on benches when I visited.

The famous Ferris wheel in Prater Park.

Noisy, brash, and representing humanity in its rawest form it is a truly neutral place within an officially neutral country where East and West can meet as easily as Christian and Turks met on the same spot centuries before, and Romans & Barbarians before them. Boats dock at the wooden quays as the sun sets once more over that epic river. I crunched on a brandy snap and watched families and businessmen alike queue up for the bumper cars and carousels. The technology changes but people really don't. Art and classical music are all very well, but this, this right here, is European Culture too.

Generations of aristocrats partying until the dawn and getting out of bed at midday had left their mark on Vienna. Streets that were quiet and leafy during the day exploded into a riot of neon light at night. Taxis lined up outside restaurants and hotels where women in beehive hairdos and glittering ball gowns were photographed coming and going constantly with their male escorts in evening dress. I too had my best black suit on, as opposed to my regular day black suit, as I was going to the opera. Mozart's 'Magic Flute', not my first choice but cheerful enough and relevant in a city that he truly loved and worked in for a long time. You can't come to Vienna and not visit the Wiener Staatsoper.

'The Magic Flute' is a silly comedy about a prince, lost in a strange foreign land being pursued by monsters and beautiful women. Half-man, half-bird himself. Mozart wrote the opera when he was living in Vienna, and it was here that it had its premiere in 1791. It is easy to see what inspired him. Scratch the surface and you can also see that the story is about two children who deny their well-meaning but authoritarian parent, who thinks that they know what is best. Again, the parallels with Mozart's own life could not be clearer. But Vienna has got me thinking about hidden messages.

I stared not at the stage but out across the giant auditorium, which glittered like the inside of a golden barrel in the darkness. I knew the words to all the songs anyway: 'Have Mercy, Have Mercy, I'm sure that there could never be such loveliness…' I scanned the audience with the little opera glasses clipped to the seat in front, but for what I was not sure. The slightly odd couplings, the men with their coats still on and the people talking furtively instead of watching all leapt out at me. As the Queen of the Night started to hurl abuse at her daughter with that incredible, almost demented top

C aria, I asked myself if there was another message here and who in the audience it was intended for. 'The Magic Flute' could easily be said to be a critique of enlightened despotism, a commentary on those nondemocratic regimes where one party rules in the name of the ordinary man on the street and freedom of the press is curtailed and used as propaganda. The Queen, stunned by the rebellious nature of her children's behaviour and the rejection of her philosophy, screams at them that mother knows what is best, and if they don't obey they will be banished forever from her lands and all bonds of nature broken. Her benevolence is contractual and demands loyalty. The allegory is not lost on the men from the East in the cheap crumpled suits.

I jumped into a taxi and went in search of my own Queen of the Night. She was waiting for me at the top of the newly opened Danube Tower, which stood 252 meters high in the centre of an artificial island in the Danube Park. It takes only thirty seconds for the high-speed elevator to reach the revolving restaurant two thirds of the way up.

The restaurant in the Danube Tower.

The great river glittered 170 metres below me in the moonlight. To the west a bright expanse of lights marked out Vienna, stretching all the way to the hills. The watchtower slowly rotated, like the moon, one side always in the light. To the east the great Slovakian plains lay in complete darkness. In two thousand years, had anything really changed?

A waiter in white cotton gloves showed me to an empty table. It was laid for two with silver cutlery on a white tablecloth. A Manhattan glass containing a 'Pink Lady' cocktail told me that Miss Seawright was already here. Perhaps the Royal Navy were building Vienna's new emperors another Ferris wheel…

Leningrad Viewer - Meopta - Reel (Vienna)

BRATISLAVA

A New Capital, 1965

Although my application for a visa to visit Budapest was rejected, it seemed that I had been deemed suitable to visit Bratislava. I wondered if this was coincidence, an administrative error, or if there is something special about Budapest that they were keeping me away from. It is best not to dwell on how such systems work. They are very vague and uncaring on the one hand and yet curiously vindictive and personal on the other. But as Miss Seawright often says, we can only work with what we're given. She usually means me. So Bratislava it was.

The River Danube is over 1,800 miles long. On its way to the Black Sea it passes through ten countries linking four capital cities. It is an artery central to Europe's development since prehistoric times, but it had been severed. It would take Richard and I just over an hour to sail The Seagull from Vienna to the capital of the Slovakian Socialist Republic. Budapest is just four hours along the river beyond that. But the pleasure cruisers lining up by the quay did not go that way. Chains blocked the river which was seeded with mines and hidden obstacles. Gunships patrolled the border and there were machine gun nests along the banks. Central Europe was looking west no more.

The Südbahnhof had only recently been modernised. It was a dirty old classical building with blackened pillars and a shattered glass roof. It was now a very clean but slightly soulless glass box. Making it slightly less clean was a dirty black steam engine with an obnoxious white star on its nose, that was belching dark smoke upwards at the roof. Everyone was giving it a wide berth in the same way that Austrians would cross the street in embarrassment to get away from a black shirt. But it was the only way to get to Bratislava and Englishmen are used to embarrassing trains.

The countryside east of Vienna is absolutely flat, like a billiard table. The Danube hides behind the long trackside grass and if it weren't for all the soot and ashes blowing from the engine, I could have smelled it. Occasionally wooden farm buildings and corrugated iron roofs popped up but there was really very little there at all, which is why it looked so dark at night. In no time at all we arrived at Petrzalka which was just a series of concrete blocks at carriage height where there might normally be a platform, and where there would normally be a station building there was a concrete fortress bristling with guns. A couple of tanks were parked neatly beside it, their barrels aiming straight at the train. We were all turfed off and there was a half-hour wait as papers and the train itself were checked. Guard dogs were walked underneath the wheels sniffing for stowaways, but the train was going in the wrong direction for that. The sad thing is that they don't understand this, they think they were protecting Czechoslovakia from corrupt Westerners trying to get in.

We were off once again and as we bent round to the south, I got a brief glimpse of the actual land border. There was a tall chain fence on the western side and then a wide strip of nothing except land mines, cleared for the machine guns. There was an inner metal fence that was electrified and had alarms and every kilometre a guard tower with sentries. Given how flat the land is you could see them stretching off into the distance like clothes pegs on a washing line. The tanks were clearly Russian even though they flew Slovakian flags, as were the guns the guards carried. Vienna knows that if it came to it they wouldn't stand a chance. The Americans wouldn't even try to save them. No, the defensive line is five-hundred miles further west in Hesse-Thuringian deep in West Germany.

I liked Bratislava immediately. It is laid out like a toy town, a large white castle high up on the hill, an old medieval section with narrow lanes at its foot. A few grand squares with Renaissance palaces and fountains and then of course the Danube itself, complete with a shiny new bridge that the Soviets had built. They had made many changes to this place since the end of the war, elevating it from a sleepy rural town to a regional capital. New buildings were everywhere, not least 'Union Park', a typically Soviet public space with geometric fountains and flower beds, squared off on all sides by multi-storey giant buildings for the Post & Telecommunications Ministry, the new 'House of Culture' and a brand-new technical university. Forests of residential tower blocks had sprung up all around the old town, and the Imperial Hapsburg Eagle that sat above the train station entrance had been enclosed in a concrete and glass cage like a museum piece. There are plenty of buildings here such as the Primate's Palace that have that typically Austrian grand style, but on the whole the town is visibly more German & Hungarian. I should say Slavic, but I'm not sure what that means architecturally. After the war the German population was forcibly ejected by the Slavs, with Russian help, but their wood framed structures, sloping roofs and spired churches are still here. A series of elegantly-fronted eighteenth-century buildings with pastel-coloured facades led me in through a maze of narrow cobbled lanes to the historic centre. Old arched doorways and gates hinted at hidden courtyards. The quiet shaded streets were coated in creams and pink, like gentle ice-cream flavours, and every so now and then a spire and a burst of green copper appeared above the roofs. It was not unlike Bath in some ways. There was hardly any traffic to speak of at all.

I emerged in a small square, which was absolutely bursting with buckets of flowers presided over by old women in headscarves. The smell of the flowers, in such a confined space, was overpowering. I wondered if I was going to be pressganged into buying some and I instantly panicked. What type, not yellow that's unlucky, how many, not an even number. I need not have worried. They saw my black suit and looked away unwilling to even lock eyes with me.

Aside from the old castle on the top of the hill, the Primate's Palace was the most exotic building in town, but even this was quite restrained, only a little more pompous than Bath's Pump House & Tea Rooms. It was built in the late eighteenth century for the Bishop of Bratislava. A 150kg iron model of his cardinal's hat sat above the triangular pediment and the statues along the roofline were meant to celebrate his qualities and achievement. There were five quite tasteful salons inside each, themed around a colour, green, brown, red and gold. It was functional rather than homely, but there was none of the Hapsburgs' extravagance here. The slight exception was the hall of mirrors, where Napoleon signed the ill-fated peace treaty with Austria in 1805. The little general, seemed to be following me around. (Actually, he was of perfectly normal height for the time and the whole thing about him being small is a subsequent vilification.) The hall was a modest size ballroom, not much larger than the one in Bath's Guildhall. The mirrored arches serve the dual purpose of making the room look larger and passing along light from the windows at one end. It was practical rather than excessive and all the better for it.

The Primate's Palace, Bratislava.

It was however a great surprise to see that the palace housed a collection of tapestries from Mortlake in England. As I have already said English wool was much prized in mediaeval times, about 45,000 sacks a year being exported for processing in towns like Bruges where workshops had access to technical innovations such as the spinning wheel and the horizontal loom. But by the end of the fifteenth century wool was also being processed to a finished state in London, especially as trade began to shift from wool to cloth. Mortlake, by Richmond on Thames, was a centre of tapestry production sponsored by Charles I and it seemed that the factory had clients all over Europe.

I was staying at the Hotel Kyjev, a sixteen-storey concrete tower block that stretched up into the sky as if daring the heavens to strike it. It towered over everything in the city, but that was not a bad thing. My room on the ninth floor had a small outside terrace which I was slightly afraid to go out onto, but the views over the brown tiled roofs towards the castle were amazing.

The hotel lobby was full of red leather sofas and oversized columns, with hints of ethnic Slavic woodwork on display behind huge flower displays. There was a very sleazy looking red lounge bar that smelt of sweat, cheap tobacco and knockoff perfume and incredibly, an open-air swimming pool on the roof. I was almost tempted to try it. Almost...

There were people queuing up to try what was billed as an 'American Breakfast' which seemed to involve a lot of fried pancake batter, but they were missing out. I ate an heroic pile of poppyseed blini, scrambled egg and cheese-filled filo parcels topped in sour cream before heading out to explore once again. Wherever you are in the world I do urge people to eat the local food – you cannot go far wrong. Cornflakes and waffles are not a good way to start the day, but perhaps if I ever get to America itself, I will give it a go and they might convince me otherwise. The coffee in Bratislava was unfortunately not great and I decided to stick to black lemon tea.

I spent the day wandering vaguely, getting the feel for the place, up the hill to the castle, where I saw young families picnicking in the woods and playing outdoors, through the lanes to the Gothic Town Hall, where I enjoyed a beer while studying some beautiful but unmarked fifteenth-century frescoes, and down to the river where I had a glass of lemonade and watched as hundreds of homemade dinghies scooted back and forth on the water, enthusiastic dads in short sleeved shirts teaching their kids to sail. Confusingly the term 'lemonade' here seemed to mean any type of carbonated drink and has nothing to do with lemons. I had some sort of fizzy raspberry concoction, which was very pleasant, but the locals seem to go mad for something called 'Kofola' which looks and smells as unpleasant as the Western original.

I felt compelled to visit the Soviet War Memorial. The grounds were a beautifully landscaped park of treelined gravelled paths that overlooked the whole town. It was popular with young couples who embraced each other on benches in the shadows or lay on blankets in the sunken lawns. There were bronze statues by local artists many of which are quite impressive, and at the centre the eternal flame burnt, forty metres above which was a statue of a Soviet soldier, but he could really be from anywhere. Everyone lost family in the war, everyone suffered. It is not a competition in any way, but the scale of the Russian loss is staggering, mind blowing, and I do feel that that needs to be taken into consideration more in international affairs by people like Kennedy and his successors. Britain and America lost nearly 400,000 soldiers and Britain 50,000 civilians. That's bad, but the Russians lost twenty-million, four million in Leningrad alone. It is not the same.

The Soviets had left their mark on Bratislava already and it wasn't just the showy buildings in the town centre, the new bridge, the war memorial and the Hotel Kyjev. They were trying to change the nature of the people that lived there. There was a brand-new university, a new concert hall, a new hospital, several new districts of residential tower blocks, a new railway station and an airport. They were keen for Slovakia to mean something real that wasn't either German or Austrian and that was completely understandable.

Above the beech trees was something else they'd left: the most extraordinary building that I've ever seen. I was looking at it, but my mind didn't know how to process what it was seeing. The Slovak Radio Building is an eighty-metre-high bright red pyramid with six floors of glass peeking out from behind a bronzed lattice. It is larger than the Pyramid of Menkaure that I had seen for myself in Egypt and about half the size of the Great Pyramid. It contains a five-hundred seat concert hall along with offices, teaching facilities and engineering equipment. It is by no means small, but it is, however, literally upside down. Quite impossibly, the entire building is balanced on the point of that pyramid. There are no external supports, and no obvious means of stabilisation at all. How it remains upright I do not know. It simply levitates like an unquestionable, supernatural statement beyond human under-standing. It represents academic socialism in Bratislava. I loved it!

A competition was held for the design of Bratislava's new 'Radio Tower', which was responsible for delivering Socialism's message to the city. The upside-down pyramid design did not win the competition but somebody in Moscow, believed to be Andropov, overturned the Slovakian Politburo's decision in its favour stating that the winning design had 'no meaning and was unimaginative' whereas this was clearly a 'bold, thought provoking and futuristic design' that the local community could be proud of as 'an addition to their town and new ways of thinking, rather than being an imposition on it'.

The Slovak Radio Building as it is today.

I ate dinner in one of the many public canteens for a change and it immediately took me back to my university days. It was a pale-yellow building with a plain tiled interior and dim tungsten lighting. Women in white aprons and starched white headscarves stood guard behind stainless steel counters, scientifically ladling out precise portions onto Bakelite trays. I had a bowl of cabbage soup, with a chunk of rye bread to start and potato dumplings for mains but hold what you're thinking because it was nothing like you are imagining, was ridiculously cheap and was phenomenally tasty. Boiled water was poured from a large jug into a thick bottomed glass to go with it. This last was exactly as bad as it sounds.

First off, the cabbage soup was not some thin watery green liquid with bits of disintegrating leaves drowning in it. It was dark orange, thick and creamy with large chunks of spicy chorizo-like sausage bobbing about on the surface. Yes, there was a background tang of cabbage but there was also plenty of melted cheese, sour cream and spices in the foreground. As for the dumplings they were very similar to Italian gnocchi, but larger and cheesier too. The sauce was yet another vehicle to show off sour cream but was full of delicious herbs and onions. Healthy it was not, filling it certainly was, and all for less than the cost of a cup of tea in England. I'd happily return!

Bratislava's Opera House, the Slovak National Theatre, is slightly disappointingly a copy of Vienna's, built in 1886 by the rather dull Viennese architect Friedrich Fellner. Two layers of cream and caramel, three sections with three windows in each layer and a bay balcony in the centre. Perhaps the Soviets will someday put a more original spin on it, or better still the people of Bratislava themselves. It would be interesting to ask the women serving in the canteen, or those selling flowers in the central square, what they thought of opera and what changes they'd like to see to their city. Modern apartments with indoor private bathrooms and modern appliances in the kitchen are understandably everyone's priority all over Europe, but I hope that the new generation of Slovaks doesn't grow up associating opera with an outdated Austrian aristocracy.

Outside the opera house, Tilgner's superb statue of Ganymede sits at the centre of a public fountain on the back of a giant eagle. His arm is reaching up with an offering to Zeus in return for eternal youth. Fish from the Danube leap all around him and his face is overcome with joy. It is a fabulous piece of sculpture, but I wonder what it means and why it is here. One has to assume that it is the Austrian Imperial Eagle and that Ganymede represents the overjoyed people of Bratislava, but that does rather fly in the face of the fact that in 1848 the city rebelled against Austrian rule and joined the side of Hungary's revolutionaries. Hapsburg pomposity does not sit well with Slovaks.

9PM. A beautiful young woman walked out onto the dark stage to muted applause; a small Slovakian brooch was attached to her long scarlet dress. She took her place at the piano holding her head up high, her blonde ponytail hanging neatly in the centre of her ramrod straight back. This was in itself theatre. She was here representing Slovakia, a nationality that before the war made up less than fifteen percent of Bratislava's population. Her position was artificial, and the Soviets were making it clear that it was they who put the Slovak minority in charge, and they could take it away. According to the programme notes she was twenty-four. That meant she was a product of their system, taught in Bratislava's Soviet-built music academy by Russian teachers. Yet she had the city's massive musical heritage to live up to, Mozart, Haydn, Beethoven, Liszt. She was an innocent civilian caught between a Western past and an Eastern future. She was undoubtedly terrified for multiple reasons but bravely refusing to show it.

The romantic composer Franz Liszt was a Hungarian, who grew up here in Bratislava and it was his piano concertos that the young Viera Janárčeková was performing that night. Liszt was a virtuoso on the piano and his compositions are famously complex and fiendishly difficult to play. I'm afraid to say that it is his 'Les Preludes' tone poem that I am most familiar with being the theme tune and background music to the 1930's serial 'Flash Gordon'. The concerto started with a stentorian phrase from the string section, replied to by the wind section. The piano butted into this conversation and accelerated away with a series of increasingly impressive cadenzas. Fist shaking turned into crushing waves of emotion, the pianist struggling to stay on top with an escalation of blazing octaves and intense arpeggios running up and down the keyboard until, completely exhausted, she collapsed. It was short, very dramatic and really quite violent, but my gosh it was good! I rarely play my own recording of the 1st Piano Concerto, but whenever I do, the striking image of that poor brave girl seated in the spotlight, centre stage in Bratislava, comes immediately to mind. I wonder where she is now…

She is doing very well for herself dad. She lives in Homburg, Germany and is composer in residence for the Lockenhaus Orchestra and Festival.

Liszt wrote many concertos for piano, but these two are the only ones he labelled as such. They are both highly unusual. According to his son-in-law, the conductor Hans von Bulow, Liszt put words to the opening phrase of his piano concerto: "Das versteht Ihr alle nicht, haha!" ("None of you understand this, ha-ha!").

My final day in Bratislava and I chose to spend it down on the river. I left town through the old fishing gate, one of the last remaining parts of the once formidable fortifications and walked along the old wharfs of the marina. An electric blue hydrofoil sat at the end of the quay, its little red pennants flapping in the wind. Two men in olive green military uniform checked the papers of anyone boarding. Budapest was just two and half hour's cruise away for those permitted to travel, but for me it was beyond reach. I never did find out why.

The Danube is not blue, but a murky shade of brown, its bottom is full of silt from the deposits of thousands of miles which constantly gets churned up as boats pass. Across the river from the Marina is the Ovsist Park. It is a wide stretch of unmanaged woodland that runs down to the water, revealing a muddy beach when the river is low. It is a fantastic playground for the kids that build treehouses here and who search the shoreline for treasure that they can recycle. The tree canopy is full of birds and squirrels dart from branch to branch. I fancy that there are wild boar and other animals amongst the bushes too, remnants of a long forgotten wilder Europe. I took out the short stubby blade on my penknife and went in search of mushrooms like an old babushka, packing them down into my suit pockets gleefully whenever I found them. Dirt paths turned to gravel ones, and small stone bridges started to span the murky green ponds that appeared between the trees. Rusovský Park was once the royal hunting ground of the Hungarian kings who moved their capital here when the Turks captured Budapest.

Walking amongst the moss-covered ruins, I was reminded that it was only fairly recently in the late eighteenth century that Hungary and the Slavic lands fell into the Austrian orbit. Before then, for almost six-hundred years, this crossroads at the heart of Europe had been part of the Arapine kingdom that had stretched across the Carpathian Mountains north into Poland, east into Romania and south into Italy itself, making it the largest country in Europe, and one of the richest. Suleiman the Magnificent wanted access to those riches and the Danube itself, forcing the kings of Hungary to move their capital as close to their neighbours as possible and away from the front lines. In 1684 the Holy League, a forerunner of the United Nations, was formed to stop them. It included not only the Poles, the Hungarians and the Austrians, but the Venetians and the Russians too. It created a post-Roman, Christian version of Europe that completely excluded countries in the West. It was successful, saving Vienna & Venice, recovering Belgrade and Budapest and putting an end to the Turkish threat. Naturally enough, it rarely figures in the history books of Western Europe.

'Net Vkhoda!' Entry is prohibited to the overgrown ruins of Rusovsky

Slowly, from between the trees, came a derelict neo-Gothic mansion, complete with crenelated towers, aviary and 'English Garden'. The last remaining Hungarian palace in Bratislava, deserted and crumbling, but still official home to a Hungarian prince.

From Rusovsky I caught a small boat from back up the river to Castle Devin, which sits at the very point where the Morava River joins the Danube. The castle dates back to Roman times of course, but what you see is the ruin of a mighty fortress built in the twelfth century at the centre of which is, appropriately, a church and a market. The castle stood intact, proudly protecting trade on the river until Napoleon's forces demolished it in 1809. Everyone – Slavs and Celts, Hungarians, Austrians, the Romans and Napoleon's army – has left their mark on this place. Even the caves deep in the rock under the ruins are full of chalk drawings and seeds from far away. Archaeologists have found trade goods from as far away as Russia and China here, as well as more wool from Britain.

I went in search of an outdoor restaurant by the river, something like I found in East Berlin, and the smell of charcoal smoke quickly drew me to one. Men were grilling fish fresh from the river on wooden spikes while old women in headscarves did battle with large metal bowls of stew. There was a small tanker from which someone was selling pint glasses of beer to go with it and so I sat down on a wooden bench and enjoyed, for less than the cost of a packet of mints, a plate of lemon pasta with a fillet of smoked zander and a pint of beer. It was truly fabulous. Strange that there are no boats out on the water.

Castle Devin on the River Danube.

But something marred my otherwise perfect lunch. The shadow of barbed wire fell across my plate, the outline of a watchtower was reflected in the surface of my beer. For Castle Devin is where the Iron Curtain cuts the Danube, and Europe, in two. It is a travesty, and it must go, but how? How can it be disassembled when politicians on both sides still rattle their sabres noisily and nations squabble amongst themselves like children? It is not a simple question of good versus bad; the darkness versus the light. The wall exists in our own minds more so than it does in reality, and it will only really vanish when we learn that there are no such things as countries, when we have learnt how to administer ourselves, to value each other's opinions and when nationalism is completely dead.

I was sorry to leave Bratislava, it felt warm and comforting, homely almost, whereas Vienna felt cold, pompous and arrogant. I felt that I could live somewhere by the river in Bratislava with its quiet pastel-coloured lanes and hearty canteens, but I'd only want to visit Vienna occasionally, like a difficult aunt. Vienna is unquestionably a bridge between cultures, but I wonder which way round that bridge is and whether the traffic really flows both ways. Slovakia was looking to the future, a new future and a new way of life, or at least trying to anyway, whereas Austria seemed to be stuck in the past, a false past. Like Britain, Austria is almost at the point of denial, the past it imagines is not a real one, and therefore its role in the real world is somewhat fake too. I hope it finds a version of itself that it can live with, before it is twisted too far into being an international shop front or bar. The true history of this wonderful centre of Europe is far more colourful and cosmopolitan than the surface Hapsburg gloss and involves many more colourful characters and cultures, such as the Poles, the Turks and the Romanians, that really we should be taught more about. I made a promise to do more reading about the history of Central Europe when I got home. My time here had run out once more. Before I knew it the Stadtbahn was pulling into the airport and my plane was waiting to fly me back to the edge of Europe from its very heart.

I think it is briefly worth mentioning here Crown Prince Otto von Hapsburg (photo overleaf), the son of the last Austrian Emperor Charles I, and a genuine European hero. Charles was always trying to regain his lost crown, and we'd naturally expect his son to be a little resentful and bitter likewise. Not so. Otto was vehemently opposed to Hitler and his right-wing policies from the start, so much so that several attempts were made on his life during the thirties, and he had to flee to Britain. After the war he became a European politician, the first Chairman of the Council of Europe and President of the 'PanEuropean Union' which he set up. For his entire life he made it his mission to better integrate East and West, and promote better cultural understanding, sponsoring numerous initiatives on both sides of the Iron Curtain. He learnt Russian, Hungarian and Polish keeping seats on committees available for the 'Eastern Bloc' countries which became his subject specialism. By definition he was 'stateless' holding a passport from the Order of Malta. He died in 2011 and chose to be buried in Hungary, his life's work complete.

Crown Prince Otto von Hapsburg.

YUGOSLAVIA

Brotherhood and Unity, 1966

arket Socialism arrived at Heathrow in the form of DC-9, and very nice it looked too, a glistening silver plane with a smart blue tail. It was my first experience of flying in this particular airliner and what an experience it was. I was escorted to the front of the plane by ladies in smart navy-blue uniforms and shown to a very comfortable deep leather seat. There were newspapers in English, Serbian and Russian, 'Spasibo' and a glass of wine to welcome guests aboard. Better still was the cup of delicious Italian coffee served with 'borek', a little like quiche in deep fried filo pastry, after we had thundered down the runway and swept up into the blue sky. We flew high above the clouds, so high that there was virtually no turbulence. I have had rougher train rides, especially in Britain.

Unusually I had done no preparation for this holiday as my mind had been on other matters. The whole venture had in fact been a last-minute decision. I had picked up some pre-prepared travel notes from the Embassy in Kensington Gardens along with my tickets, so I spent much of the flight retrospectively reading about the country, whilst sipping an unexpectedly good Serbian Shiraz. My notes tell me that they have been making wine in Yugoslavia for longer than they have in France. The shattering of Europe into ideological zones of control complicated the logistics but getting to Yugoslavia was much simpler than it had been flying to Berlin just a few years before. We followed almost the same route that we had to Greece before turning out across the Aegean and heading for the rocky azure coast. The plane seemed to be heading towards the dark shadows of the Montenegrin mountains, before turning sharply and descending over sun kissed valleys of vineyards and landing almost on the beach itself. What an entrance!

Dubrovnik's Hilton Imperial Hotel.

The Imperial was a magnificent Victorian style hotel right on the seafront. It was rather luxurious, and I felt ever so slightly guilty, but I was beginning to get accustomed to fancy hotels. I drank an excellent cup of tea in the gardens and watched the sun set over the water, just soaking in the quiet atmosphere.

It was the shortest of walks, from the hotel to the old town, past a couple of small coves where crystal clear water foamed over white pebbles and across a small footbridge before passing in through a gap in those thick walls under the glare of St. Blaise himself. There were hardly any tourists, and nobody spoke English. The little town was all the better for it. I followed no particular route, ambling down first one winding alley then another, every one of which seemed to contain a view that I could sit and stare at for hours. In the absence of an easel and some paint, I decided to acquire a sketch book at least, but from where? There were few shops of any kind here let alone an art suppliers.

I took all day making a slow circuit of the city's ramparts, stopping here and there and descending into the town for a coffee or a light snack. No more borek, but side plates of fresh fish served in butter, with salad plucked from the plants in the gardens that had been created in the midst of the crumbling city walls. I sat so quietly that the locals soon forgot about the strange man in a dark suit. Even in the market square watching the police control a queue for potatoes no one worried about me.

Dubrovnik, or Ragusa as it was known during its heyday, is quite unique, at heart just a small church, with an easily defendable harbour in a very beautiful setting. It was an important community in the Byzantine Empire before becoming in the Middle Ages a naval power in its own right, yet another one, and finally the capital of the Republic of Radusa, which I have always thought sounded like a type of stew. Caught between the mountains and the sea, the growth of the town was limited to what we see today, giving it a quiet charm that its bigger rivals such as Venice simply don't have. There is no wheeled traffic allowed within the old city walls, leaving visitors with the constant awareness of the sea that surrounds them. It is lovely rather than beautiful and in many ways I prefer that – and I much preferred the temperature here to that of Greece.

At the end of the Placa is a straight street that runs from the Square of St. Peter to the fortress, its flagstones polished as if they are wet. There is a small square containing the Town Hall, a couple of old palaces and the cathedral. The last remnants of the Habsburg aristocracy that tried to restore the city's former independence. What were Austrians doing here? Standing in front of buildings no bigger than the Georgian townhouses of Bath and a church far smaller than its abbey, it seemed as ridiculous for anyone to try and make this funny little town into a state, as ridiculous as it would be to attempt to make Bath a country. A nation? No, but an independent authority as part of a wider integrated union, perhaps… That after all is what Dubrovnik had been for hundreds of years under Byzantine rule.

The great walls encircle the town completely, a maze of alleys and stairways climbing up the hill, little doorways, little balcony gardens, family groups sitting on the steps with elders chatting in the shade of an old cypress tree. It is an enchanting place. From the ramparts the roofscape was glorious. Not only the great sea of tiles from brown, through orange to red of every conceivable shade, but a whole separate world, four storeys up, of flats and large roof gardens, where dogs and sometimes cattle roamed. I saw two women talking quietly, sitting in separate gardens not four feet apart, but with a sixty-foot chasm between them. The sun shone and sparkled on the silvery stone, the sea that incredible almost luminous blue splashed gently against the flat rocks and little pebbled beaches outside the town. The small boats in the harbour bobbed up and down and the great arches from which ships were once launched and that gave the world the word 'Argosy', threw their cool shadow over the town. It was truly delightful.

Back at the hotel someone had found me some paper. It was cheap material, almost thin enough to see through and unbleached, but it would do.

Oil Painting of Dubrovnik Town & Harbour.

At this time tourism was only just beginning seriously and many places, now resorts, had no hotels, or perhaps just one very old one. There was no concept of the 'Dalmatian Highway'. The tourist agency 'Atlas' was, let's be kind, uneven in its service, and luxuries such as Kodak or Aspirin were unknown to shopkeepers. But on the other hand, a more intimate connection with the country was possible than could be experienced today. Back then visitors, foreigners, were special guests. I remember going into a small cafe, a 'Kafana' as they are called, in a small town in Montenegro while waiting for a bus. Dark faces with huge moustaches looked at me, in my suit, fiercely. A splendid, bearded patriarch, stomped over, a sharp knife glistening in his belt. He indicated that there would be no payment for the little cups of black coffee in his village, and that he would be insulted if I didn't try some 'zimnica' on a slice of bread. Such generosity was common, especially in the countryside. I offered a toast, 'To Brotherhood!' and shared out my Dunhill cigarettes in exchange. They found the filters most curious.

At Cetinje, the palace of Nicholas (Montenegro's only king) was closed. The custodian was having a coffee in a café opposite. He was amused that my name was also Nicholas and greatly admired my tie, which was silk. I had another back at the hotel, and in the same spirit of brotherly generosity I offered it to him. So it was that a couple of minutes later I stepped, sans tie, into the royal palace.

The museum was interesting historically but not architecturally. My host looked increasingly uncomfortable as I walked quickly from room to room, looking around casually but focusing on nothing in particular. In truth it was rather eerie being alone in a huge building with forty-foot-high ceilings. He decided that it had not been a fair exchange. I had given him a silk tie; all he had offered me was a substandard palace. We stood at the door awkwardly. 'Come with me,' he said, holding the tie carefully as he turned the keys in the lock. I followed him to a livid blue Zastava police car that was sat there quietly with a moustachioed officer behind the wheel.

'Poydem!'

After a tour of the historic town centre, the monastery and a beautiful little church with a fence made out of the barrels of captured enemy rifles, we drove out to the rugged mountains where I was lined up in front of a gated cave where other militiamen patrolled with guns. For a split second I wondered if they planned to rob me and dispose of my body here. It seemed unlikely, and certainly unwise. The Lipa cave complex is one of the largest in Yugoslavia. It had been of strategic importance during the Austrian occupation and King Nikola himself was known to take foreign dignitaries there. Today it is one of the biggest tourist attractions in the area, but at the time it was not open to the public. The caves are much larger than those of Cheddar Gorge that I was familiar with, and I saw only a small portion of them. They did not contain the prehistoric artwork that I'd seen in the Pyrenees, but were fascinating, nevertheless. My police guides were fantastic, although I couldn't shake the feeling that they were leading me down to inspect a dismembered body.

After about an hour we returned to the surface to find a free lunch that the squad were tucking into. They insisted on giving me a lift all the way back to my hotel in Dubrovnik, which made for a few curious looks and doubtless some gossip. My host had certainly paid for his tie!

The hotel had organised a coach for the small group of us willing to venture further than the beach. A few I recognised from the tables at breakfast but at least two of the tourists taking their seats seemed slightly out of place. Shifty. The woman sat near the front and stared forward the whole time not looking at anyone or anything as far as I could tell. She wore large sunglasses and a headscarf so may have been a celebrity ignoring the riff raff. I wouldn't know. The man sat at the back of the bus with a newspaper, chewing on a cheap paper cigarette and reading the same pages over and over again. I noted them and sat down to enjoy the view. The coast immediately south of Dubrovnik was lovely and unspoilt. It rolls up and down gently like a boat on the sea, up through woods covered in spruce trees then down into the next cove with yet another little village. At Mlini the flowers came right down to the sea, where a curved stone wall sheltered the little fishing boats. I had a splendid meal in a little taverna on the harbour front, called the 'Konoba Lanterna'. The fish had been plucked straight from the water that morning by the men who sat at the bar grinning expectantly. I wouldn't have changed a thing about the place, and yet they were only too keen to show me the sites where the foundations of two enormous hotels had been pegged out. I had my reservations, but they seemed too happy for the future for me to not want to share them.

The woman with the headscarf and sunglasses had temporarily disappeared, but I noticed, predictably, that the man with the newspaper had not eaten.

The Ikarus bus climbed gingerly up the narrow road as it snaked up the cliff face, gingerly not because the engine was struggling with the slope, but because the bus was clearly brand new. The driver was evidently trusted and competent, but it was obvious to me that he was terrified that he was going to scrape it on one of the many protruding sections of rock. He looked frantically around every time we hit a pothole, the woman in the headscarf tutting and taking notes. At the top of one hill, he stopped completely despite the fact that the road was clear. It was curious but I did not mind. The view was fabulous. The man with the newspaper glanced at his watch and continued reading in a bored fashion. Boom! An incredible bang echoed along the valley making everyone jump. Rocks rolled down the hill and crashed across the road. The larger pieces were dragged to the side, and then once again we were free to go.

Much to my surprise I saw that many of the workforce were children. Teenagers and young adults dressed in shabby dungarees swung sledgehammers with their bare hands as they sang. A sort of happy chain-gang. These youth brigades were a fundamental part of growing up under Socialism and were seen as both a rite of passage and building community spirit. Such projects joined up to form what was known at the time as the 'Highway of Brotherhood and Unity'. They would live to tell their children stories of shovel-inflicted blisters, of solidarity and joy. I was glad to see, however, that at least a few professionals were involved in building what was to become the start of the 'Dalmatian Highway'. So loud and continuous was the blasting, that it sounded like an artillery barrage.

At Kotor the tarmac petered out altogether and the bus lurched over a cart track across the fields, apparently making for a little village. There was no other traffic at all. At the village a ferry was to take us across the fjord. It was a curiously-made craft consisting of two wooden hulls strapped together with a flat wooden raft across the top. The ferry sank deeper and deeper into the water. Given how terrified our driver was of scratching the bus I wondered what reaction the authorities would give if the bus actually sank? Even behind her dark glasses I could tell that the woman in the headscarf was appalled. This really amused me. The bus now looked far bigger than the semi-submerged ferry. It overhung it on all sides so that from the windows I stared straight down into that dark green water. No boat was visible at all from inside the bus. I could hear swearing and cursing outside and the sound of wrenches being bashed against pipes. I imagined the water pouring in through the pneumatic doors. The woman in the headscarf would be one of the first to get sucked down into the icy depths. I could picture it now, the frantic screams, and all that would be left of her treachery would be the immaculately written notes floating on the surface of the fjord.

An outboard motor roared angrily. The man with the newspaper seemed to have noticed nothing.

The road, a proper one, round to Kotor was lovely. The little houses along the side of the fjord each had its own little harbour. Byron had lived in one of them when he wrote that, 'At the birth of the planet the most beautiful encounter between land and sea must have been on the Montenegrin coast.' I am inclined to agree, although I assume that Byron did not arrive here on such a precarious raft.

Budva Harbour as remembered by my father.

At the head of the fjord, right under the shadow of the mountains lies the little mediaeval town of Kotor, another Venetian possession, another jewel in the Byzantine crown. Once it was a great port, the beginning of the trade route to Istanbul, but now it lies, almost entirely forgotten, overgrown with weeds and moss. Large thick ramparts surround the seaward side, inside them the now familiar pattern of a long rectangular piazza, a town hall, cathedral and that most important place of focus, the clock tower. Streets with low arcades seemed full of cats sheltering from the sun, while the wide jetty was lined with palm trees. I sat in a Pescaria in front of the old Romanesque cathedral and enjoyed a delicious plate of pasta and a local red wine, ignoring the angry glares from the cats and the UDBA spies alike.

The city has seen intense fighting over the centuries, and it is remarkable that it is preserved so well (it is a UNESCO World Heritage site). The Venetians fought continuously with the Turks over the city for nearly four-hundred years, before it was captured by the Austrians and became part of the Hapsburg Empire. Both the French and Russians invaded it, and the British in 1914. The Italians invaded in 1941, until the British invaded again in 1943 and removed them. It became part of Yugoslavia in 1947, triggering the longest period of peace it has probably ever seen. Since the early 2000s it has become a stop on the Mediterranean cruise circuit, over 1000 people passing through the town each day.

Beyond Kotor the road swings inconspicuously off to the right, passing a brand-new factory. This is the beginning of 'The Serpentine', one of the great roads of Europe. Twenty-four hairpin bends give the road its name, blasted out of the rock by Austrian engineers to connect the town with military positions in the mountains. By bus it is five kilometres from its start to the edge of the Montenegrin plateau, yet the longitudinal distance is just four hundred metres. In that time, it climbs seven hundred metres vertically. It starts in mid-summer warmth under palm trees in the region of Croatia but finishes in Montenegro with snow still lying in the hollows beneath rocks. What few trees there were, were bare. Most of us braved the howling wind to take in the incredible view. The man with the newspaper and the lady with the headscarf stayed on the bus.

The green shoulders of the mountains ran down to the sea, no longer the deep green it was during the ferry crossing, but now an impossible blue. To the right, snow-capped mountains, to the left a coastal plain stretching off into the hazy distance, perhaps even to Istanbul. It was an extraordinary place, the crossroads of a continent that we have almost forgotten. As I sat reflecting upon all this, there was the slightest of sounds and suddenly, materialising from the grey background, came a long train of mules. The people that accompanied them were so drably dressed that they blended in and were as silent as the beasts they led. Silently they disappeared up the original path into the mist. I felt that I had seen ghosts from long ago, the start of a mediaeval caravan embarking on its long trek, and perhaps, when I looked down at the town, I would see galleys in the harbour far below.

It was from this position on the 1st October 1991, that the Yugoslavian People's Army first opened fire on the World Heritage sites of Kotor and Dubrovnik, during the war of Croatian independence. The bombardment provoked international condemnation and became a public relations disaster for Serbia and Montenegro. We should not be surprised that different cultures arise in ports along a shared coast, from those found in the mountain hinterland. My father was always clear that such differences are to be embraced and are certainly no basis for artificially drawing national boundaries.

Montenegro means 'Black Mountains' but it also implies 'bald' or 'bare' for nothing grows there. There is little soil, just loose stones like gravel. When peasants here come to market, they tend to carry back a basketful of earth or two from the coastal plain. With this they build their little fields and patches of cultivation, usually about four metres in diameter and try and grow their vegetables. According to locals it is the only place where a fox can starve to death. This is a land where agriculture needs state aid. But there are limits to what Market Socialism alone can achieve here in this bitter, proud, but fascinating land. It is what I think of when I hear Rimsky Korsakov's 'Night on a Bare Mountain'.

We ended our journey in Budva, another Venetian town on a sandy promontory. The town is rumoured to have been founded by Cadmus when he was exiled from Thebes and items from antiquity have been turning up on this beach for decades, including a bronze helmet from the fourth century B.C. now displayed in a local museum. Generations of defensive wall structures stagger their way back up the hill to the citadel. Like Kotor it was a Venetian holding until 1797 after which, like Kotor, it passed between the Austrians, the French and the Italians. As part of a united Yugoslavia the area has finally found peace. In recent times Budva has become a tourist resort, and the tiny village of St. Stephen is effectively a single hotel. Instead of a room, guests rent a cottage. The Town Hall is now a restaurant, the church its reception. Instead of a live village you have a fossilised shell. Tourism was getting close to Budva.

In the opposite direction from Dubrovnik, lies Mostar, in the region of Bosnia-Herzegovina (such a lovely name), and I was keen to see the famous bridge. With its steep polished stones and its slender arch over the turbulent stream it was every bit as graceful as it looks in all the photographs.

The 17th Century Ottoman explorer Evliya Çelebi wrote that the bridge 'is like a rainbow arch soaring up to the skies, extending from one cliff to the other... I have passed through 16 countries, but I have never seen such a high bridge. It is thrown from rock to rock as high as the sky.'

'Stari Most' The Old Bridge Mostar.

The bridge is Turkish, although it is built on the Roman foundations of an older bridge and unites the town's two sides by spanning the Neretva River. At the time of its construction, it was the widest man-made arch in the world. Its architect, charged under pain of death to construct a bridge of such unprecedented dimensions, reportedly prepared for his own funeral on the day the scaffolding was finally removed from the completed structure.

Beautiful though it is, Mostar has always been an industrial city, the narrow road over the bridge connecting the ports of the Adriatic to the mineral-rich interior. Plastic, tobacco, wine, aircraft and aluminium are all produced here, and several dams have been constructed to harness the wild power of the river. As a result, the city has expanded rapidly. Money was clearly flowing into it, not least from Moscow, and an extensive programme of renovation was underway in the old town, which they were more than keen to show us. The bridge is unsurprisingly in the heart of the Turkish quarter where all the houses were of different colours and had balconies overhanging the street. I was invited into one such house which was being restored. The fig tree in the courtyard was overlooked by a beautifully carved balcony. Cushions were scattered there, and in the living room tiny cups of coffee were served, not bitter like it had been in Dubrovnik or Egypt, but of an intense smoothness that I had never previously experienced. There were big mosques there that said nothing and little mosques where one precious illustrated copy of the Koran is proudly shown. Some women still wore the traditional baggy trousers. In the neglected cemetery the strange Turkish head and footstones leaned out at different drunken angles. I would like to go to Turkey one day, it being an important part of our history, but I doubt that I will have the time.

The Communists refer to mosques and churches as heritage buildings and religions as 'legacy' practices, but here they are tolerated equally, and what a fantastic heritage they are. It is all too easy to stand in the great cathedrals of Rome and Paris and say that Europe is Christianity, that the Holy Roman Empire is what defines us, but that would be to ignore the truth, for what is Europe without the Byzantines, the Venetians and the Ottomans? The Gothic architecture style that defines most of our medieval cathedrals was based almost entirely on Turkish ideas. To ignore the role of the Serbs and the Turks is to ignore that of the Austrians and the Franks. They are part of our family and a welcome part of our story.

From Mostar it was on to Sarajevo high up in the mountains, time for a quick stop and dinner before the overnight ride to Belgrade. Sarajevo is tucked inside a long, thin valley and surrounded on all sides by forested mountains. At almost every crossroads and street corner you are rewarded with a glimpse of an idyllic picture-postcard backdrop. The city skyline was unlike any other city I had seen. Mosques and minarets mingled freely with onion domes and the spires and towers of both Orthodox and Catholic churches. If religion was a legacy, then Sarajevo was a time capsule. It was an incredible mix of cultures, a melting point where religions met, and the Turkish and Austro-Hungarian empires clashed. Even on one street the contrast was acute, a mosaic of Western shops to the right, a bazaar to the left, cafés and bars serving beer on one side of the street, hookah pipes and coffee on the other. Swarms of pigeons accompanied us as we were ferried around the Baščaršija, the ancient market in the centre of town, and with stalls blocking out the sight of the mountains we could easily have been in Cairo. The Gazi Husrev-beg Mosque would also have felt at home in Egypt, but here we were, and here was the 'Latin Bridge'.

The bridge, despite its name, is Turkish, like the one at Mostar, and although more modest, is equally beautiful. You can see that a more confident architect has drawn this bridge mathematically rather than via engineering. To prove his point that the arches themselves would hold the load, circles were additionally cut out of the buttresses that held up the bridge. This 'proof' now adorns the city's coat of arms. It is a magnificent achievement. Sadly, the bridge is more famous for another reason.

On the afternoon of June 28th, 1914, a Bosnian revolutionary, Gavrilo Princip, threw a small bomb into the open topped carriage of Archduke Franz Ferdinand, heir to the Austro-Hungarian throne and fired shots from a pistol. The bridge is narrow, and the Archduke and his wife had no chance of survival. Less than two months later Austria declared war on Serbia, and by extension, Germany declared war on Russia, France and Britain. The bridge is now officially named in Comrade Princip's honour, but I'm not sure that that is entirely appropriate. The Great War was an argument long in the making, the result of conflicting Imperial expansionism and was hardly the poor boy's fault.

There is no railway over the Yugoslavian mountains, so it was by bus that I made the overnight journey to Belgrade. It was cold and bumpy, a huge contrast from my flight into Dubrovnik, and I didn't sleep at all. My companions huddled beneath their coats. None of them was either making notes or reading the newspapers.

Belgrade is as much a mix as everything else here. I had no high hopes for it, but I was proved entirely wrong. It was very refreshing.

It had rained overnight, and the flagstones of Republic Square were glistening. Water still dripped from the leaves of the maple and linden trees planted around its sides and caused the pantographs of the trams to sparkle and crackle. You could smell the water in the air, but also a sense of excitement. Belgrade was built where the Sava River joins the Danube and so the city is naturally split into three sections. Old Belgrade sits on the right bank of the Sava and dates back to the Roman era. It is full of the mediaeval and Romanesque buildings and the Ottoman influence that I had seen elsewhere. The Austro-Hungarian town of Zemun sits opposite it on the left bank with its Danube port. It is full of nineteenth-century and art deco buildings, pedestrian boulevards and the most tasteful of cafés. The area north of the Danube, twice the size of the other two, is 'New Belgrade', where most of the residents live and work. It is the home of Brutalist architecture, large parks, art museums and new Soviet tower blocks. Republic Square and the Fortress Park next door lie where the three Belgrades come together. The Square does not appear to have been planned, like it might be in London or Paris, and is completely informal. Even at that time of the morning it was full of smartly dressed young people, busily going about their daily lives. The buildings are a jumble of different styles and heights, the statue of Prince Michael is not placed centrally in the square. It should have been annoying, but it wasn't. I made a note to come back to the theatre and the National Museum later and continued walking down into the riverside park that surrounds the fortress.

It was cooler down by the river, but already the day was heating up. The rain still clung to the pine trees and long blades of grass, but they had begun to steam in the shafts of light that filtered through the grey clouds. Pensioners and middle-aged women were out walking small dogs, while businessmen in grey suits sat on benches and talked earnestly. Information boards and wooden benches were set out all along the winding paths, while neat squares of red crocuses lined themselves like soldiers waiting for the sun.

I zigzagged up the steep slope past picturesque fountains, statues, and ancient structures to the old citadel, passing in through the gates of its thick city walls. Although the ruins date back to the Roman era most of the buildings date from the fifteenth century when the despot Stefan Lazarević made Belgrade his capital. I viewed the remains of the Dormition Mother of God church-cum-mosque and the observatory in Stefan's tower, as well as the 'Roman

Well' which is neither Roman nor a well. Although plague was a major issue for the Ottomans in mediaeval times, the fortress has not fallen to military attack and one can see why. Even during the Great War all the Austrians could do was fire at it from the river or fly over and drop bombs. It still remains proudly obstinate.

'Brunch' was in a kafana in Skadarlija, an area in the Zemun part of the city with a real bohemian feel to it. Artists and musicians drifted round the tavernas, playing the accordion and drawing in chalk on the stones. There was a stall selling books and several selling paintings on little offcuts of card. The smell of wet leaves, coffee and strong tobacco filled the air. A jazz quartet played quietly in one corner. Nobody spoke a word of English, but it mattered not a jot. A coffee and a local newspaper were offered without even asking. There was no menu, but a series of small dishes of grilled vegetables and cream cheese rapidly appeared. I had been looking forward to some of that deep fried cheese in filo pastry but it was not to be. The wine – I'm afraid to say – went straight to my head.

With a name like 'The Hotel Moscow' I had expected my hotel to be one of those huge Soviet monoliths that are all concrete and glass with no character at all. I was therefore surprised to see an Art Deco building on a busy corner of downtown Belgrade. Built in the style of the Russian secession, its dining room and lounges were light and airy, decorated halfway in period brown tiles, halfway in white, with high ceilings, square columns and brass chandeliers. The ceilings were embossed with gold relief and tasteful geometric plasterwork, the floors a soft cream marble. My room was decorated in an old fashioned but quite tasteful way, with floral walls and dark wooden furniture, but had a balcony with a pleasing view out over the busy intersection. I noticed that a small pile of reading material had been placed on my bed.

I took my time at breakfast, ensuring that I once again caught up with that heavenly borek, and the Hotel Moskva did not disappoint. There was an excellent buffet of fresh meat and cheeses as well as French patisserie and the option of an 'American breakfast', while 'French', 'Italian' or 'Turkish' coffees were all on the menu. I had reserved a whole day to enjoy the National Museum which even at that time had more than 400,000 exhibits and a fabulous collection of many types of art, and was looking forward to it, when a white-suited young man appeared at my side to inform me that I had received a letter, but clearly not one that could be delivered to the table. The books I had ordered in advance, but who was writing to me, here in Yugoslavia? I had visions of a long list of complaints from the woman in the headscarf on the bus. It turned out that the letter was a short note from Miss Seawright who wanted me, no, was instructing me, to meet an acquaintance of hers who was also in Belgrade for dinner. How small the world is. To be honest I felt annoyed that someone had interrupted my holiday. I was slightly surprised that the Grande Dame wasn't here herself. Interrupting me was normally her job. But although she travelled widely, she never ventured behind the Iron Curtain.

The museum is housed in what was once a bank just to one side of Republic Square. Architecturally it is a dull and slightly pompous mix of cement columns, brick walls and shallow copper domes, that one might find acting as a council building in many rural towns in England, but its collection is extraordinary. It is unfocused to say the least, a clear statement that Belgrade itself has been influenced by all these cultures. Naturally the museum includes Serbian art from every era but also extensive collections of French, Dutch, Flemish, Italian, Russian, German, English, Spanish, Hungarian, Romanian, Bulgarian, and even Japanese and Chinese art. It was hard to know where to begin or what to look at.

The large nationalistic pieces such as the Coronation of Tsar Dušan left me as cold as ever, and instead I was drawn to the miniature icons in the Italian Collection, lost works by Titian, Raphael, Credi. But what I remember most about the museum in Belgrade are paintings of a series of 'shady' looking characters, characters that reminded me of the couple on the bus, and others that I had seen following me on the streets of Belgrade. Dega's furtive looking 'Man with a Soft Hat', after something to quench his thirst, van Cleve's man with a rosary about to swallow an unpleasant deal. Then there was the desperate uncertainty in Borovikovsky's portrait of the rebel leader Karageorge, who had just been elected as the leader to stick it to both the Turkish Sultan and the Austrian Emperor.

Perhaps I was getting used to scanning the people around me out of the corner of my eye and subconsciously categorising them. On every corner someone in a crisp white uniform was ready to offer official assistance, just as a man with a newspaper lurked in all the shadows, and somewhere, someone, always a woman, would be scribbling it all down. I knew the game well enough. None of these 'otbrosy' were worth worrying about. It was the ones that thought about what should be written down, and had people to write it down for them, that you needed to look out for.

Coffee with a slice of opera cake in a piece of grey greasy paper, multiple layers of orange and pistachio cream and filo pastry all wrapped in chocolate, then back to the hotel to freshen up, pick up my freshly laundered suit and head out to my new mysterious friend.

The Colonel was staying at the Metropol, an edgy building designed as the Central Committee building for the League of Communist Youth and only recently converted into a luxury hotel. A huge fountain greeted guests, and inside all was glittering glass and colourful curves. Tito himself had stayed there, as did many visiting heads of state and celebrities. My dinner guest looked distinctly out of place there in his old woollen jumper, heavy cotton shirt and square knitted tie, sitting on a brightly coloured plastic chair in this glitzy hall, cool kids in sunglasses and flunkies with flutes of champagne on silver trays spinning all around us. He shuffled a magazine and nervously stroked his neatly clipped pomaded beard.

'I hate this place.' He grunted. 'I'll get a taxi and we'll do our talking over dinner.'

If I'm honest I did not enjoy dinner, which was best described as functional, nor did I get much pleasure from Milan Ristić's Second Symphony afterwards. I do not imagine that the Colonel did either, as pleasure of any sort seemed to be something that he had long since forgotten. How he knew Miss Seawright I didn't like to ask. He didn't seem to be her type at all, far too quiet and not enough gold braid, but Miss Seawright is a lady of great depth and semi-infinite resources. I know that she only pretends to be a stereotype, so we don't ever get too close to the real her. I don't think that anyone else in the whole world has a better idea of what's underneath than I, and I will never betray her. In truth I would much prefer to have shared dinner with the old battle-axe, despite the society gossip, the pink gins and the endless smoke from her beloved Sobranie. For her part she is completely tone deaf so may not have found Ristić's work as troubling as I did either. The Belgrade Philharmonic are one of the top orchestras in Europe, but even they couldn't make it work for me. It leans towards being clever, and atonal as much modern music does, which is fine, if you then deliver something of substance with it, a message or a moral at least, but I found the symphony too superficial, too brassy and rather more like a film score than a serious piece of classical music.

Still, at forty-three, I can no longer claim to be 'with it', and Belgrade struck me as a city for the cool kids of tomorrow, rather than for yesterday's hangers-on. The young fashionistas were everywhere in their short cut clothing, and so serious too, but there was nothing that I saw that night as we drove into Student Square, that suggested the protests and violent uprising that would happen on that very spot just two years later. What did they have to complain about? This was a generation that had not had to fight for what it had, had not had to struggle, the 'baby boomers', the generation that, as Macmillan had said, had 'never had it so good'. Here, they had been brought up in new apartment blocks with ensuite bathrooms, were fed and educated well. They had luxuries that no other generation had ever had, sports and leisure facilities and a promise of work and housing for the future. Life here was wonderful even if it was built on money borrowed from both Great Powers, money that Yugoslavia didn't have and couldn't pay back. Harsh? But fair. But we cannot tell our children off for being ungrateful, we should just be happy that they do not have to endure what we did, and we bite our tongues... I had great hopes for the future Belgrade and Yugoslavia in general, which seemed to have put centuries of conflict to one side and found a meaningful and productive peace in the sunshine.

One final gem before I left. The house of Nikolai Tesla. It's a small museum in an aristocratic 20s townhouse, crammed full of his possessions, notebooks and works. Unfortunately, visitors are not allowed to just browse through them for ideas, but there are several working models, including of the infamous Tesla coil and I was just dying to have a go. A group of Serbian children were all standing in line orderly, reluctant to volunteer for any experimentation when a strange Englishman in a dark suit pushed his way to the front and grabbed the silver ball enthusiastically. I kissed the cold metal sphere, and the shock blew my glasses clean off. My hair, already turning grey, tried to leap off my head. I have never laughed so hard, and like a child was desperate to do it again.

Belgrade's most famous scientist and the original 'Tesla Coil'.

Maybe in some small way I have inspired at least one small group of Serbian children to become scientists rather than protestors.

Leningrad Viewer - Meopta - Reel (Yugoslavia)

PRAGUE

City of a Thousand Spires, May 1967

The Tupolev 104 flew through the heavy clouds, its high-pitched jet engines whining, water streaking past my window. There was plenty of champagne on board for those that chatted around me excitedly, but I made do with a lemon tea and a perfectly respectable, if slightly dull, meal of bread, soup and cold cuts of sausage handed out of the hatch. We landed, a rather fast landing in my view, in the pouring rain, a grey concrete building topped by the red letters 'PRAHA' slowly sliding out of the gloom and parking itself alongside us. Prague is a really beautiful city that I would happily go back to, but it was foreboding from the start.

There is little to see of the 'city of a thousand spires' until one is almost upon it. It lies in the centre of a broad plain and tends to wrap a blanket of fog and mist around itself, both meteorologically and metaphorically. Only when we crossed the Manes Bridge and passed the Rudolfinum did I even know that we had arrived. The resemblance to Belgrade, or to Zemun at least, is obvious, and familiar Austro-Hungarian architecture greets you at the door. It escaped relatively undamaged from the war but hundreds of years of industry have left its buildings blackened by smoke. It is a city of mediaeval merchants' buildings, a busy bustling chaos of cottage industries along the river. Twin black spires, like witches' hats, puncture the skyline menacingly and loom over the town.

It was raining when I arrived and misty most mornings, yet even in the sun it felt cold and damp. It seems laughable to say so, but there was something that was very peculiar and unnerving about Prague, different even from East Berlin, something almost spooky!

I was staying in the Jalta Hotel in a room looking directly out onto Wenceslas Square. It was a work trip, and I wasn't paying. The hotel was surprisingly busy given that it was only June. It was serving politicians, diplomats and businessmen, all of whom seemed to be crowded round its circular wooden bar talking noisily over a Pils. Everyone it seems drinks beer here. I had been spoiled for breakfasts on my previous trip and breakfast at the Jalta seemed a little dull by comparison, but food is one of Prague's most admirable qualities and the innumerable cafés, restaurants and street stalls more than made up for it. Prague's main square is large. Trams run up and down the middle and at the edges it is lined by linden trees and newspaper kiosks. A statue of the 'Good' King himself stands in the middle staring sternly back down the hill. He may well have told his servant to follow in his footsteps, but woe betide any of them that stepped out of line. Stamp collecting is popular in all the Eastern Bloc countries, and under the watchful eye of the old King I bought a packet for an old, kinglike friend along with a map of the city and a newspaper for myself. Few people in the city spoke English at the time, but German was very common.

Despite its width most of the square lies in shade; the sun blocked out by the tall buildings that surround it. At the top of the slope is the largest of these, the National Museum. Like many of Prague's buildings it is built out of dark stone, in a pompous Austrian style and has over the years, including during the war when it received direct hits by bombers, been darkened further by layers of smoke. Up close it is a dark chocolate colour, but from the square it just seems like an immense wall of black, blocking out the light. It was covered in scaffolding when I visited which added to the austerity, but inside it unfolds like a great jewellery box.

It is primarily a teaching museum, intended to educate the average man on the street about Natural & Political History. I found the mediaeval panel paintings, sculptures and reliquaries fascinating but merely sauntered around the rest, peering in the dusty glass cases. Far better, from my perspective at least, was the Sternberg Palace which sits in the grounds of the Royal Palace at the top of the hill. It holds the Holy Roman Emperor Rudolph II's collection of European Baroque art including Dürer's 'Feast' and work by Brueghel and Rubens. Beneath exquisitely painted vaulted ceilings lay innumerable treasures. I was particularly drawn to 'Portrait of a Girl' from the 4th century and the miniatures by Norbert Grund.

I was, ostensibly at least, in Prague to attend a book fair and writer's conference so I had dinner back at the hotel while I prepared. I had reread all my Kafka before going of course, his work was still largely banned in the country at the time, and more recently a copy of Milan Kundera's 'The Joke' which I had obtained with great difficulty for the bookshop.

I decided to forgo breakfast, heading out instead into the old town where I could undoubtedly find something to eat among the many cafés and bars. It was summer but still the cobbled streets seemed gloomy and dark as if the narrow mediaeval lanes just could not shake off their otherworldliness. The grey form of horses appeared out of the mist, wriggling in their harnesses and pawing nervously at the ground. Could they sense something too? Were they even really there? This was a world where time did not seem to be entirely linear or continual. I looked up at the famous astrological clock and watched as its parallel universes slowly came together. Behind me an ominous dark shadow made its presence felt, two black horns ripping at the clouds, a large black mouth dripping with malice. It was only the 'Our Lady before Tyn' Church, but I half wondered what monsters might burst from its mouth when the clock's stars aligned?

I have noticed that time is very important to the citizens of Prague. They are ever so slightly obsessed with it. Not in the way that Germans are. No, it is not punctuality that they care about but the concept of time itself. It is as if they object to it, and if they cannot stop the flow, then they must fill every moment of their day with tasks and plans. But time does not flow continuously in Prague, nor does it flow in straight lines. They have broken it somehow.

A pile of manure on the cobbles suggested that the horses were real and there in the present day. They were lined up along one side of the Square in pairs to pull carriages for the tourists. I walked past them and saw notes scrawled on a blackboard advertising a Mozart recital in the Jesuit church. I like Mozart, who doesn't, but I didn't fancy sitting bolt upright in a pew in church listening to it. I doubt that Mozart himself would have fancied it much either. He came to Prague in the spring of 1787 and his opera 'Don Giovanni' premiered here. He was hugely popular and even wrote a symphony just for the city (his 38th) known as 'The Prague Symphony'.

I could smell pancakes frying and followed the smell down a small lane barely wider than a car. An old man with a cart was frying what they call 'Palacinky'. They are Austrian but are given a Slavic name. A delicious mix of chocolate, cream and strawberry dripped out the other end and threatened to spill over my suit and tie. I refolded them and ate them quickly.

The mist still lay over the river, leaving the Baroque statues that lined the famous Charles Bridge standing in mid-air. They seemed to hang their heads in sadness or shame. I didn't know which. I hurried off to the Clementinum.

Charles Bridge with its baroque statues.

The Clementinum is a series of mediaeval buildings clustered around the chapel of St. Clement in the Dominican monastery. Under the Austrian Empress Maria Theresa it became a university and the country's central library and book repository. Its hallways and chapels are Baroque masterpieces, marble floor to painted ceilings stacked full of books in exquisitely carved bookcases. It is also an observatory and contains rooms and towers used to scientifically determine noon and the rotation of the stars. There are collections of globes as well as maps and the prize possession the Vyšehrad Codex, an illuminated copy of the Bible from the eleventh century. I had dinner near the bridge too, by then its large lamps glowing brightly. An ancient door in one of the towers creaked open to reveal a narrow circular staircase leading down, not up. I thought we must be sitting in the river itself. Bare tables were laid out under the barrel-vaulted brick roof, sunflowers stood in earthenware jugs. Food was not so much ordered but shoved at anyone sitting on a bench without food in front of them. I had something that was somewhere between a thick soup and a casserole. Potato and pork knuckle floated in a green liquid under a carpet of stewed cabbage. Large tankards were topped constantly with a pale beer. It cost virtually nothing. My companions I noted talked earnestly, but quietly hunched over their food. They did not look each other in the eye as they spoke but only before or afterwards, as if exchanging gossip and only slowly approaching the truth by a law of averages. There was much to gossip about. The President, Novotný, was extremely unpopular. The economy was growing too slowly. Stalin had been dead for fourteen years, but the process of de-Stalinization had barely begun. The government had been slow to make simple decisions, to modernise or do anything for themselves. The rest of Europe was recovering, even East Berlin was struggling bravely to its feet, but in Prague they just seemed to be waiting. Time seemed to be standing still, except that of course, it wasn't.

The city is perhaps even more beautiful at night than it is in the day. The dirt disappears from the buildings and the large tungsten lamps make their outlines sparkle and their faces glow amber. The spires that stick up threatening like black teeth during the day seem to stretch upward, hopefully towards the stars at night. It is a city that is full of ghosts and there are plenty of people offering walking tours that go in search of the 'Headless Templar Knight' or the 'Headless Maid', or the 'Begging Skeleton'. The sound of horses' hooves echo mysteriously by the Devil's Stream. One of them is real at least. The 'Iron Man' stands on Platnéřská Street silently waiting for his true love. He is quite touchable and photographable. His betrothed was unfaithful while he was away at war, so he remarried, causing his former fiancée's father to kill himself. Seeing what pain he had caused, he returned to his first love only to find that she had killed herself too. Mad with grief he killed his new wife before committing suicide. There is something about the story that seems to me to be particularly apt.

Another moon passed over the Clementinum. The Basilica of St. Peter and St. Paul pricked at another starlight night from its position high up on the hill, and finally I had the chance to explore Prague for myself. Just beyond the Charles Bridge lies the Malá Strana, which means 'Little Quarter'. In mediaeval times this is where German and Italian merchants lived and worked, across the river from the Slavs, at the foot of the castle, where their employers could keep a close eye on them. The area contains the State Senate palace at one end, the castle at the other and all stages of society in between. Two excessive Rococo churches are on this street, their insides so florid and gaudy that they made me feel physically sick, but between the two, as the road bends up the hill, a little market formed. Women in shawls and dusty cardigans line up with their string bags, men in dungarees and flat caps plod around trestle tables poking piles of cabbage, paper cigarettes lolling from toothless gums. The struggle to survive was as real now as ever. I wondered what these people made of the Baroque palaces and intemperate churches that surrounded them. They are, as I said earlier, defined as 'legacy buildings', now 'heritage'. But I wonder if such ornate buildings were ever meant for the common man. How different was it for them than for those that sold cabbage on the same spot, five hundred years or more before? Time after all often stands still in Prague.

I climbed the hill to the Castle stopping in a busy café halfway up, full of writers and other bohemians talking over pots of tea. I did not have the faintest idea what they were saying but the recognisable stench of scandal was in the air. I moved on quickly as soon as I had finished a very English cup of tea and a strange, sweet cinnamon pastry wrapped around a stick like a kebab. I ate it with a spoon and fork so that everyone realised that I was English, rather than Russian, and the conversation started to flow once more.

The castle is no longer a castle, but a series of very pleasant Romanesque and Gothic buildings and palace. Everyone who has ruled over Prague, from St. Wenceslas himself to Hitler has called it home and added their own mark. As a result, it doesn't actually look like anything close up. Even the Czechoslovakian Communist Government ruled from there, which seems particularly ill-fitting. No wonder the ordinary man in the street grumbled.

It is said that upon seizing power, the Nazi Governor of Czechoslovakia Reinhard Heydrich, grabbed the state jewels and placed the crown of King Ottakar upon his head. Rumour also says that anyone who usurps the crown of Bohemia will die within a year. Less than a year later Heydrich was ambushed by British SAS and Czech resistance forces in Operation Anthropoid. He and his family were executed shortly after. The repercussions of this were particularly unpleasant, but the importance of Czech industry to the Germans prevented indiscriminate killing.

In the middle of the rose gardens sits St. Vitus' cathedral. At over a hundred metres tall it is in my view a little too large for the location, a little bit awkward. Its Gothic exterior feels more like a deluge of brown water from the sky rather than a sculpture of magnificence from heaven. The nave is a relief after the horrors of the St. Nikolas church at the foot of the hill, but the ornate rose and the Chapel's stained glass left me wishing that they were simpler. The little St. Wenceslas Chapel on the other hand is a delight, its walls covered in rich paintings from the life of the Saint, the low ceiling ribbed with gold leaf that picks up the flickering light from the candles.

Down the hill to wander through the famous/ infamous Jewish quarter where Kafka himself once lived. It was a quiet area of leafy irregular shaped courtyards, narrow lanes and high walls which speak clearly of ghettoization. There has been a significant Jewish presence in the city since the tenth century when moneylenders helped finance the growth of trade along these rivers. Narrow streets of workshops with names like 'Goldsmiths' Street' bear testament to the professions that were based here. They were a delightful burst of colour in this otherwise rather grey town. There are six synagogues in this small sector, two of which are exceptional. The Old-New synagogue dates from the thirteenth century and was one of the town's first Gothic buildings. It looked more like a warehouse than a place of worship; a steep pitched roof decorated with teeth made it look like it was wearing a bishop's mitre. Inside it has a high ceiling with a fine ribbed and vaulted roof, reminiscent of many English churches and cathedrals. High above the Ark was a large red flag, proudly bearing the 'Star of David'. Far from being a relic from historic persecution, the banner was awarded to the Jewish community by the Emperor Ferdinand III for their help in the defence of Prague during the Thirty-Years War.

The 'Spanish' Synagogue or the 'Geistgasse-Tempel' as it was known by its German speaking congregation is a delightful Moorish style building standing next to a small park. Unlike the plain but beautiful Old-New Synagogue, its interior is an imposing mix of Arab and Byzantine styles. Every inch is covered in blue mosaic or gold leaf. The effect, standing under the copper-coloured dome is of being inside Aladdin's lamp.

The sun was blazing as I emerged onto the river front. Youngsters were sunbathing out on wooden pontoons, and a procession of German and Austrian Mercedes buses made their way into the square. The Church of Our Lady Before Tyn made a face, turning her nose up in distaste. I was almost tempted to take my jacket off, but there was still a coldness clinging to the old town.

I went for a walk in the Petrin hills, catching the funicular railway from the other side of the river. Once royal vineyards, the hill is now covered in trees. There is another rose garden at the top and ponies offer rides for children. The Czechs, like the Germans, enjoy their outdoor activities and several were running or performing some sort of exercise beneath the trees. At the top of the hill was a radio tower, intended to look like a little Eiffel Tower. There was a queue to go up in it and look back at Prague stretched out below us, but I was not sure that I'd see the same city that the tourists did. Little wooden huts 'Imbiss Stands' were serving food and, of course, beer. I purchased myself a picnic, open faced sandwiches with ham, cucumber and pickles, and a hardboiled egg. I sat down beneath the laurel trees and took out my notebook and my stubby red pencil. This was the setting for Kafka's 'Description of a Struggle' where he has an unworldly conversation with a supplicant, a fat bureaucrat and a drunk. I felt that I had met these people. There was time for pre-theatre dinner at the Triton restaurant across the square from my hotel, then a concert at the National Theatre. The restaurant was in a cellar that had been designed to look like an ornate cave, with stalagmites and stalactites, sculptures and discrete lighting. This on its own would be peculiar, but the addition of pseudo-Greek sculptures and Roman mosaics made what was intended at the turn of the century to be pompous and classy, look bourgeois and quite ridiculous. I drank a glass of Morovian red which went straight to my head and ordered a beef sirloin in a cream sauce. It sounded normal enough, so I was surprised when it arrived covered in whipped cream, with lemons and cherries, looking more like a desert. I had to check if other people were eating it or if this were some joke for the Englishman. In actual fact, the lemon cut through the thick cream and the sharp and sweet cherry went beautifully with the steak. I wondered how such a dish had ever come about, what the Edwardian Era chef had been thinking. It was an insight perhaps into the bizarre world of the rich Austro-Hungarian aristocrats that ruled here before Comrade Princip fired his gun at the Archduke in Belgrade all those years ago.

That night's performance was Bizet's 'Carmen' which seemed a slightly peculiar choice for the city, but it was a cheerful break. Prague's finest were there for the occasion including the President who was surrounded by armed guards. The Russians, who never really felt they should approve of the original opera, had got themselves into a bit of a flap about the new Carmen ballet that was supposed to be touring Europe, although I had heard that it was very good. The Czech president, Novotny, seemed to be unable to act without instructions from Moscow so he didn't yet have an opinion about the ballet and didn't know whether to allow it or not. The choice of Carmen as the opera was almost certainly some sort of challenge to his authority, a deliberate asking of awkward questions. Rumour had it that he was too dim to see that. The astronomical clock was ticking…

I was keen to get out of town and so I took a bus out into the countryside and on to Brno. Industrial complexes stretched all along the river. There were no large red posters with the face of Marx or Novotny here, the only thing the billboards were advertising was Skoda. Slowly the river plain gave way to rolling countryside, with red houses and ancient farmsteads buried amongst the green hills.

We inexplicably stopped in a village for some union rule, and I took the opportunity to look around. There were grapes and vine leaves painted around the doors of many of the old houses, and decrepit wine presses in their front yards. But it wasn't just wine fermenting in the cool dark cellars of these buildings. The area had been famous for its glass making since Roman times, and most of these houses doubled as family workshops. These days the raw materials are made in communal state-run factories. Glass rods arrived here on the back of flatbed lorries, but it was down to the local community to decide how it was finished and who made what. Timetables and progress against targets were posted on information boards by the shiny new post office. Instead of learning how to make glass at home, children were now learning in the central technical schools. Few returned to the villages to work, so the rural population was ageing and becoming bitter. I decided to buy a paperweight as a souvenir. I deliberately overpaid and let the old lady keep the change, making her gasp up at me in toothless wonderment.

Nowhere has the concept of nationality seemed quite as meaningless as Czechoslovakia. For a start it is not one country, but three: Bohemia, Moravia and Slovakia, each of which has a quite distinct character to its geography and even its own language. Under the current regime each is administered separately, and a proposal is on the table to split the country into three, each with its own capital. However even within a region there are major differences, and most cultures are cross-regional. No matter the country, all along the Danube the churches have exactly the same style of tower and spire but venture ten miles from the river and the style starts to change. Prague was clearly dominated by the Austrians, but less than an hour out of the city we could easily have been in the 'Black Forest' of southern Germany.

Cesky Krumlov

A mediaeval town at a bend in the Vltava River, held in the embrace of its castle's ramparts. Its brick walls and tiled roofs glowed invitingly in the midday sun. It is unquestionably a German town and until the end of the war, eighty-five percent of the population spoke only German. With the forced expulsion of Germans from Czechoslovakia many of its factories and streets fell silent. The town was quiet when I arrived, uncertainly awaiting its future. Mercifully the local brewery was still functional. I enjoyed a lunch of pork knuckle and dumplings, washed down with a dark beer under the arches in the town square and dozed for the rest of the journey.

Cesky Krumlov.

We arrived in Brno and I immediately liked the place. After the shady narrow streets of Prague, Brno's seemed wide open and full of sun. Red & cream trams slid quietly down the cobbled streets, past pastel-coloured buildings from the seventeenth & eighteenth centuries. Fountains bubbled, and flowers seemed to be everywhere. I sat in the town square, known as the 'Vegetable Market' with the evening sun sparkling in the water of the Parnas Fountain, the spires of the cathedral of St. Peter & St. Paul poking over the top of a row of buildings painted cream and brown like the coaches of the Great Western Railway and smiled. A cup of coffee appeared, brewed in a large copper barrel that looked like Kaiser Wilhelm's helmet, followed moments later by a deep-fried filo pastry dessert topped with cinnamon and sugar.

I had timed my arrival so that I could go and see Prokofiev's 'Romeo & Juliet' at the Mahen Theatre, or the 'Deutsches

Stadttheater' as it was known until the war. It was in this very theatre that the ballet first premiered in 1938, and it has been a favourite there ever since. Surprisingly the theatre also claims to be the first building in Europe to be lit by electricity, Thomas Edison himself coming across 'The Pond' to oversee the work in 1881.

Brno's skyline.

Some will associate the city of Brno, or Brünn with its concentration camp or with the 'Death Marches' that thousands of prisoners were forced to undertake. The city positively 'welcomed' the arrival of the German army on 16th March 1939. In a census from 1935, thirty-six percent of Brno's residents declared themselves to be German not Czech, and like Cesky Krumlov, nearly everyone spoke German as their primary language.

Wehrmacht arrives in Brno.

Brno was an industrial city and there had been large armament factories there making equipment and ammunition for the German military since the turn of the century. The Red Army reached the city on 26th April 1945. A month later 27,000 German residents were forcefully expelled from the city and marched to the Austrian border. Between 1500 and 5000 died en route.

There was just time for a quick look at the castle before catching the train back to Prague from the ornate Art Deco train station, whose fine white columns, elegant hallway and station clock would be just at home in Paris. There was no time to visit the site of the Battle of Austerlitz which saved Europe from domination by Napoleon. It lay just a short taxi ride from Brno, but I was told that there was nothing to see there of the famous battle, nor any cafés worthy of my attention. In complete contrast to Brno, the Central Station in Prague is a gloomy building, with its grey face, beady little eyes and a gawking black mouth.

This account of my time in Prague has been very one sided, and my experience was heavily coloured by the thoughts that occupied me while I was there. Dark thoughts. Unlike anywhere else I have travelled to, Prague was the only place where revolution was clearly in the air. It is, of course, a very beautiful city and very gracious to its many guests, so I will leave this entry with a happier memory of it. The Vltava River, or the 'Moldau' as the German speaking people of Czechoslovakia call it, and who are we to judge what is German and what is Czech? It starts high in the mountains of the Bohemian Forest and flows through the Czech plains, over rapids to reach, at last, the capital itself. Its personality is brilliantly captured in Smetana's Symphonic poem 'Ma Vlast'.

The movement starts with light, rippling leitmotifs that represent the emergence of the river as two mountain springs, one warm and one cold. Water from the springs then combine to become a mighty river, symbolised by a thickly orchestrated, stately theme that recurs throughout the remainder of the piece. Farther downstream, the river passes jubilant hunters, portrayed by a horn melody, and then passes a village wedding, signalled by a passage in polka rhythm. It then enters a gorge where, according to legend, water nymphs (suggested by serene and mysterious melodies) come out to bathe in the moonlight. With the morning light, the main river theme returns, though it soon breaks into tumultuous dissonance as the river enters the St. John's Rapids.

Beyond the white water, the river reaches Prague, to grand arpeggios of a regal hymn. After fading to a trickle, the piece, and the journey, comes to an unambiguous close. I tried to find a recording of it in Prague itself, but there were few shops selling records at the time, in fact there were few enough places that were obviously shops, and a piece as patriotic as this might have been a questionable item to sell openly, so I was only able to buy one after my return to England.

The 'Vltava' steamboat.

I boarded the 'Vltava' steamer at a concrete quay just down from the Charles Bridge. It was just coming up to ten, and the air was just beginning to get warm. I had had a good breakfast, including a mix of both Eastern and Western European items, and was in no hurry to eat or drink again. I took my place on the open deck, folding my suit jacket on the orange wooden bench, and took out my pencil and notebook. It was difficult, as you have seen, to separate my feelings about Prague, from my actual thoughts, and that was something that both Vltavas were going to help me with.

The unimaginatively named 'Vltava' was a vintage steamboat that slowly cruised through the river valley. She smelt of oil and woodsmoke, a little like the trains of my youth, and it is easy to imagine Edwardian aristocrats with their moustaches and parasols promenading along her decks. In truth she is not quite so old, having been built in 1940 in a Nazi military shipyard. I am tempted to imagine SS troops goose-stepping around the decks with large moustaches and pink parasols, but I won't. Still, we must forgive the 'Vltava' for things that she could not control, just as we must reluctantly forgive the citizens of Brno who welcomed the German army in, and more understandably, the citizens of Prague who forced the German population out after the war. It is how we go forward that counts in life, something that many still find difficult.

The Vltava went forward slowly, cautiously, and quietly, but move forward she did, under the railway bridge, past the twin spires of Vysehrad Castle high on the hill, past the long thin uninhabited islands that floated mid-stream. Soon heavily wooded hills began to rise and fall, all along the left bank. There was no noise at all apart from the singing of the birds and the gentle lapping of the water around the hull.

'Would I like a beer?' A smiling face in a grimy apron interrupted my thoughts. No, not right now, but I accepted a tea, black with lemon. The order had the desired effect. I was trouble. He brought my glass and then left me alone. The sun sparkled brightly off the surface of the water, and I could see little beaches full of ducks sunbathing in all the sandy inlets along the riverbank. Beavers and coypu played in the river while swans watched us glide silently by. It was a haven for wildlife, but it has not always been so, for this was for hundreds of years a busy trading route full of river traffic. We passed a working harbour just beyond a bend in the river, a sudden smell of diesel and oil filling the air. There was a shower of sparks from someone welding on the quay next to a semi-submerged barge. But in only a few moments it was gone, and we were once again alone with the wind and the birds. The river widened and divided. The water seemed a darker colour and shade began to fill the valley. The trees were denser here, with just a few orange roofs and church spires poking above them.

Another village appeared at the next bend, an isolated community of typically-German-looking houses and workshops. Several of them were being repaired and a large cement mixer stood in the street. The river narrowed again, trees hung out over the water. The banks rose on both sides, and we entered a rocky gorge. The river began to zigzag frantically, plunging its namesake alternately into sunshine and shade. The engine roared and suddenly we were confronted by a huge concrete wall blocking our way. The crew of the Vltava, busied themselves with ropes as we drifted to the bank.

The dam at Slapy was built by Russian engineers after the war, to supply electricity to Prague and the remote villages that we had just passed. In doing so they created the Slapy reservoir upstream of it and the associated outdoor centre so popular with Czechs today. We had an hour there for lunch, most of which I spent inspecting the dam itself and touring the massive generator rooms.

Although the Austrians created grand buildings in the major cities like Prague and Brno, it is clear that the towns and villages of Bohemia are predominantly Germanic in nature, the product of German merchants and engineers settling here over hundreds of years. But that is not sufficient cause for it to become part of a state called Germany, not least because Germany itself is not a real place. The people of Bohemia and the Rhineland have much more in common with each other than the Rhineland has with, say, Bremen or Berlin. Just as the people of Bavaria have a closer connection to their Austrian and Italian brothers than they do to the people of the Berlin or Cologne. Countries are in my view a complete nonsense, but that also means that it makes no sense to split Czechoslovakia into the smaller independent regions of Bohemia, Moravia and Slovakia just because they are different from each other. Communities have always benefited from the intermingling of culture and the redistribution of wealth, and nowhere is that demonstrated clearer than here on the River Danube.

But that Iron Curtain has come down over Europe, splitting our community in two, effectively orphaning whole countries. Bohemia drifts like one of Prague's ghosts, decapitated, cut off from its parents and family, wandering zombie-like in the wilderness. Moscow has other things to attend to and cannot spoon-feed the republics. Nor is that its role. Novotny needs to make more of an effort, to get the country working again.

Time is broken in Prague, city of ghosts and spires. But the town square clock is ticking and time does not stand still, not even here.

Prague's 'Astronomical Clock' watching and waiting silently.

Less than six months after my father's visit the Czech President, Antonin Novotny, was forced to resign in the face of mass opposition even from within the government. His successor, Alexander Dubcek, was elected on a platform of reform and was referred to as 'Socialism with a human face'. He was strongly supported by the Kremlin initially, who thought Novotny a poor leader. But reforms got out of control and by June 1968 Dubjeck was calling for an end to one party rule and the Socialist system, a complete non-starter with Moscow. Despite the head of the KGB's request to work with Dubjeck, or his replacement, (Andropov's threat was very blunt), Brezhnev gave the order for the tanks to roll in.

The Warsaw Pact countries all supported the invasion, four of them sending troops; however, such a heavy-handed approach caused other Socialist states, particularly China, to distance themselves from Soviet foreign policy. Andropov referred to the affair as an 'unfortunate and unnecessary slip on a ladder'.

Warsaw Pact tanks enter Wenceslas Square on 21st August 1968.

Leningrad Viewer - Meopta - Reel (Prague)

THE RHINELAND & THE TYROL

The Country That Europe Forgot, 1968

We are, mercifully for you dear reader, nearing the end of my travels overseas, and you will be expecting me to be building to some enlightened conclusion or devious plot twist. I wish it were so. The truth is more humdrum as I, like Britain's railways, was finally beginning to run out of steam. I had learnt a great deal about Europe, about my context, and about myself. As a result, the desire to seek out new places and have new adventures had subsided a little.

In addition, I had been in a bit of a 'funk', as they don't say anymore, since the autumn of the previous year, bordering on depression. I was forty-five and life was beginning to pass me by. I still wanted to fight for something, to rally against the injustices I had seen, but I didn't really know what or who to fight for. I understood the world better than many, and yet still I was doing nothing to improve it. I was growing soft, settling into bourgeois ways and although I no longer lived with my parents, my domestic situation had hardly changed. My mother still cooked my dinners and I was still alone.

I was comfortable with the past, but I was losing faith in the future. Only seven years before I was sure we were entering a new age, where the 'white heat' of technology would save and unite the world, but progress was slow, both at home and abroad, while the great ideas that I had held up almost as religious truths were coming into disrepute. Seeing the situation in Czechoslovakia, where I had been just a few months before, descending into unseemly violence certainly contributed to my glum mood. This was not the future for our children that any of us believed in. The bookshop kept me busy, as did various small projects for the Admiralty, but it did little to occupy my mind. What could I do from behind the counter in twee middle-class Bath to alter the path of things? Was I doomed to watch from the side lines as the world was driven forward by others?

I did not have a television, but my parents did, a large colour one that my father had purchased for the horse racing, and I had sat in their lounge horrified as I watched Russian tanks rumble into Wenceslas Square, parking outside what had been my hotel. I had not believed that it would come to this, I had thought some deal could be done. Everyone did. I was in shock. My father, who only normally read the Racing Post, was grumbling about Harold Wilson, who was struggling to push reform through parliament. He tapped his newspaper:

"You need to take one of your trips, old boy." He said changing the subject. I disagreed. Holidays were at the back of my mind. What I needed was a purpose in life. He snorted, as if the very idea that any of us had a purpose was arrogance personified. We were playthings in the hands of the gods. For him life was chaos to be enjoyed while it lasted, and if one could pick out a pattern in the chaos, or a bit of previous form, then as an opportunity to be cashed in on. What I needed was a woman, his solution to everything, and to be fair the solution had worked very well for him.

'How about Arabella in the four-thirty at Goodwood?' I was confused as to what he was talking about. He leant forward in his high-backed chair and pushed the paper into my hands indicating an article about cruising on the Rhine, that was clearly a thinly veiled advertisement for Mercedes buses. I remembered the giant three-pointed star revolving slowly on top of the Kaiser Wilhelm Memorial Church in Berlin, and the same glinting symbol on the long black nose of the open top cars that Hitler had always paraded in. I wanted no part in adding to the coffers of that organisation.

'No thinking, no planning,' my father continued, blissfully unaware of my mood or perhaps blissfully disinterested in it. 'Just sit back and relax like a normal person would and let it all go by. You never know, you might meet a young lady, looking for an educated older man.' I made a face, and my mother slipped silently out of the room. My father was a different sort of person from me, a far simpler, but more gregarious one. He would have been perfectly happy to be cooped up with the same group of people on a bus for a week and would have been chatting heavily or sharing stories with his neighbours in minutes. I almost envied his straightforward outlook on life. Although he had been horrifically gassed by the Germans in the First World War and was ill for most of his life thereafter, he was undeniably happy. I however took much more after my mother and was more introverted and withdrawn. She always said that she was happy, but I wasn't always convinced. She had given up a lot to be with him, including ambitions that had been filtered down to me instead.

I looked down at the newspaper. I had already visited Germany three times, and I am sure that if it had been anywhere else, I would have said no. But Germany wasn't really a holiday, it felt like a responsibility, a work still in progress, and the ticket price was very good value. At worst it would present an opportunity to catch up on some reading material. I went to join my mother in the kitchen and sat on a stool munching a ham and pickle sandwich as I listened to her thoughts. Dad meant well, but only she and Miss Seawright really understood me.

Ostend looked very much the same as it had the last time I had seen it as the ferry came in, but there was only time for a quick drink before the coach left for Holland. It went via Brussels, where the Atomium, built for the trade fair ten years earlier, still gleamed above the trees. From there it was on to Liege. Here, I kid you not, the bus went into a broadside skid right into the opposite traffic lane. (Liege, what a terrible place to die!) It was not, I thought, the best advert for Mercedes-Benz. However, luck, and lots of frantic activity on behalf of the drivers of the oncoming lorries avoided a collision. After a stop at a café to let our quivering nerves quieten down, with drinks courtesy of the bus company, we proceeded to Maastricht.

Maastricht was a splendid old Dutch town with several fine old buildings in the grand square. A brass band contest was being held of all things, and there must have been twenty bands competing at least, all jolly and red faced. My hotel must have been the centre for the celebrations, and I could have sworn that the winners came back to the room next to mine to celebrate, such was the noise. They like a good celebration in Maastricht. Located as it is at the point where

Germany, Belgium and Holland all meet, they've been toasting international peace treaties on the Saint Servatius Bridge with a slice of the local limburger cheese and wine from the Louwberg hills since Roman times.

On the 7th February 1992 twelve nations, including Britain, signed the Treaty of European Union in Maastricht's town hall. Building on the Treaty of Rome, it resolved "to continue the process of creating an ever-closer union among the peoples of Europe", creating a council of ministers, centralised legal and security controls, and the provision for a single currency and financial union. But as my father has demonstrated, Europe is a concept much larger and more complex than membership of an exclusive club of twelve wealthy western nations, and the treaty, though noble in spirit, has proved to be an idea slightly before its time.

From Maastricht it was on to Bonn. How would it have changed? I was not sure what sort of country I would find. In my previous brief visit I had seen the wreckage of a country, not just physically destroyed but annihilated mentally too. What would I see this time, now Germany had begun to stabilise and sort itself out? The shallow Germany of West Berlin? The tragedy of East Berlin, the mediaeval towns of the Sudetenland or something else entirely? Who had the Germans chosen to be? Sadly, we bypassed Charlemagne's lovely town of Aachen, where the founder of the Holy Roman Empire lies buried in an area that is both French and German in equal measure. It does not need to choose between them and would be historically wrong to do so.

Bonn had changed a lot in the past 14 years since I had last seen it. It was still a quiet backwater, but instead of simply being a rundown rural town with rubble in the streets, it had become a kind of model village, full of fake buildings, artificial parks and doll's houses. From my elevated and detached position in the coach I looked out at its citizens. Gone were the hungry, haunted faces that roamed the streets, replaced by quiet people diligently going about their lives, keeping their heads down. The sullen confused children that I had seen all those years before had now grown up into sullen confused adults. The sun shone innocently enough on the square with its scrubbed clean, white concrete buildings, a series of international flags flying over the Bundestag like sandcastles. The city seemed like a mass of flowers, not unlike a hospital ward, whose every surface was covered in vases of gifts from visitors. They are tended meticulously, as is the whole town, in neat rows in public gardens, and in private gardens behind carefully locked gates. Like the town's citizens, no flower is out of line here.

It is not like West Berlin in some ways, with its brashness and politics, but here everything is quiet, understated but equally artificial. Even the people who rule here are proxies for the real power which sits elsewhere. It is a children's playground, a safe house. A front of no real substance.

Across the river was Koenigswater and high above that the Drakonfelds, fearsome mountains looking innocent and cheerful across the sparkling water. A café sat beside the wide road with red and white umbrellas lined up along the railings giving earnest couples the chance to enjoy the view. It serves American ice-cream, Marlboro cigarettes and Coca Cola. I have no inclination to partake or to join my companions. Germany needs this sort of commercial rubbish to survive in the short term, but I hope it doesn't seep too deeply into its veins.

So began the journey up the Rhine. It was quite fascinating. The Dutch section, and bits of the Ruhr I had seen before, but now, after Bonn it began to change, to become more open. The Lorelai Rock was disappointing, the legend killed by the proximity of the main road and the power of the modern diesel engine. But irrespective of what was, or was not, on the bank, the river itself, with its endless traffic was a constant source of interest to me. Tours and indeed cities passed, Remagen with its famous ruined bridge, blackened and full of bullet holes, Koblenz where the dirty brown Rhine is joined by the blue Mosel River. Now it was a country river, its banks covered with vines, the occasional castle poking through the trees. Still the river traffic flowed; great barges, small barges, pleasure steamers, ferries, little boats all swept along or fighting against the broad, relentless current.

It was the river Rhine that created 'Germany' in Roman times, and once again in mediaeval times. It was clear to me that it would be the Rhine that would eventually rebuild Germany once again.

So on to St. Goarshausen, a pleasant narrow-streeted town with timber-framed houses under the gaze of the formidable Katz Castle. Here a pleasant Fräulein in the approved national costume handed out an enormous, packed lunch. There is a plethora of rules in Germany when it comes to lunch as with all things. A side salad is mandatory for health reasons, as is some form of hard-boiled egg, which is solemnly eaten although nobody likes it. The girl was scarcely old enough to have been alive during the war, and certainly was not old enough to remember it, yet her life was already controlled by a terrifying hierarchy of new social laws concerning how Germans should behave if they were to avoid the mistakes of the past. I couldn't help feeling that it had been the blind following of rules had been part of the problem.

I say that she wore 'national costume' but there is of course no such thing, the traditional folk costumes differ greatly from region to region. She was dressed for the tourists' benefit rather than for historical accuracy and that was who Germany was choosing to be for a while. It had not hurt Switzerland after all.

An assortment of authentic period costumes all from areas of modern Germany.

Dirndls, and to a certain extent lederhosen, are twentieth century inventions based on earlier everyday attire. In Bavaria where the cornflower is common, they are stained pale blue, in the Rhineland predominantly green.

Shorts are more common in the southern farmlands, and knee length britches in more respectable regions and towns.

As you might expect there is a lot of politics in who can wear what. The town halls have great ledgers documenting what professions were given the right to wear what dead animal pinned to their hat or lapels. As a computer consultant, I was permitted to wear the attire of an Italian Gunpowder expert, which apparently involved a lot of dead badger.

From its middle the Rhine looked very wide. I sat by myself in the bows, drinking in the sun, slowly succumbing to the temptation to open my lunch. The best ever, beating even those memorable feeds in Switzerland! Chicken breast, pâté, cheese and crisp rolls, butter, tomatoes, lettuce and two oranges. There was a bottle of lemonade and a bar of chocolate, and of course the ubiquitous hardboiled egg. I was a happy man and I left not a crumb of it!

A little fort appeared in the middle of the river, another castle on the right side. Vineyard after vineyard, castles preserved, castles ruined, the hills opening and lowering, slowly becoming gentler. Still, I sat there perfectly content to absorb the glorious panorama as history floated gently by. There was something deeply satisfying about seeing the mixture of old and new, houses and industries being created and recreated continuously as time flowed alongside the river. Here was a people, fully integrated into their context, a context almost unchanged in two thousand years. The trip ended far too soon.

The coach, when it appeared again, took us on to Mainz. I thought that this would be a pleasant place to stay and a fitting end to the day, but that was not for us. We joined the autobahn near Darmstadt and switching into overdrive we roared south. Our coach, which until then could quite frankly have been any regional bus, finally showed us that it was after all a Mercedes. We passed Heidelberg, which I would also have liked to have seen, the castle on the hill gleaming in the sun, through endless tunnels of trees in the Black Forest, the engine whining hypnotically. Just as I thought that this was going to go on forever, we left the motorway, plunged down a country road, not literally this time, passed peasants that Beethoven would have recognised, turning the hay in the late sun and came at last to Emmendingen and the Hotel 'Zur Post'. Here in a vast dark wood-panelled hall with antler and polished hunting horns on the walls, we had a gargantuan dinner with huge tankards of beer. I fell gratefully into bed.

The next day was more leisurely as we drove across the corner of the Black Forest, the road switching back and forth as we climbed and descended hills continuously.

Freiberg was followed by a splendid, wooded road and quite an impressive gorge with a name like 'Hell's mouth'. Then through more woods, ablaze with colour, arriving at the Swiss frontier at Schaffhausen. Here we were introduced to the Rhine once more, but a different version of it, unrecognisable from the fat brown industrial one I'd met before.

The Rhine at Schaffhausen.

Sleek, fresh and almost turquoise, it burst angrily from the mountains, foaming at the mouth. I could not see it initially, but as we walked down through the woods, the roar of the falls grew louder until suddenly they were there. Not high, but very, very wide and with a sheer force that stunned my senses.

Across Switzerland to Liechtenstein and to the splendid tourist trap of Vaduz. Up to the fine mediaeval town of Felkirk at the foot of the Arlberg Pass, that I had gone under by train in 1959. Down the steep road to the Inn Valley to the village of St. Anton and the hotel where we were to stay. The tour part was over, and I was already exhausted.

I would not choose St. Anton again for a summer holiday; there is quite a lot of traffic, road and rail, and the place itself is very tourist conscious. It is a skiing rather than a climbing resort. The valley is fairly straight with further ones up which you could escape but nothing of great interest at either time of year, unless skiing is your thing. That said, I used my time well, throwing myself into an energetic routine of walking, climbing hills, eating strawberry flan and drinking beer. The fields were full of flowers and the little chapels on the slopes were always garlanded. Growing naturally out of the rocks or in the fields, they were far more beautiful than the formal flowers I had seen everywhere in Bonn. I had seen in other places how people, often unable to express themselves in other ways, channelled their thoughts and emotions into flowers in some way or other. They bring brightness and colour in dark times and represent hope. Only days after the guns fell silent, they began to appear in the rubble and I had seen whole beds of them growing in the ruins of buildings in East Berlin, on previously hidden surfaces now exposed to the sky. I picked a few, for no particular reason; an uneven number of course, avoiding any yellow ones, and I fixed them to my lapel. The sun broke from behind the clouds and I felt my spirits lift for the first time in months.

The chairlifts I was not impressed by. One carrying me upwards through the mist suddenly stopped and I was left sitting there in a fog so thick that I could not see the ground below me. For a few minutes I was totally isolated. It was not a pleasant experience. The cable car to the Valluga was however one of the great mountain lifts of Europe.

The first stage of the Vallugabahn is straightforward, a large car, sufficient to take twenty people or so, swung up to a shoulder of the mountain through the tops of the trees and over the short grass. The second stage was from this shoulder to another at roughly the same height. This resulted in a vertiginous sag in the middle of the cable as I swung incredibly high over sheer rock. For both reasons it was breath-taking. The third and final stage was in a car no larger than a telephone kiosk which went to within a few feet of the 10,500 ft summit, out through an ice cave to the same brilliant blue-white light, the deep blue sky, the blinding snow and that piercing wind that sears the lungs. All around were peaks. To the east they stretched away to the heart of Central Europe and beyond, all the way to Montenegro and Slovenia; the same vast spectacle that I first saw from Interlaken back in '53. I felt that I had come full circle.

Cable car over the Valluga valley.

I did one excursion from St. Anton. It was to Merano in Italy. I had had a long day previously and could do with a rest, and a splash of sun seemed like no bad idea. Expecting little, the day turned out to be a pleasant surprise. Italy has consistently come to the rescue in my life. We went down the valley to Landeck then up into the pass, steep mountains dusted in green rising on both sides. The road was hewn from the valley that went towards St. Moritz; mountain streams crossed by frail wooden bridges like that at Altfinstermünz.

The road rose in a steady gradient. One side of it, officially Austria, the other Switzerland. Where in the tarmac they met I did not know or care. The bus lawlessly but pragmatically, stuck to the middle. A sharp turn left into a small cleft guarded by a tower and then it was over the bridge into what surprisingly is officially Italy, even though everyone drinks beer, speaks German and wears lederhosen. We skirted alongside a large lake, the campanile of a drowned village sticking up out of the water. Down again through a long valley to Merano.

Merano – once capital of the country of Tyrol.

Merano is a naturally pretty city, in a beautiful setting. At its heart is a mediaeval trading town that has grown wealthy over the ages. It has a pleasant climate and its streets seemed full of rockeries of blooming mountain flowers. Franz Kafka, who we last saw in Prague, lived here and I can see why. It is a surprisingly small world. A nineteenth-century esplanade ran along one side of the Empress Elisabeth Park down to the bank of a little stony river. Blinking in the midday sun outside a small café it was strange to think that this sleepy little town was once the capital of a country that now no longer exists.

The Empress Elisabeth Park is named after Elisabeth of Austria. She first visited Merano in 1870 and returned many times after, transforming it by association into a spa town for the aristocracy. She is herself, meanwhile, remembered for her lack of pretension and her charity, making it all the more poignant that her life was pervaded by tragedy. Her only son died in a murder-suicide and she herself, heartbroken after a chain of sudden bereavements, was fatally stabbed by an Italian anarchist, Lucheni. Only because he had not been able to reach his intended victim, the Duke of Orléans, and heard in passing that an empress was nearby.

From 1253 to 1848 Meran was officially the capital city of the Principality of Tyrol, a country that included all of the land now artificially split between Italy, Austria, Switzerland and Germany. It was the 'Counts of Tyrol' and the Habsburg princes that paid for the roads to be built through the passes and for the bridges that span the mountain streams. They grew rich from their investment and funded the construction of many churches, all with the Baroque layout and black onion dome that we see throughout the mountains and giving rise to the 'National Anthem' of the region, 'The Holy Land of Tirol', which everybody here learns at nursery school.

The ancient footbridge at Altfinstermünz.

At the heart of the town there is a fine old Roman bridge, a reminder that for thousands of years, trade, and knowledge have flowed through this region, its mountain passes as vital as the rivers further north. Only when the State of Tyrol opposed Napoleon's invasion of the Holy Roman Empire, preventing French reinforcements joining Napoleon's army from the south, did European imperialists see the strategic importance of the area. The European powers raced to divide it up. Even the Russians invaded it!

On 10th September 1919, the country of Tyrol was signed out of existence by the same piece of paper that created the artificial nation of Czechoslovakia.

I remembered how, after the war and university, I had been so keen to stretch myself by going and climbing the great mountains of Europe. I remember looking up at the Eiger and thinking I must get to the top of that ferocious wall. But now I knew that being in the mountains, being amongst them, was more important than trying to get to the top of them. I had no desire to plant my flag on them, I wanted them to embed themselves in me. That is perhaps why we travel, we are empty vessels, until we are filled by our experiences.

The peaks seemed to prick up like cat's ears, but I was no longer afraid of being alone with the gods. They seemed to be grinning mischievously at me. At forty-six I was getting too old for this. 'Not a climb, just a walk…' they seemed to be saying to me. 'One last time…' It was hard to resist, not least because I too knew that it would be the last time. I am not religious, but I lit a candle in the St. Nicholas Church, where else? and headed out.

I paused on a rock to ease my breathing and quiet the thumping of my heart. I am not well. My limbs ached. I was out of practice. Behind and far below me the village houses, full of people going about their daily lives, looked like toys, carelessly scattered on a green crumpled carpet. I found myself looking back at them more and more. Looking backwards, not forwards. It was increasingly like this now. I wondered what it would be like to call such a place home. I would like to think that it was not unlike Somerset in some ways. Part of me knew that 'home' is what I was still searching for. I looked up, the long hard part of the climb was over. One final push and I would reach the shoulder of the mountain. But I had no desire to reach the top. I could do it, easily, for old time's sake, or out of bloody-mindedness of which there was no shortage. But I just didn't want to, I didn't need to. I wanted to be in the valley, not sat on top of a barren rock. To the east the gorge stretched away, to the west the Alps loomed, not menacingly but undeniably, like fate. Breathing deeply, I seemed to expand in that great openness, mind drinking in every peak, every glacier, every tiny, warm red roof. I noticed two summits set apart like the dark spires of the evil churches of Prague.

377

I wanted to laugh and point it out, but there was nobody to point it out to, and nobody that went to Prague with me. I was alone.

I walked on, not taking great strides aggressively up the slope, but slowly, casually following the gently undulating contours, almost as if I had a companion with me. We were high enough. A small stream bubbled gently down the hill and across the valley the 'witches' hats' mountain shone in the sun. The snow, blueish white, seeming so close in the clear air. It was the perfect spot for lunch. A can of beer in the ice-cold stream, ham rolls, an apple and of course the ever-present hardboiled egg. I took my shoes off. Time for an hour's sleep on the soft moss under the scented pines. I was surrounded by mountains and sun and not a sound save the gently bubbling stream.

There were tears in my eyes when I woke, and I was not sure why. The real world seemed a long way away, but I knew that I must return to it. Crunching a mint, I followed what will become the river Rosen, down the slope as it leapt from stone to stone, making sudden little twists like a child skipping down a hill occasionally checking backwards on its parents. Suddenly it turned and plunged into a dark ravine. The sides were not steep, and I followed it nervously, like a parent, slipping and sliding as I went. Just as I was beginning to query the wisdom of this action, a path of sorts opened up on my left. I found myself at the head of the Rosenschutte Gorge. The Gorge is a gigantic cleft between two mountains, full of trees. From this high point the great green carpet of leaves fell away and down into this plunged the brook. After a short rest I followed it down. The stream sprang out and downward, flashing gold and silver in the sunlight, crashing into a pool a hundred feet below.

Back once again at my hotel, it is a slightly different version of me that was standing at the bar. The walk had taken just over nine hours, but it was well worth it. There would be stiffness for sure, but nothing that a hot bath and a glass of brandy won't fix. Except that it won't fix what was really wrong.

I wished that it hadn't been a Mercedes. The coach back seemed far too fast, every field, every river ripped brutally away from outside my window. I knew that I was not returning but had no idea how to say goodbye to the continent that had given me everything. I tried to imprint every moment of it on my brain and in my heart, so I would always have it with me. We stopped at various cafés, where I sat, surrounded by people and yet still utterly alone, and tried to imagine all the while that I was back in that mountain valley in the sun, or somewhere else with that perfect sense of stillness, warmth and peace.

It was hot in Paris, overwhelming after the coolness of the Tyrol. There were relatively few signs of the riots that had rocked the city in May. Workers and students had risen up in protest. There had been reforms, especially for women, and De Gaulle was now gone. That was a good thing and France was better for it. It could finally grow up and be itself, but I was sad at more violence on Europe's city streets.

After dinner I strolled down to the opera to see Turandot and have a final drink at the Café de la Paix. The tale of Turandot is a great one. It is violent and greatly disturbing. There are parts where I feel sick and want to cry. But the opera, although it has an end, is widely acknowledged to be incomplete. The ending that it does have, not only doesn't tie up the loose ends, but isn't really consistent with the behaviour of the characters up to that point. It is as if the composer could not commit publicly to the real ending, as if he was unable to reconcile his loves, very much as in his own life. The story contains both rape and murder, so forgiveness and a happy ending seem unlikely, but musically the melody must resolve. Real life however, is not like opera, it does not always have an ending, happy or otherwise, often it just peters out.

I left Paris for the last time, still unsure what I felt. Everything told me that I should like it, but that in turn made me less inclined to do so. It tells me that it is wonderful, the most beautiful and cultured city in the world, special. But I know that Paris is a liar that cheats on everyone. Like Turandot it has a beautiful body but an ugly heart. It has been raped and it has in turn murdered. A darkness wraps itself around the city like its famous black stoles. Perhaps I would feel differently if I were here with someone that I loved, but as it is, I must leave it for the next generation and its many children now returning home from overseas. I hope they find love in it and that Paris too, one day, finds what it wants to be.

View-Master™ Reel (The Tyrol)

SICILY

Kingdom of the Sun, 1969

We have finally reached the last of my journeys abroad, and I genuinely knew before I went that it would be my last. We have covered a lot of ground and by now you will have formed your opinion of me. If it's critical than I'm sure you're not wrong. I like a good laugh, and never more so than at my own expense. There is after all no bigger a critic of me than myself. I had been travelling every year for sixteen years, looking for something, testing myself, like I had in the mountains of Britain even before I travelled to Switzerland. I had in those journeys found what I thought that I was looking for, I had essentially found myself. I knew who I was, I knew what I liked and where I'd come from. I was at rest. But I was lonely.

My trip to Sicily was unlike any of the rest of my travels abroad, it was what we would recognise as simply a holiday. In my eyes it is particularly badly written as a result, and I apologise for that in advance. My desire to climb and conquer had gone, my desire to test and travel gone too, but the enjoyment gained from sitting in the sun after a splendid meal and looking out at the sea had not. I was happy with my own company, but I also knew that I wanted to share that experience with someone. My search for that stillness and warmth, that sense of peace, was not quite over yet.

I had been preparing the books for the Bath Grammar School for Girls prizegiving when an elderly gentleman entered the shop, leaning on a walking stick that appeared to be made from a vine tree. He was a well-known archaeologist who had written several books on Ancient Greece, fortunately two of which I had in stock and close at hand. They had been invaluable during my trip a few years earlier, so I was very keen to help with whatever it was he had come looking for. He was, it turned out, heading out to Sicily for a short field trip and wondered if I'd be interested in accompanying him and his daughter, who apparently was a bit of a handful. Quite why I was qualified to deal with such a thing I was unsure, and I clearly pointed out to him my lack of experience with female companions that were a handful or otherwise. He laughed strangely, in that slightly condescending way that academics do when in the company of one who understands nothing about their subject. Miss Seawright sometimes laughs at me the same way. She was initially as sceptical as I was, but after a bit of thinking and research, thought that it would be good for me and urged me to accept, especially if the old man were paying for at least some of it. Miss Seawright has a very devious mind and is able to follow even the most tortuous logic, playing one side off against another and juggling multiple opportunities without dropping a ball. But I do not have her skills and doubted whether I could legitimately go along with what appeared to me to be some sort of scam. I wondered later how much she knew of what was going on.

'If you have moral doubts about it then be very clear of your intentions up front.' She responded. 'That way if they lose out financially it's nobody's fault but their own. But, if I were you, I'd just enjoy it.'

I was sure that there would be plenty of unwelcome extra costs for me to pick up, whatever their original investment in me was.

For whatever reason, within a few weeks, I found myself climbing slowly, perhaps even reluctantly, up the steps of a BAC One-Eleven behind this elderly gentleman and his young female companion. We turned not to the right as I normally did, but to the left, where I was ushered through the soft curtains and into first class. I have to say that I don't really understand why people go 'first class'. For my generation it is simply amazing that one can fly from one end of Europe to another in just a couple of hours, a luxury in itself. In that time, you are invariably offered free newspapers, your choice from a range of exotic drinks, and often a perfectly acceptable meal. I find it extraordinary that people pay twice the price of the standard ticket to sit on the same plane and get there in the same time, with a slightly bigger seat, free peanuts and an additional glass of a prescribed and rather unpleasant bottle of fizz. I will never understand people.

Drinks were brought round, which for my septuagenarian host meant champagne. I rarely drink the stuff, especially in planes which I find dehydrating enough anyway and for a moment I considered explaining to him how the lack of oxygen and lower pressure in the cabin would affect the behaviour of the bubbles and the taste. He, however, was already toasting the stewardesses and although scientific advice had a time and a place, I could see that this was not it. Graciously I accepted a small beaker of the nameless liquid, it was indeed very bland. I quickly ordered a tomato juice to replace it. My companions were witty and intelligent and their joint enthusiasm for archaeology, which they discussed the whole way, was quite infectious. I hardly got the chance to read the paper and didn't even get started on the crossword. His daughter had grown up playing on her father's dig sites, so naturally she had entered the family profession too. They were overseeing a dig in Morgantina, where a three-thousand-year-old Greek city was being extracted, slowly, from the rock. I had visions of another Pompeii, which I had enjoyed wandering around on my own many years before.

We were met at the airport by a car and chauffeured to our hotel which, like everything else so far, was first class and very well appointed. I had scarcely unpacked my reading material and changed my suit, when a knock on the door politely informed me that it was time for dinner on the terrace. Dinner was lovely, but in truth I can't remember it at all. The whole thing was all very civilised, but I literally hadn't had a moment to myself all day and was beginning to get a little frustrated, so I used my host's age as an excuse and left the party early, for a party was what I feared dinner would turn into.

The next morning after breakfast on the same terrace, we set off for Messina, catching glimpses of the sea as we followed the coast road, little lidos tucked into every bay. 'Perfect for a quick dip' my companions assured me. I wouldn't have thought that the old man would have been into that sort of thing but who knew? The Mediterranean lifestyle was known to have innumerable health benefits, and as a resident of Bath I knew the healing powers of water better than most. I thought no more of it. On to the Bay of Nassos where the Greeks first landed in Sicily. I could see all the way across the sparkling water to the hills of Calabria and Reggio across the narrow straits. The harbour was bursting with life and movement. A cruise liner was berthed further up gleaming white in the blazing sun, two small grey naval vessels next to her. A hydrofoil tore in from Reggio and a train ferry backed cautiously out of the harbour. Add to this a host of small craft and people everywhere. I wanted to explore. But no.

We were met by more servants and lackeys fawning over us, this time with 'elevenses', tea, scones and honey and cakes courtesy of the University of Palermo who were giving a talk on the history of the island. I temporarily set aside any moral objections and filled my plate. Suitably fortified, I headed in to find out more about the people who had come to colonise and conquer all those years ago. It was only fair in return for the excellent cake. However, I got the distinct impression that this was not what my host or his daughter had anticipated. It was an incorrect answer to an exam question that I hadn't even noticed. She had already seen the Treasure of Attarouthi in the flesh, she said, and wasn't interested in hearing someone else talk about it. Did I detect a certain rivalry between opposing academics here? They slunk off while I went in.

Messina's Cathedral as it appeared hastily patched together after the war.

There was no sign of either of them when I emerged, so I made my own way over to the cathedral. Only a few parts of it had survived centuries of earthquakes and the terrible bombing during the war but it had been quickly rebuilt using concrete. For many this was a travesty, but I rather liked it. Why shouldn't Messina have a concrete apex on its cathedral? Most churches are a mixture of bits built in different styles over the years anyway, it's just that to the untrained eye it all looks 'old'.

It was new, bare inside, but of such perfect proportion that it carried an artistic grandeur about it. It was of course significantly different from any of the basilicas that I would see later covered in mosaic, but none the worse for it. Beyond it stood a little Norman church that had also somehow escaped the destruction. It was strange to see such a familiar object, essentially something from the quintessential English village, here in the hot dust of Sicily. It was difficult to grasp that the Normans, the same culture of William the Conqueror, beloved by schoolboys all over England, was so at home here in the Mediterranean, in a land that his relatives ruled for hundreds of years.

After the fall of Rome, the islands off the coast of Italy came under the protection of the 'Eastern Empire' and the majority of the churches and cathedrals here date from this Byzantine period. But Byzantium was slowly bled dry by Arab forces and by the turn of the first millennium Arabs had captured Sicily and Barbarians had invaded Italy from the north. The popes called for mercenaries to come to the aid of Christendom and the Papal States, and there were few organised, military societies quite as mercenary as the Normans. Richard II, (William the Conqueror's grandfather) was the first to send troops to Italy, and over the next hundred years the lure of Byzantine gold drew more and more of them. Robert Guiscard, who liked to be called 'the Fox' or 'the Weasel' invaded Sicily in 1061 with a force of fanatical cavalrymen. They landed at night and took the Saracen forces by surprise. Caught between the mountains and the sea the Arabs were easy pickings for the heavily armoured and fast-moving Normans, who mostly ignored the Pope's pleas and grabbed as much land for themselves as they could.

Robert went on to capture Malta and southern Italy itself, leaving his younger brother Roger to rule Sicily in his place. Roger's bloodline continued to rule Sicily until 1443 when it was captured by Spain. Sicily only became part of Italy in 1860.

The next day we pressed onto Palermo via the North Coast. Yet again my host had arranged a most magnificent hotel. It was right on the seafront with splendid views and had a huge swimming pool that his daughter was very keen on trying. My room looked out on a cloistered garden full of exotic plants, the sea's presence felt but not seen. I was looking forward to relaxing there with a good book that I'd brought along for the occasion. Booksellers are not generally well-off individuals, and my shop was certainly not a profitable establishment. There were places of course like the Waterstones just up the road that made a pretty penny selling the latest pulp thriller, but that had never been the intention for Seawright's Bookshop. We were a cultural enterprise rather than a commercial one and subsequently my funds were always running a little short, if I thought about them at all. So, I was surprised quite how generous my host was able to be. Archaeologists were surely amongst the poorest of academics, whose work needed constant sponsorship. What then was happening here?

My hosts were keen to show me around the capital. Palermo was noisy, baroque, and grandiose, with two opera houses, and a cathedral. It was wealthy but yet poor at the same time. The city had some fine buildings but not necessarily ones to admire. Perfectly pleasant, especially for its middle and professional class citizens, but one only had to peak around the corner of the dusty backstreets to see the poverty and crime that lay just below the surface. Behind the stuccoed nineteenth-century apartment blocks and the ornate churches lay street after street of lean-to shelters where families lived without water or electricity. The police didn't go there nor did the Catholic Church. It was a lawless world, or rather a world separated from the normal one that policed itself. Grim stony faces peered out from a door in a shack made from a Cinzano billboard. I quite like the drink with lemonade, but now I can't look at a bottle without thinking of these poor people. Beyond the shantytown, Mount Etna smoked threateningly in the background, ready to wipe it all out. I wondered if Pompeii had been like this, but I didn't think so. Pompeii had been bursting with life, bold, brave, blasé until the last second. This was a destitute district, its semi-forgotten residents, doomed. The people who lived here didn't seem to care, they had more day-to-day concerns to worry about.

Palermo cathedral is a riot of gold. It sits ill with the crushing poverty that lies all around it. What efforts was the church making to help the poorer citizens of Palermo, what was it doing if anything to oppose the Mafia or just to give people a chance in life? You could see the priests scurrying away, heads down, eyes almost closed, shutting out the poor, but how did those who eked out an existence in the shantytowns react when staggering out of their hovels and into this blaze of golden extravagance? I felt angry on their behalf.

Palermo's magnificent cathedral.

My companion joked that I spent more time looking at buildings than with her. It seemed an odd thing to say, especially for an archaeologist and I wondered what her point was. Surely the whole point of me accompanying them on this trip was for them to show me their world? Wasn't it? I had the nagging feeling that the answer was no. My father would be telling me that real life was passing me by and once again I was slightly missing the point of it. This trip clearly had a hidden agenda, and it was an agenda that had a significant budget.

Another fabulous dinner, but this time the conversation was a little more awkward. My host was heading out to the dig site early the next morning so excused himself, while his daughter had firmly booked a spot by the pool for the two of us for the next day. The whole of the next day.

How does one spend a whole day by the pool when there is an entire island of literal treasures to be explored? The sky and the beautiful light helped certainly, and I tried my best. I had brought books to entertain myself and borrowed a couple of paperbacks and magazines from the hotel, finding to my delight an old stack of 'National Geographics'. I went and fetched trays of drink, black tea for me, with lemon, and occasional tomato juice, with just a dash of Tabasco, a "Gin Rickey" or something called a "Mint Julep" for her. In truth she hardly used the pool at all, a few half-hearted strokes the couple of times she went in, and even then, she spent most of the time talking to me, or rather at me. I steadfastly refused to undo even as much as my suit jacket let alone my tie. I fear she had me confused with someone completely different. Had her father meant to extend his generous invitation to me or someone else? Conversation was awkward and I was rather relieved when she went back to reading silently, although I got the impression that she was displeased with me.

Lunch on the terrace was grilled fish and a chance to break the awkwardness that seemed to have developed between us. I suggested a walk. She jumped at the opportunity but in retrospect clearly had misunderstood once more. We had scarcely gone up the hill from the hotel into the treeline before she asked how much further it would be. I was surprised that one who had spent her childhood scrambling over rocks would tire of the outdoors so quickly. It was cooler in amongst the trees and the path meandered. She seemed to like this more and I confess her attentions became a little annoying but what could I say? As we scrambled up a path, I offered her my hand as she fretted about tearing her pants on some rocks. We emerged near the summit of the Shrine of St. Rosola, the Patron Saint of Paloma. It was quite unplanned on my part but there were fabulous views over the rocks and down to the magnificent sea. We walked silently down to the shoreline where fishermen held sea urchins in a leather glove, before cutting them open as a snack. I suggested a paddle or a look in the rock pools for crabs. She thought that I had lost my mind.

> As if the Sea should part
> And show a further Sea—
> And that—a further—and the Three
> But a presumption be—
> Of Periods of Seas— Unvisited of Shores—
> Themselves the Verge of Seas to be—
> Eternity—is Those—

It was worth a shot, but it turned out that my companion was not familiar with the works of the American poet Emily Dickinson which surprised me a little, because during that awfully long morning by the pool I had been doing some thinking. My companion had grown up on her father's dig sites which meant that she was born and grew up here in Sicily, and because of her age that must have been during the American occupation. She had ordered American cocktails from the bar, that were quite unknown to me, and drunk filter coffee at breakfast, much against my advice. She had boasted about having seen the Attarouthi treasure 'in the flesh' a hoard that I now knew, from the talk I attended, was displayed at the MET museum in New York. And finally, she had referred to her trousers as 'pants', a textbook mistake. Yet there was not the slightest trace of a southern drawl in her voice or an East Coast twang. As we walked back along the shore, I thanked her for her attention but made it clear that I was not interested. Not because she was American, but because she was not my type, not that I know what my 'type' is. But my 'type' would be a little more honest about herself. Sadly my 'type' had been taken a long time ago.

Confrontation over, suddenly all the tension and unpleasantness between us was gone. She even laughed and apologised. The whole thing had apparently been a setup and she had just been doing her job in it for a free holiday as much as I was. I stress that although it was subsidised, I was still paying for much of mine. So much better that we could now just enjoy ourselves, as ourselves from here on. I asked if there was no archaeology to be done back in Virginia, to which she said that they had no history there, let alone archaeology.

I wonder what the Powhatan or the Algonquian people would have to say about that.

As we walked, we came across a puppet theatre. It was not one of the tourist attractions, but a genuine, poor, working theatre. It reminded me a little of similar things I'd seen set up in the back streets of Bristol when I was a child. There were four or five rows of wooden benches, a small proscenium arch made of old cloth, and a large barrel organ. This instrument was turned by the younger member of the family. When he grew tired the music slowed, and a larger sized boy took over.

The puppets, about four foot high, were operated by iron rods, the manipulation matching the voices. The knightly deeds, the slaying of Saracens, the rescuing of damsels all proceeded with great zest. Swords and shields clashed with great realism, and heads literally rolled. For such a stylised art form, the level of excitement it generated was enormous. Thirty, maybe forty young men who might have been terrorising the neighbourhood or fighting rival Mafia clans, roared their encouragement from the benches, then disappeared off into the night, some perhaps inspired to do who knows what… Gallant deeds perhaps, one hopes… The proprietor, himself a traditional puppet-like figure, was surprised to see tourists in the audience, a young lady and a man in a black suit no less and insisted on giving us a behind the scenes tour. His younger siblings had emigrated to America thirty years before and had no doubt found their fortunes, or somebody else's fortune, but he had stayed here, running the theatre that had been in his family for generations on this very spot. My companion acted as my translator and got to play with the puppets herself. We were surprised to find that by the time we had left, it had gone midnight.

Having had our talk, I saw surprisingly little of my companions. Her father busied himself with the business of managing his dig at Morgantina, and she, well she just seemed to fade away and focus her interests on something, or perhaps someone else. But it was all perfectly amicable, and I felt much the better for it. I wanted company, but not any company at any cost.

The sun glinted on the chrome of the observatory as we fought our way through the traffic of Palermo. We crossed a pass, guarded by a fort, out into the bare landscape of the country after the lushness of the plain. Norman Sicily fell away, and the landscape returned to that I associated more with Greece. On to Partinico where Dolci lived and worked. The town had been devastated by an earthquake the previous year and the inhabitants were still living in temporary Nissan huts. Very little attempt was being made to help them or restore order. It was a real case of survival of the fittest. People had dug themselves burrows in the rubble, and families sheltered together under scraps of tarpaulin. I saw neither priest nor policeman as I passed through, nothing in fact that implied any sort of official help or support at all, and I wondered how long it would be before this whole place became just another Mafia fiefdom.

Soldier sifting through the rubble of Gibellina.

On the night of January 14th 1968, a magnitude six earthquake struck Sicily. The photograph below shows the town of Gibellina, in which nearly 25% of the population lost their lives and 100,000 were made homeless. A year after the quake, two thirds of victims still had not received any government compensation. Ten years on 60,000 people were still living in temporary accommodation and to this day not a single family has been placed in new housing.

The Temple of Segesta stands alone, quite alone, in a sea of blue sky. Like myself perhaps. It was good to have time by myself again.

I could breathe again. The air was fresh but warm, it smelt of the sea, but also of warm earth, pine and slightly of lavender. True there was a restaurant, and a car park at the bottom of the hill, but they were in a fold of the ground and couldn't be seen. The hill itself rose from the fields of waist high clover. It was clad in short grass and shrubby bushes. These gave way to bare rock, silhouetted against that brilliant sky. A rough path wound upwards toward a shelf on the hill, and there stood this glorious temple, unfinished but unruined. It was golden brown, its columns not yet sculpted with grooves. It was Doric in style, but not as heavy as some. It had no inner sanctum, it never had a roof, its walls were never painted. Its balance was near perfection, but it was the setting that made it incomparable. Standing in the Stylobate, all that you could see in that vast panorama is ancient. There were   no churches, no houses, just the red and green fields and the huge sky. Only the wind and the past were here. Virgil's 'Aeneid' says that the town of Segesta, which this temple was meant to serve, was founded by colonists from Troy, but the old men in the café say that archaeological evidence shows that the settlement is much older than that and that it was inhabited by the Elymian people. Quite why the temple was never completed is unknown. Perhaps it was on a similar lovely day when the workmen just sat down on the grass with their sandwiches and decided that the temple didn't really need flutes cut into its columns or a tiled roof. Who could blame them if they did? I'm sure it works just as well as any of the other temples that I have seen and it is certainly nearer to the gods than most. I took my jacket off and slung it over my shoulder in solidarity with ancient laziness.

On the opposite hill, within easy walking distance of the temple and the restaurant, lay the remains of an amphitheatre, built with typical Greek flair in a dramatic setting overlooking the Bay of Castellammare. It seemed however that others very much appreciated the ancient Greeks' work too. My host was in charge of a dig here, and this is what I had come out to see. Trays full of earth were set out on trestle tables in the sun and in them were Roman coins, beads and all sorts of everyday debris, even a sandal. Where the Greeks, Phoenicians, Carthaginians & Trojans went, our old friends the Romans were sure to follow. But it was not the Romans that we were apparently looking for. In the grass behind the ancient stage a long trench had been dug, a cross section of a marked-out area of the hill that the Muslims called 'Cebel Hamid'. A hoard of Byzantine and Arabic coins had been found here amid the ruins of a mosque. One end of the trench was used as a rubbish dump and it was here that the inexperienced were placed, myself included.

I had enormous fun that day, 'playing in the dirt'. There were just enough things being turned up to keep me fascinated. Every item I pulled out of the ground was a delight to see, however mundane. I dusted them off, marked their position and took them to be assessed all very solemnly. Sea birds wheeled far above, the quiet smile of the glinting sea encouraging us. My prize for the day, a shard of green Seljuk pottery from twelfth century Persia. Proof how interconnected the world was even back then. I felt a surprisingly intimate connection to this bowl that had somehow gone on an amazing eight-hundred-year journey and found its way from ancient Arabia to present day me.

The next day I went on an expedition to see the hill town of Erice, above Trapani. The bus ground its way up into the hills, giving impressive views over steep cliffs. There was a heart stopping turn and the sea could be seen glinting below, the town's sickle shaped breakwater extending into the sea. There is something curiously different about Erice, but at first it is not easy to establish what is unfamiliar. There are two castles, one, founded by the Normans upon the ruins of a former Roman temple, interesting monuments and sights including the gardens of the castle, the Dome of the Assunta, the Spanish District and plenty of religious monuments (Erice was once called 'Town of 100 churches'). But gradually you will realise that what is missing is quite simply the people. They are there alright, but very rarely seen, a glimpse of a shadow by a door, the sound of radio music, a small Fiat disappearing around a corner. Outside the Town Hall I once saw five men at the same time, but I was told that was exceptional.

The residents of Erice are a strange people. That part of the island is known for its dour and grim personality – the city of Trapani, far below, has no nightlife or entertainment at all, the product perhaps of poverty and exploitation. It should be remembered that however wide its organisation may stretch and showy some of its international activities may be, the roots of the

Mafia are here, deep in the land of Western Sicily. Among these, the people of Erice are the remotest of all. They live alone high on the top of their mountain. The fog blows in from the sea and can linger there for days. Invaders have come in waves, so the inhabitants have developed this closed, communal life. Generally, three or four dwellings share a courtyard, with a single shared staircase to the upper floors. A small heavy door gives access to the road. No windows look out, there are no pavements. The road itself is patterned elaborately with cobbles which shine like silver as the road winds between blank walls. The doors of course are shut, but should you open one, the courtyard becomes a living room and people will appear at the doors and welcome you with courtesy and interest.

Even today Erice's streets are mostly deserted.

I did not find anywhere to eat in the town so took a taxi across the flat salt plains, to the vineyards of Marsala and the undulating countryside of the South Coast. A 'baglio' was recommended to me, a type of Mediterranean house with a spacious courtyard, draped in hibiscus and dotted with citrus and olive trees. Upturned barrels were set out on the patio and being used as tables. A friendly welcome and I was led out of the heat of the day down into a cool cellar. It had a high barrel ribbed roof reminiscent of the water cisterns built beneath Roman cities and not dissimilar to many great cathedrals. Row upon row of large barrels were neatly parked on each side, chalk marks covering their fronts.

The Marsala style of wine was created by English wine merchant John Woodhouse, who like me was from Bristol. He opened his first production centre here in 1770, primarily to supply the British Royal Navy. Nelson famously ordered 500 barrels of the stuff a year, and his body was preserved in it on the way back to England after Trafalgar. I wonder if he was one of Miss Seawright's relatives? What a small world it sometimes is.

With a thud, back into the present day as my coach crossed from the country road onto the first opened stretch of motorway down to Syracuse. The place was in uproar, the city was in the throws of an election. The streets were full of people chanting and waving banners, Communist Party versus the Separatists. This was a world where poverty and desperation had forced people to the extreme left or right. It seems odd that we are able to send men and women into space but are unable to deal with relatively simple problems on the ground. Why with all our science haven't we eradicated poverty and hunger? It's easy enough to share resources, why does it have to be every man for himself? Traditional parties have fled the battlefield in Sicily. Here the Italian Movement of Unity, which is really an old Fascist party, faced off against the PCI. Support for the Italian Communists was very high, due to crushing poverty and poor governance, but the Mafia backed the right-wing parties and the Americans made an anti-communist stance a precondition of financial aid. I feared that there would be an anti-democratic military coup here, just like the one in Greece.

The PCI General Secretary was trying to campaign here, but he received regular death threats and feared for his life. If I'm honest, the whole place was ripe for Robert Guiscard to return with his Norman cavalry. I worry that our politics too are becoming a childish fight of left versus right, good versus evil, East versus West. It's this kind of foolish tub thumping, and seeing the world in black and white, that led us into two World Wars. Not that I blamed the locals, they've been let down by everyone, Church and State included. Poverty is everyone's problem. Tackling it is clearly not something that can be left to local politicians, we need such things to be managed at European level sharing the cost across borders, rich countries helping the poor. I'm not sure how I can help.

Syracuse is a perfectly acceptable city but nothing to write home about. I went for a walk along the seafront to get away from all the noise. There was a shallow sandy slope and it was easy to see why the Americans chose to land their troops here. The bay was now planted with papyrus and ducks bobbed about on the surface. It would have been nice to sail here in The Seagull, but it's too far a trip for someone with my meagre sailing skills. This is where Nelson loaded his ridiculously large order of Marsala on board his ships, floating the barrels on the surface of the calm sea. All along the shore, fishermen sat mending their nets as they did in Nelson's day, but the nets were nylon now and couldn't be so easily mended. The US Sixth Navy's flagship, the Puget Sound sat where the Victory once did, doing I know not what. I hope it was something innocent like loading huge barrels of alcohol onboard, but I suspect not.

A new glass terminal had been built at the end of the quay, where white cruise liners disgorge crowds of people who have spent half a year's salary on a week-long cruise; and the money barely reaches the shore.

One thing in Syracuse was pleasantly memorable, however. The rather florid facade of the Cathedral concealed a surprise. The main body of the Church had been built inside an ancient Greek Temple, reusing the stone. It was strange to see the great Doric columns that I was so familiar with, set into the nave walls, separated by elaborate Spanish wrought iron gates. For hundreds of years, it was also a mosque and it had been this that had saved the columns. The mix of styles and historical con- tinuity within the one building appealed to me greatly.

Roman columns inside Syracuse.

I was coming to the end of what I already knew was my last trip abroad. It had been pleasant on the whole, but unnecessary. I had enjoyed it less than my other trips and had learnt very little new. I started searching for the customary concert to add to my memories. The Theatre Massimo in Palermo would have been the place to see one, but I had missed my chance. Neither my host nor his daughter were interested in such things. But where there is a will there's a way. I walked through the steep streets checking notes outside café terraces and asking locals for suggestions in my best Italian. The Greeks, the Romans, the Ostrogoths, the Byzantines, the Arabs, the Normans and the Spanish had all left their touch on the language spoken here. Their language is very much the proof of their multicultural heritage, very much as English is of ours. Vowels are dropped, soft consonants doubled, harsher sounds and definite articles worn away. Their accents sound like the sweeping of the sea on the sand.

Who was this strange Englishman wandering the streets in a dark suit and tie on such a hot day? Un concerto? La musica classica? Si. Naturalmente...

The town square in Syracuse.

Outside the unmistakably Venetian Town Hall a concert was taking place, with an orchestra of entirely plucked instruments, double bass, mandolins of all sizes, guitars, zithers, balalaika and so on. As darkness fell the strange haunting music rose over the town. It was

397

Mozart, but in an unfamiliar guise, arranged for local instruments, dropped into a minor key, more in keeping with the sad songs that Sicily is known for. I was delighted how the people of the region had taken something so well-known and made it their own, and Mozart would have been pleased as well, I am sure.

My last day, and time to face the reason why Sicily exists at all, its creator, a constant background presence, and what will almost certainly be the cause of its eventual destruction. The volcano, Etna.

Mount Etna

The trees ended abruptly at the head of a cliff, where two-hundred feet below a little river wound its way through the rock, following the ancient magma flow. We followed a narrow twisting path down the cliff, witnessing the deep cracks in the stone through which rainwater poured. It was a solid bed of lava two-hundred feet thick. I put on waders, stepped into the crystal-clear water and began to walk up into the Alcantara Gorge like a child on a rainy day jumping in puddles.

The Alcantara River cutting through hundreds of feet of lava.

The current was swift, and the lava sand on the bottom shifted continually under my boots like fate. The gorge twisted. Suddenly all sight of the entrance was lost. I had become its plaything. As the stream narrowed, so the current increased. It was only sheer bloody-mindedness that got me to the other side.

From the Rifugio Sapienza I caught the cable car, the 'Funivia' up the next section of the mountain. I passed just over the tops of oaks, beeches, pines, and chestnut trees. There was an amazing diversity of plants growing on the slopes. Soon dark ridges loomed above me. It had been hot and sunny when I had set out, but it had become cold, and mist now clung to the slopes. At the cable station we were told that clouds of poisonous gas were sweeping down from the summit and that we couldn't go up, but a guide would lead us to a subsidiary cone.

The climb was surprisingly steep. As I struggled, I thought back to my expeditions to climb the Eiger and the Matterhorn all those years before. I had become a different person, an older one, a softer one. I was approaching fifty. My feet disappeared in the fog; my nose was frozen. I wanted my scarf and gloves, I wanted a hat, I wanted a climbing axe and a good pair of boots. 'Come on Nicholas, put your back into it...'

The great bowl of the crater was coloured with every conceivable colour of ash, from white, yellow, to livid red, browns and black. The floor was rocky and uneven, closing in the centre to a giant gash. Steam rose constantly through it. We descended into the crater very cautiously. The rock was hot to the touch, and I wondered just how far below us the magma was. Like a child I walked to the edge and stared down into the hot darkness, tightly clutching my glasses. They steamed up instantly and I saw nothing. Like a child, I also dropped a stone in and listened. Of course there was no sound. Stupid I know. The steam played tricks on my vision. It always seemed to be somewhere else, never where I was. It blurred the edges of things and left them ever so slightly out of focus as it condensed on my lenses. It was warm and humid, comforting like a steam room. Our guide measured the air constantly. It was easy to forget that the air was poisonous, and the warm fuzzy feeling and blurred vision was actually my body starting to shut down. It was time to move.

At the lip an unpleasant surprise awaited, gale force, biting cold winds. My vision was instantly restored, but it took me a moment or two to realise it. It was snowing. Horizontally. We pressed on across a desolate monochrome landscape, snow covering the black rock, grey clouds obliterating the sky. It was impossible to speak even if I had wanted to. This was unlike any planet that I knew, this was no longer Earth. It was utterly barren; not a thing grew anywhere. Unequipped for such an environment our guide turned round and brought us back down the slope. Almost as suddenly as opening a door, the clouds cleared, the wind dropped, and the sun returned. A cup of hot chocolate at a café at the cable station quickly restored me. That night, at dinner, (which I took with a larger than usual glass of red wine) I looked up the Volcano from the warmth of the terrace. It seemed a little brighter, the crown of burning ash glowing higher into the night sky. A waiter, seeing where I was looking, said: 'He is restless. He will erupt soon you will see.'

Just three months later he did.

I stood in the same spot at breakfast, as my suitcase was loaded onto the coach, taking in that final panorama, Italy visible as a smudge in the distance. The beautiful curve of the Bay of Naxos glittered on my right, on the left a series of small villages clung to the slopes, behind me the plain leading back, and up to Etna, emitting a gentle stream of white up into that infinite blue sky. All life, everything that Earth was, seemed to be included in that glorious view, creation, evolution, culture, business and death. As I stood motionless, lost in wonder, a great bird swept over my head on silent gliding wings. It held in its beak a long writhing snake that coiled back upon itself. An omen, I thought, of the most classic sort. I am a man of science, and set no store in such things, but I knew that it was beautiful, dangerous and epitomised Sicily. I knew too that it was time to go to wherever my future lay.

View-Master™ Reel (Sicily)

THE MOON

One Small Step, 20th July 1969

At seventeen minutes past nine, Apollo 11's lunar module touched down on the surface. It was a warm Sunday evening; the French doors were open, and the sun had not yet fully sunk below the horizon. I was sitting with my parents in their back lounge with a spread of cold cuts from lunch and cheese from the local market laid out on the little table in the corner. My father was sat bolt upright in his high-backed chair opposite the big television, nursing a beer, a blanket stretched over his knees. My mother, as always, sat beside him, nursing my father in turn. Both now over seventy, they were very much still in love. I was hopping about with excitement, like the birds that flitted around the bird bath on the patio, unsure what to do with myself, as the dark shadow of the Eagle's leg reflected off the moon's dusty surface. Nobody had any idea if the surface was even solid, not me, not my father, not the Eagle's pilot Buzz Aldrin, nor anyone else at NASA. Lunik alone knew that it would be alright, but she was no longer talking.

For a while they drifted towards a crater from which escape would be difficult. Armstrong fired the thrusters manually to steer the ship away, but they had just seconds of fuel. Six-hundred million people across the whole world watched live, terrified, but as a single community, as their words were echoed live across the solar system.

'Contact light…'
'Out of detent… Engine Stop. Engine arm off.'
'Mode control to Auto. 413 is in…
Houston, Tranquillity Base here. The Eagle has landed…

Roger, Twan—Tranquillity, we copy you on the ground. You got a bunch of guys about to turn blue. We're breathing again. Thanks a lot.'

It was to be another three hours before the lander's hatch opened and Commander Neil Armstrong started to climb out. The coverage was continuous, the BBC's first all night live broadcast, with James Burke, Patrick Moore and Cliff Michelmore providing commentary and analysis. The sun disappeared, the moon came up and the French doors were shut, but nobody thought about going to bed, not even my father who regularly dozed off. They were watching in Moscow too. Suddenly there were roars of approval all over the world and spontaneous cheering up and down the street which could be heard even over the television.

'That's one small step for man, one giant leap for mankind...'

The BBC's live coverage of the moon landing.

So, mankind has made it to another world, and I am as overjoyed as everyone else on the planet, but there is a question nagging at me.

What we will do with that world, when we have made such a mess of this one? We, both East and West have spent so much, an impossible, clearly never to be repeated one-off amount, on this two hours and thirty-one minutes of extra vehicular activity. What more could we have done with that down here in our world?

The media are treating this as an American achievement, a victory for Capitalism and of course it is, but in truth the launch system was designed by Germans, much of the communications and computing equipment was British, the materials used were German and Italian, the life support system mostly French and the Space Suits, flight paths and so much experience was Russian. This is an international achievement.

The Americans oppose Socialism everywhere and use the Space Race as an example of Capitalism's superiority, but who says that this is where the finishing line is? Now that we have got there, we will be building bases on it and people will begin to live on the moon. I worry that in fifty years' time that too will look like Berlin, half covered in sleezy neon lights and Coca-Cola, perhaps with shops full of heavy china and dark furniture that nobody wants to buy, while the other half lies in darkness and silence, a barbed wire fence with laser towers stretched between them. It is hard to see how Capitalism and the 'every man for himself' culture will work on the moon. There are limited resources, and everyone will have to play their role in the community, 'from each according to their abilities, to each according to their needs'. I have tried not to be political in this travelogue, but it is hard to see that there is any solution that is sustainable in the long run other than Socialism, but the Socialism of the future needs to be a different type from what I have seen in this decade. It needs to separate itself from Nationalism. We need a new moderate, considered form of Socialism; a new kind of 'European Socialism'.

HOME

A Place in Context, Bath 1970

I was back in the bookshop, in the city that had become my home, surrounded by a context that I understood and revelled in. It was a beautiful day, and the US military had just approved my application to supply a reading library at one of their facilities. I had a mug of tea in one hand, and a cinnamon bun by my side.

The post had brought me a selection of space stamps from overseas to add to my ever-expanding collection, and I'd received a letter from a very old and dear friend. He is much wiser than I and tells me that despite everything, the world is exactly where it was meant to be, that people everywhere are fundamentally good and trying to do their best, and that the future we have dreamed of is in our hands and is certain, even if not quite 'just around the corner' yet. Furthermore, he congratulated me on my recent news and sent me a most honest and heartfelt handshake along with his best wishes. It meant a lot. I trust in him completely.

The doorbell jingled merrily and the familiar figure of a British actress, who had made her name in America after the war, appeared. You know as well as I do what she was going to say.

'It's a lovely May morning and here I am, once again in the gorgeous city of Bath.' She smiled with obvious excitement. Well, I was excited too, but being in the city of Bath, beautiful though it is, was not the reason why as well you know. After decades wandering in the wilderness, I was finally engaged to be married and to someone who had been here in my home city the whole time.

My fiancée was someone I had known, albeit vaguely, for years, someone who I had handed prizes to nearly every academic year.

The granddaughter of a great Admiral no less, one of Miss Seawright's closest associates. She is funny and clever, and although she disagrees with me about nearly everything, there is a rebellious streak of nature in her that I like, and I think I can work with. Miss Seawright says that I have no chance of controlling her and laughs heartily. What the girl sees in me I do not understand. Everybody that knows me is delighted. My father so much so that he offered to buy us our first house, to 'get us started', accidentally letting slip that he thought that it would never happen to me. My mother is more reserved and assures me that owning a house is not a cardinal sin, provided that one uses it well, shares it with others and isn't left 'in hock' to the banks for life.

I was delighted to be getting married, eager to start a new life with someone, and excited at the thought of settling down, and possibly having children of my own that I could share my experiences, and limited thoughts with. It had taken me a long time to get to a position where most others started out. Had I learnt anything to pass on in all that time?

The omen seen from that rocky outcrop in Sicily was now perfectly clear. I was the restless serpent struggling on the ground with no sense of direction, and I had finally been swooped up and taken to my place in the universe, my context.

I asked in the introduction of this travelogue the question, 'Why do we travel?' and of course the short answer is, to see the world, to see new things, and to learn. The deeper and more poignant question is, why do we feel the need to do this? Others may have their own answer to that but, for me, in order to be settled and comfortable and to have any real sense of direction in our lives we need to know who we are, where we've come from, and why we are here. We need to ground ourselves in a context, understanding our place in the universe. That we are tiny, transient and inconsequential; a mirror at best, reflecting all that has gone into making us.

So here I am, sitting at an American typewriter full of Arabic symbols and Egyptian paper, using mediaeval German technology. I am in my office at the top of a Victorian era shop, built from material from the Welsh hills, used by French refugees in a Roman city made wealthy by German aristocrats and Georgian society. I am surrounded by people speaking foreign languages, by records of classical music by composers from all over the continent, and by travel books and fine literature from all over the world. My Moka coffee pot, bought after my first trip to Switzerland, full of Dutch coffee from Indonesia is by my side, as is a Viennese cinnamon swirl, and a sheet of Russian space stamps. A Belgian waffle maker that my future wife won't allow in the house sits on a shelf opposite me remembering good times as do many other of my souvenirs.

I was very lucky. I grew up in an extraordinary place, in extraordinary times, but there again so did you, so did everyone, ever. The world is, and always has been, an extraordinary place. What made me different was that I was wealthy enough, lost enough and maybe lonely enough, to spend twenty years looking for my context. It proved an incredibly rich one, but it is one that we all share. Now that I had finally found it and found myself, I had no need to travel further.

It has been the greatest sadness of my life that our European family has been split in two by ideological forces, Nationalist sentiment and misunderstanding, despite the horrors of two World Wars. As I write, the situation seems to be getting worse, rather than better, despite, or perhaps because of, rising standards of living and liberalisation in the East. I worry what will happen to Berlin, Bratislava, Prague, Belgrade, maybe even to Vienna and Istanbul, but only in the short term. Things will return to their rightful state eventually. But neither Germany, nor Europe, can move forward until the family is united. Only when Europe is one and its government has been federalised can issues like poverty be centrally tackled and eliminated. The situation cannot be sustained and yet I cannot see it being resolved in my lifetime. We need a Europe that is built on going forward together as a family, not on alliances against fears that do not, and never have, existed. In short, we need the past back. As for me, I will have to content myself with the knowledge that the future and the past are both clear and it is only the present and the short-term future that is confused. I wish all my European siblings well.

My father got married on 29th October 1970.
He had three children, born in 1971, 1976, and 1979.
He did not go abroad again.

407

THE AUTHOR

Ex Spinia Uvas
Grapes from the Thorn

Gordon Nicholas was born in 1923 in the St. Paul's district of Bristol where his father ran a small grocer's shop. He was brought up on his uncles' farms and in their biplanes, one of them being a pilot at nearby RAF Upavon. He attended Bristol Boys Grammar School before getting a scholarship to Clifton College. He served in the Somerset Light Infantry Signals Division during World War II, before being released from active service in 1947.

A collapsed lung and relatively poor health prevented Gordon from serving on the frontline during the war, but despite this he developed a passion for mountain climbing, conquering all of Britain's tallest mountains between 1947 and 1953. The Alps were a logical next step, and he went on to climb the Eiger and many others.

Gordon graduated from university in 1953 and travelled across Europe for nearly twenty years in search of adventure and a desire to understand the world better. He was endlessly consuming knowledge, interested in everything and read voraciously with a large stack of books on the go at any time. Charming, quiet, cultured, immensely knowledgeable and slightly cheeky, he was the perfect front man for Seawright's bookshop in Bath where he was the manager for many years. He met many famous visitors to the city and became quite a local celebrity in his own right, speaking not infrequently at the Guildhall and acting as an independent advisor on both architectural and cultural matters.

Gordon did lots of work for Bristol charities, and informally for the Admiralty in Bath. He worked as an editor on the famous publication "Jane's Fighting Ships" and was a consultant on many other projects behind the scenes. He created a book lending scheme for military personnel all over the country, setup the Bristol Astronomic Society and founded a small commune for the unemployed on the edge of the city at Tadwick.

After the bookshop closed, he was offered a position working for the MOD at Fox Hill, where he was a project and team leader in the Goddess programme which used state of the art computer aided design to minimise the sound of warships passing through the water.

Much to both his and his parents' surprise, he got married at the age of 48 and had three children, all of whom are proud Europeans.

Index of Reel Images

View-Master images all © Sawyers or Meopta under license.

Switzerland	2009, 2056, 2012
Holland	1917, 1915, 1905
Belgium	1981, 1952, 1950
Pyrenees & Provence	1415, 1405, 2670, 1442
Paris	1401, 1402
Cairo	3301, 3306
Rome	1601, 0352
Brussels Trade Fair	1990* 3
Venice	0301, 0302
Florence, Pisa & Italy	1610, 0281, 1609, 1612, 1615, 0282
Châteaux of the Loire	1701, 1702, 1703
Brittany & Mont St. Michel	1431, 1432
Greece	2151, 2152, 2160
Vienna	2325
Yugoslavia	6803
Prague	Meopta 06-10, 06-5, 06-6, 02-2
Germany	4072, 1566, 1505
Sicily	0551, 0552, 0553

Eastern Bloc images copyright of Meopta.
Gordon's paintings digitally reimagined as required.
Additional artwork provided by Bill Hyde.

Printed in Great Britain
by Amazon